Mini-Reference

Things Everyone Needs to Know

To	*Do This*
Start Windows (from DOS)	Type **WIN**, press Enter
Leave Windows	In Program Manager, click File, Exit Windows, click OK
See all currently running programs	Press Ctrl+Esc
Get help	Press F1
Close the active window	Press Ctrl+F4
Start a program	Double-click its icon
Run a DOS command or program	Double-click the Main group icon, double-click the MS-DOS Prompt icon

Things to Do with All Windows

To	*Do This*
Make window full-size	Click Maximize button
Make window an icon	Click Minimize button
Restore window to partial-screen size	Click Restore button
Move window	Drag window by its title bar
Size a window	Drag its border

Things to Do with Program Manager Windows

To	*Do This*
Open a group window	Double-click its group icon
Close a group window	Click Minimize button
Create a new group	Click File, New, Program Group
Move an icon to another group	Click icon, press F7, click group name, click OK
Copy an icon to another group	Click icon, press F8, click group name, click OK
Delete an icon	Click icon, press Del, click Yes
Cascade windows	Press Shift+F5
Tile windows	Press Shift+F4
Save setup (of Program Manager)	Hold Shift key, click File, Exit Windows
Check available memory, operating mode	Click Help, About Program Manager

Mini-Reference

Things to Do with File Manager

To	*Do This*
Open a new drive window	Double-click drive icon
Display files on a different drive	Click drive icon
Copy file	Hold Ctrl key, drag file
Move file within same disk drive	Drag file
Move file to a different drive or directory	Hold Alt key, drag file
Copy a floppy disk	Click Disk, Copy Disk
Format a floppy disk	Click Disk, Format Disk

Things to Do with Programs

To	*Do This*
Start a program	Double-click its icon
Leave a Windows program	Click File, Exit
Leave a DOS program	Varies; use program's usual exit routine
Switch to a different program	Press Alt+Tab
Put a program away temporarily	Click Minimize button (program reduces to an icon at the bottom of the desktop; it's still running)
Use an "iconized" program	Double-click its icon at the bottom of the desktop
Make DOS program a window	Press Alt+Enter (requires Windows running in 386 Enhanced Mode)
Return DOS program to full-screen	Press Alt+Enter (requires Windows running in 386 Enhanced Mode)

Popular Keyboard Shortcuts

To	*Press This*
Close dialog box and accept changes	Enter
Close dialog box but cancel changes	Esc
Open program window's Control menu (long dash)	Alt+Space bar
Open document window's Control menu (short dash)	Alt+Hyphen
Maximize program window	Alt+Space bar, X
Minimize program window	Alt+Space bar, N
Restore program window	Alt+Space bar, R
Close program window	Alt+F4
Show Task List	Ctrl+Esc
Switch to next program	Alt+Tab

I HATE WINDOWS™

Gordon McComb

I Hate Windows

Library of Congress Catalog No.: 93-83299

ISBN: 1-56529-214-6

95 94 93 6 5 4 3 2

Interpretation of the printing code: the rightmost double-digit number is the year of the book's printing; the rightmost single-digit number, the number of the book's printing. For example, a printing code of 93-1 shows that the first printing of the book occurred in 1993.

Screen reproductions in this book were created using Collage Plus from Inner Media, Inc., Hollis, NH.

I Hate Windows is based on Microsoft Windows Version 3.1.

Publisher: Lloyd J. Short

Associate Publisher: Rick Ranucci

Publishing Plan Manager: Thomas H. Bennett

Operations Manager: Sheila Cunningham

Acquisitions Editor: Chris Katsaropoulos

Dedication

To Mercedes and Max. You two are my best work yet.

About the Author

Gordon McComb has written over 40 books and 1,000 magazine articles. His specialty is computers, and he has written about them for over 13 years. He has written a lot of normal stuff, too, for publications like *Popular Science*, *Omni*, *Video*, *Family Handyman*, and the *Christian Science Monitor*. He writes a weekly syndicated newspaper column for *Copley News Service* and is the west coast editor for *PC Upgrade* magazine.

When he's not writing, Gordon visits antique stores, collects magazines and other junk from the '50s and '60s, and putters around his San Diego home wondering which half-finished job to put off until next week. He lives with his long-suffering wife Jennifer, children Mercedes and Max, two dogs, two cats, and two computers.

Credits

Title Manager:
Shelley O'Hara

Production Editor:
Barbara K. Koenig

Editor:
Heather Northrup

Technical Editor:
Lynda Fox

On-the-Spot Technical Editor:
Timothy S. Stanley

Book Designer:
Scott Cook

Illustrations:
Jeff MacNelly

Novice Reviewer:
Sandra Naito

Editorial Assistants:
Julia Blount
Sandra Naito

Production Team:
Julie Brown
Laurie Casey
Michelle Cleary
Bob LaRoche
Jay Lesandrini
Caroline Roop
Linda Seifert
Phil Worthington

Indexer
Joy Dean Lee

Composed in Goudy and MCPdigital by Que Corporation.

Acknowledgments

And to think that all this started when I had lunch with my agent, Bill Gladstone. Thank you, Bill, for connecting me with Que to do this fun book, and for suggesting the chile rellenos.

My thanks to Shelley O'Hara, product director and Keeper of "The Vision," for seeing this book from start to finish and making innumerable suggestions on how to make it better. If you spot a good idea in this book, it was probably Shelley's—though I'll gladly take the credit! Also, special thanks to Rick Ranucci, the Reader's Advocate, for making sure I didn't slip into techno-ese—a dirty habit, I know.

A tip o' the Windows icon to Chris Katsaropoulos and to the many other "behind the scenes" editors and experts at Que who made this book possible. It's nice to work with professionals. Mucho grass to friend and fellow writer Chris Van Buren for letting me steal some great concepts from his Windows book. And a special salute to Dan Gookin, who proved to publishers that computer books don't have to be dry and boring.

Last, and you better believe not least, thanks to my wife, Jennifer, for letting me stay up past my bedtime to write this book. We'll take that vacation now...promise.

Trademark Acknowledgments

Contents at a Glance

Table of Contents

I HATE WINDOWS!

I HATE WINDOWS!

I HATE WINDOWS!

I HATE WINDOWS!

I HATE WINDOWS!

I HATE WINDOWS

Introduction

"Which one do you think I should use?" the voice on the other end of the line asked, "a 16 ounce or a 24 ounce?"

My father, who had just started to use Windows, was of course referring to a 16- or 24-ounce hammer. He wanted to bash in his computer after wasting several hours trying to get Windows to work for him.

"I hate Windows!" my dad complained before we hung up the phone.

That he did. And yet, over the months, Windows would grow on him. He'd learn to use it and make it behave. He'd never become an expert, but that wasn't his aim. In the end, he got the better of Windows and became its master.

Though Microsoft Windows is supposed to make using a personal computer easier, parts of it can make you feel like you're trudging knee-deep in the muddy waters of truly stupid PC programs. This book is aimed at clearing up those dirty waters and bringing into sharp focus the steps you can take to control Windows. No longer must Windows control you.

A Book Just for You

If you feel like my father—you dream about blowing up Windows and your computer in devious and creative ways—this book is for you. If you've tried Windows, but discovered that it almost has a life of its own, you'll find this book indispensable in overcoming the roadblocks keeping you from using your computer.

I Hate Windows is for users who want to get work done. You don't live and breathe and eat computers, and you aren't interested in spending much time on the why. Far more important to you is the how.

While *I Hate Windows* is for beginners, it's aimed primarily at those who are new to Windows, not computers in general. No, you don't need to be a computer expert, but I expect you to know such things as how to turn your computer on, and the difference between a keyboard and a monitor.

Some of this very basic stuff is covered in Chapter 21, but if you want more information than that, I suggest that you first read *I Hate PCs*, which will give you a solid background on what personal computers are and how to use them.

Why This Book Is Special

This book is special for many reasons:

- It treats you like a smart person who doesn't have the time to bother with the technical gobbledygook found in the other books. I get right to the point here.

- ▼ It concentrates on what you need to know, when you need to know it. You don't have to read through chapters and chapters just to learn how to start Windows.
- ▼ It highlights things you gotta know about. That way you're not likely to miss really important stuff.
- ▼ It wraps up less important but interesting tidbits in boxes. You don't have to read the boxes if you don't want to.
- ▼ It uses special icons:

This icon alerts you to shortcuts, tricks, and time-savers.

This icon flags skippable technical stuff. If you are the curious type, read the material marked with this icon.

This icon warns you about those pitfalls and traps to avoid.

This icon warns you that you're about to learn technospeak.

This icon points out when Windows is likely to do something frustrating.

- It uses a light dose of humor and fun to make it easier to learn about Windows. By the same token, this book isn't a stand-up routine, because that would defeat its purpose of teaching you what you need to know about Windows in the shortest amount of time.

- It was written, edited, and published by people who use Windows every single day. This is not a book whipped up by part-time Windows users, who themselves only learned about it from another book.

- It was tested by real, honest-to-goodness beginning Windows users, just like you. When these users spotted something they didn't understand, they told us and we rewrote it.

PART I

The Basics

Includes:

1: Windows

2: Starting Programs

3: Arranging Your Programs

4: Making Windows Pretty

5: For Keyboard Lovers Only

CHAPTER 1

Windows

(The Promise of a Better Tomorrow)

IN A NUTSHELL

- What is Windows?
- Starting Windows
- Opening a window
- Starting a program
- Exiting Windows

In the next few pages, you'll be introduced to Windows, learn how to start it, play around a bit, and safely get out before you do too much damage! Just kidding about the damage. Proceed without fear.

What Is Windows?

(You had to ask, didn't you!)

Windows is a program designed to make using a computer easier. Windows is a *graphical user interface*, or *GUI* (pronounced "gooey"), which is just a fancy way of saying that Windows uses pictures instead of commands. Rather than operate your computer by using hard-to-remember commands, you do what you want by pointing to pictures.

A Short History Lesson on DOS

If Windows is the beauty, DOS is the beast. DOS (rhymes with "boss") stands for *disk operating system*. DOS communicates to the different parts of the computer—the monitor, the hard disk, the printer.

Your personal computer uses DOS as a kind of traffic cop. DOS directs the bits and pieces of information as they whiz about inside your computer. Your computer needs DOS.

The ugliest trait of DOS is that it was designed a long time ago, when most of the people using computers were engineers, scientists, and pimply faced kids who'd grow up to be billionaires. What came *out* of the computer was more important than how the various scraps of data got in there, so these technical types didn't mind learning the special secret code of computers. Heck, they reveled in it.

To get the computer to do something, its operator (they weren't called "users" back then) would type a command. If the operator didn't know a command or forgot an important one, tough luck. The computer was an unforgiving partner, responding only to the exact incantations its masters had programmed into it.

So DOS is a relic from the past, designed for a different kind of computer user. For one reason or another, it's still around to haunt us, vexing entire populations and bringing the world to its knees. Okay, that's a bit of an exaggeration. But DOS is cumbersome to use; requiring you to memorize all sorts of arcane commands and weird symbols.

Enter Windows

Windows shields you from DOS in two ways. First, Windows takes a visual approach by using a desktop metaphor. The windows in Windows are supposed to be like papers on a desk—an exact but adequate metaphor. Just as you can have many pieces of paper on top of your desk at once, with Windows you can have many different windows open at the same time.

BUZZWORDS

WINDOWS

Note the distinction between Windows (with a big W) and windows (with a little w). Windows is the program; windows are areas on-screen.

Second, instead of making you remember a long list of commands like DOS does (boo...hiss...), Windows provides a way for you to *see* the things you can do with your computer. You pick the job you want to do, and then sit back.

Checklist

- With Windows, the programs you run on your computer appear in windows. It should come as no surprise that that's where the name "Windows" comes from.
- Despite all the features and amenities that Windows provides, it still needs DOS to operate. The reasons for this are technical and involved. Trust me, you don't want to know.
- Good news: you can still use DOS programs with Windows.

The Preliminaries

I know that you are anxious to get started, but before you crank up Windows, you first have to be sure that you're ready. Check your crash helmet and then be sure that

Checklist

- Windows is already properly installed on your computer's hard disk. If it isn't, try following the instructions in the manual. If the task seems too daunting for you, enlist the help of a knowledgeable friend.
- The Windows on your computer hasn't been tinkered with. You can customize just about every aspect of Windows, which is terrific for fine-tuning it just the way you want. It's not so great if you're trying to teach someone about Windows. If your Windows doesn't look like the Windows described in this book, you might want to

reinstall it or have that knowledgeable friend of yours undo all the changes so that Windows is back to its original, out-of-the-box form.

- You have a mouse connected to your computer. Without a mouse, Windows is mean and stubborn and not worth the trouble.
- You are at least a teensy-weensy bit familiar with your PC, namely that you know how to turn it on, insert diskettes, use the keyboard, and all that.

MOUSE

A mouse is a mechanical device you slide around your real desk to move an arrow pointer on Windows' electronic desk.

PC

PC stands for *personal computer*. And no, "personal" doesn't mean the computer has to be friendly (you know better by now). It means that it's intended to be used by one person instead of shared by everyone in Iowa.

On Your Marks, Get Set, Start Windows!!

The best way to learn about Windows is to play around with it, so let's do just that. First, turn on your computer. Though all computers start up about the same way, where they end up afterward is anyone's guess. Your

computer may start up and then strand you at DOS's dreaded C:\> prompt, or it may display a menu of things for you to do. Or it may automatically start a program like Word for Windows.

Here's how to handle the likely start-up scenarios with deft, wit, and charm:

- The computer starts and Windows does too. You didn't have to do anything; your computer did all the work for you. Skip, skip, skip to the next section.
- The computer starts and leaves you at the C:\> prompt. This prompt—the DOS prompt—lets you know that the computer is ready for a command. To start Windows, type **WIN** and press the Enter key.

EXPERTS ONLY

Who-cares-how-you-do-it Dept.

WIN, win, Win, wIn…who gives a flip how you type it? In this case, your computer doesn't care about capitalization, so you can type WIN in any style you like. By convention (that is, the way most books and software manuals do it) the commands you type at the DOS prompt are shown in all uppercase letters. However, there is no rule that you must type DOS commands in all caps. Follow your heart.

- The computer starts and leaves you staring at some type of "what to do next" menu. Whoever set up your system decided what this menu should contain and how it should look. If the menu contains an option for starting Windows, choose it (you may have to press the Enter key after making the selection). If there is no Windows option but the C:\> prompt appears, type **WIN** and press the Enter key.

- The computer starts and automatically runs a program. If this happens, you must first leave that program. Exactly how this is done depends on the particular program. If you're not sure, you'll have to look at its instruction manual for guidance. If you feel adventurous, you might start pressing keys to see what effect they have. Good candidates are the Esc (Escape) key and the F7 function key. If neither of those work, press the Alt key and then press F and then X. Once you're back at DOS's familiar C:\> prompt, type **WIN** and press the Enter key.

Give yourself a pat on the back if Windows starts.

Uh-oh. Nothing happened!

You type **WIN** and press the Enter key, but nothing happens. Or worse, your computer tells you that you've done something wrong. Relax. It happens to the best of us. If your computer responds with its all-purpose error message, "Bad file or command name," be sure that you are typing the WIN command correctly. Try the command again. If an error persists, Windows may not have been installed correctly, or Windows may be stashed away in a place your computer can't easily find. You'd best get the help of a friendly, knowledgeable friend, because there's no telling what's wrong at this point.

It looked like it was starting.

Should Windows start to run but then quit, you may have serious problems. After you type WIN and press the Enter key, Windows should display a copyright screen with a big "WINDOWS" in the middle. If you see that, things are going okay so far. After a few seconds, this copyright screen should disappear, and the computer screen may momentarily blank

"I HATE THIS!"

out. This is normal. But eventually—say within 20 to 30 seconds—the screen should change to a lighter color. Within about half a minute or so, Windows should start entirely, and your hard disk should stop making wheezing and clacking noises. If the start-up process doesn't proceed in this manner, something's wrong with Windows or your computer, and you'll need to have someone take a look at it.

Getting from Here to There

Looking at the Windows screen may be a little intimidating at first, because there is no obvious way to start communicating with the blasted thing. Do you pick up the mouse and start speaking into it, like Scotty did in the movie *Star Trek IV*? Not if you don't want to look silly.

No, instead you use the mouse as your "finger" to point to the thing you want Windows to do for you. So, take mouse in hand and move it around the table. While you move the mouse, the Windows pointer arrow should move in exact unison. Congratulations! You've already mastered 75 percent of using Windows. (Really!)

The technique you're employing goes by a highly technical name called "pointing the mouse." Here are the other key mouse techniques:

Key mouse techniques

▼ *Click*. Point at something with the mouse and then quickly press and release the left button on the mouse. This is how you select things in Windows.

- *Double-click*. Point at something and then press the left button twice in quick succession. You use this method to select things in Windows and to start programs.
- *Drag*. Point at something, press and hold the left mouse button, and then move the mouse until it is where you want it. Release the mouse button. One of the things you use dragging for is to make windows larger or smaller.

EXPERTS ONLY

Tidbits about mouse buttons

Your mouse will have either two or three buttons on it. The left button is the one that does all the work. The right button isn't used very much. If you are left-handed, you can switch and use the right button for clicking, double-clicking, and dragging. Read "12 Super Simple Ways to Customize Windows" in "Quick and Dirty Dozens," toward the end of this book.

If your mouse has three buttons, you need to know that Windows never uses the middle button. But even though Windows ignores it, you can still put the middle button to good use. You can practice Morse code. Or how about tapping the rhythm to "Girl from Ipanema."

The Windows Desktop

There isn't too much to see in the Windows screen. Everything is kept in one big window, titled *Program Manager*. Behind the Program Manager window is the big, blank background. (You may or may not see the background, depending on how big the Program Manager window is.)

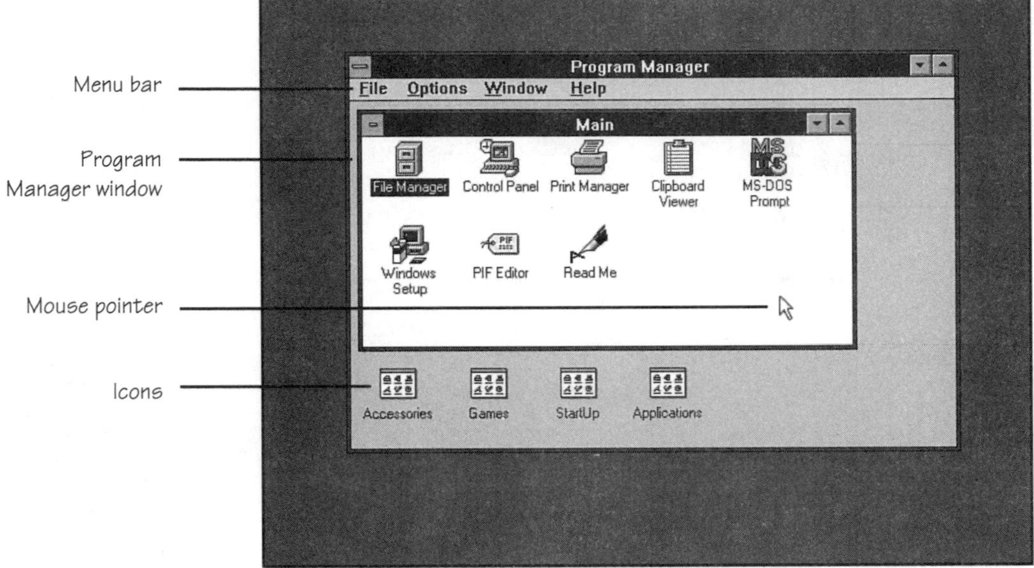

Along the top of the Program Manager window, you see a menu bar. You use the menu bar to order things, to tell Windows what to do.

Along the bottom of the window are square little pictures called *icons*. Windows uses different types of icons to represent different things. The icons shown here are storage icons, or *group icons*; they contain other stuff such as programs. To look at what's inside a group icon, you open it (coming next).

ICON

An icon—from the Greek term *eikon* (an image or representation)—is a small picture that Windows uses to represent something else, such as a program, a group of programs, or a document.

I HATE WINDOWS!

@☆#!
"I HATE THIS!"

Memorize this

You might confuse the two, but the Program Manager basically *is* Windows. You can't run Windows without running the Program Manager. If you exit the Program Manager, you exit Windows.

Opening a Window

(Finding the goodies)

To see what's inside an icon, point the mouse over one of them—say the Accessories icon—and double-click the left mouse button (click twice in rapid succession). Don't worry if nothing happens. It means you didn't double-click fast enough. Try again.

If you did it right, the icon should open up into a window. Odds are, there will be even more icons within the window you opened. These icons represent programs you can run.

Parts Is Parts

Each part of a window has a name, and although you won't be tested on this later, you should recognize the names. Then, in the next section, when I say "click on the title bar," you'll know what I mean.

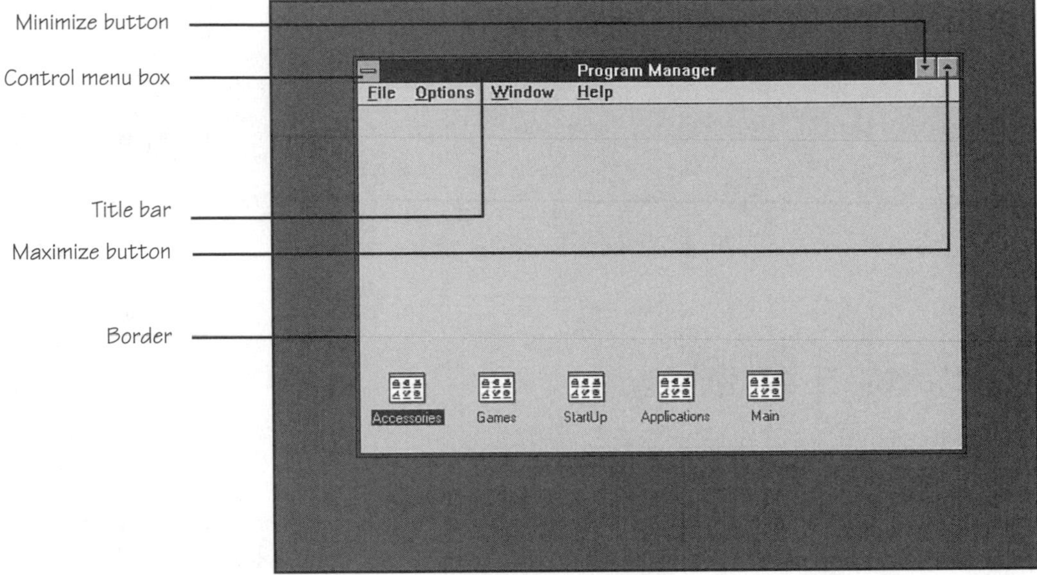

Checklist

- ▼ The title bar displays the name of the window.
- ▼ A border is just that—the border of the window. You can use borders to resize the window.
- ▼ The Control menu box looks like a mail slot and lets you control the window. Every window has one. You'll get the lowdown on window control in a little while.
- ▼ The Maximize button and Minimize button are covered in the next chapter. Hold your horses.

Rearranging Windows

With the window open, you can now move it and change its size. There's no great need to move and resize a window, but it will make you feel like you've accomplished *something*. Also, moving the windows around may appeal to your aesthetic sense.

To move a window, place the mouse pointer along the very top border (the title bar). Press and hold the left mouse button and move the mouse around the table. The window goes with it. (This is called "dragging," remember?) Release the mouse button when you're tired of moving the window.

To change the size of a window, carefully place the mouse pointer on a border. Notice that the mouse pointer changes shape from a single-tipped arrow to a double-tipped arrow. Drag the mouse (press and hold the left button and move the mouse) to change the size of the window.

Closing a Window

To close the window (turn it back into an icon), double-click on the Control menu box—it looks like a "mail slot" and is in the upper left corner.

CONTROL MENU BOX

The Control menu box is the mail slot at the upper left corner of a window. Double-clicking this box closes the window.

Starting a Program

Windows is primarily a tool for starting other programs. Starting a program in Windows is as easy as double-clicking on a program's icon. Try it out.

Windows includes it's own calculator program. To run this program, find the icon labeled *Accessories* and double-click on it. The icon opens into a window to reveal what's inside.

Next, find the program icon labeled *Calculator*. To start the Calculator, double-click on its icon, appropriately shaped like a calculator.

The Calculator window opens on your screen. You can punch some numbers in if you'd like, just to see how the thing works. Just use the mouse to click on the Calculator keys.

When you're done messing around, close the Calculator by double-clicking on its Control menu box. To close the Accessories window, double-click on the Control menu box for that window.

Saying Goodbye to Windows for Now

You've had fun, yes, but now it's time to bid adieu and say "farewell" to Windows. To leave Windows, click on File in the menu bar. The File menu appears. Find the Exit Windows command at the bottom of the menu, and click on it. (By the way, you're not only learning how to exit here, you're also learning how to use the Windows menu system.)

TIP

Instead of using the Exit Windows command, you can double-click on the Program Manager's Control menu box and then click on OK to exit.

To make sure that you really want to leave, Windows double-checks with you by popping up a dialog box. This box contains two buttons: OK and Cancel. Click on the OK button. Windows complies with your request and, within a second or two, you are out of Windows and back at the DOS prompt, the black screen with C:\>.

BUZZWORDS

DIALOG BOX

A dialog box appears when you make certain menu selections. The dialog box is usually double-checking to make sure that you really want to do something or is asking for more information.

Once back at the DOS prompt, you can restart Windows, you can turn your computer off, or you can leave your computer on and just stare at the screen for the rest of the day.

CAUTION

Don't turn off your computer unless you are back at the DOS prompt. Why not? Because of lots of technical reasons—*good* technical reasons. Just take my word for it.

Shoe
By Jeff MacNelly

STOP LOOKING AT ME THAT WAY...

ACK!! I CAN'T GET THIS STUPID COMPUTER TO WORK RIGHT!!
MUST BE THE HARD DRIVE.

WHAT AM I SAYING?! I WOULDN'T KNOW A HARD DRIVE IF IT FELL IN MY COFFEE..

I'VE TRIED EVERYTHING.

I'VE PUNCHED EVERY KEY.

EVERY COMBINATION OF KEYS...

THERE'S ONLY ONE THING LEFT TO DO.

THE LAST RESORT:

READ THE DIRECTIONS.
6-23

CHAPTER 2

Starting Programs

(We Have Liftoff!)

IN A NUTSHELL

- What programs do I have?
- Where did the icons come from?
- Starting programs
- Tinkering with the size of your windows
- Exiting programs
- Running two or more programs
- Switching between programs

Perhaps the biggest and most important job Windows does is run other programs. This job is handled by the ever-faithful Program Manager. This chapter introduces you to the Program Manager. First you see which programs you have; then you learn how to run them.

PROGRAM

A program is a set of instructions your computer uses to perform some task. The computer follows each instruction in turn until the program ends, sort of like instructions on how to get to get to Uncle Lou's house: "Go down I-81 until you see the old dairy, turn left, go 5.2 miles, hang a right at the swamp...." Instructions in a program are in code, so only your computer can understand them.

The biggest frustration with the Program Manager is that it's so flexible. You can open more than one program, and you can open a program in more than one way. You also can arrange your windows in more than one way. There's not just one plain, simple scenario. But take heart. This chapter helps you make sense of all the possibilities. And once you experiment and see that "Oh, this happens," you'll quickly get the hang of Windows.

Which Program Icons Do I Have?

You know, it's a lot easier to simply point at something with your finger and say, "Gimme one of them," than to have to describe where it is, detail by detail. Pointing may not always be polite, but it's a faster way to tell others what you want.

Ditto for Windows. When you want to start a program, you just point to an icon and double-click on it with your mouse. Simple. Elegant. No mess.

There are two kinds of icons you can see in Windows' Program Manager: program group icons and program icons.

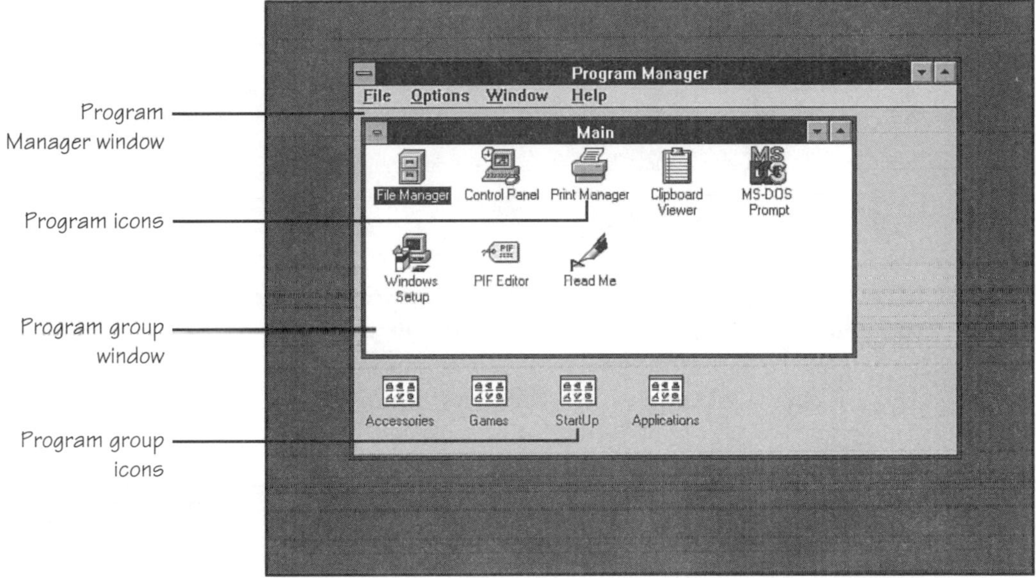

Program group icons look like little windows. These icons are simply containers: they store program icons inside them. The name of the program group appears below the group icon. If you double-click on a program group icon, a new window appears—a group window. Inside the group window are the program icons.

Each program icon represents a program. The name of the program is right underneath the icon. If you double-click on a program icon, you will start that program.

Program Groups Help Sort Out the Mess

When you install Windows, the Program Manager starts out with a small collection of program groups and places selected program icons inside them. The groups keep your program icons separated by category so that you can find them more easily.

TIP

There is no reason to keep the same program groups Windows first offers. In fact, it's an instant give-away that you're a Windows greenhorn if you don't change the program groups! The next chapter tells you to how personalize your program groups.

The program groups are named to give you a better idea of what kind of programs are inside them. The name appears below the program group icon. Here's the original, out-of-the-box collection of program groups Windows gives you when you first install it:

Checklist

- *Accessories*. This program group contains a bunch of simple programs, like a basic word processor and a graphics "painting" program. These accessory programs are supplied with Windows.
- *Main*. This group contains a collection of programs that supports Windows in one way or another. These programs come with Windows.
- *Games*. This program group contains two games: Solitaire and Minesweeper. These programs are supplied with Windows.
- *StartUp*. This program group doesn't contain anything, unless you or someone else puts a program icon in it. Programs in the StartUp group automatically run themselves when Windows starts.

- *Non-Windows Applications*. This program group may or may not appear in your Program Manager window. It contains popular DOS programs that were located when Windows was first installed on your computer. The group won't be there if your computer doesn't have any DOS programs, or if you decided to skip that part when you installed Windows.
- *Applications*. Like the Non-Windows Applications group, this program group may or may not be in your Program Manager window. It contains Windows programs that were located when Windows was first installed on your computer.

BUZZWORDS

APPLICATION

An application is a type of program you use to create something, like a letter or a spreadsheet. The word *application* (or "app") is often used simply as a synonym for *program*. There are two types of applications: DOS applications (designed to work with DOS) and Windows applications (designed to work with Windows). You can run DOS applications in Windows, but you can't run Windows applications if you just have DOS.

Where Did the Icons Come From?

Where do icons come from? Do they appear during a full moon? Do elves put them there? No, nothing as magical as that. Program icons are placed in the Program Manager by Windows, by a Windows program, or by you.

Windows Put Them There

When you first installed Windows, it snooped around your hard disk looking for DOS and Windows programs such as Excel or Word for Windows. When it found a Windows program or a DOS program it recognized, Windows created an icon for it.

Checklist

- DOS programs are placed in the Non-Windows Applications group icon.
- Windows programs are placed in the Applications group icon.
- During installation, Windows also added the Accessories, Games, and Main group icons. Inside these groups it put icons for its very own programs, like Write (a word processor), Solitaire (a card game), and File Manager (a file and disk management program). You didn't have these programs before; they came with Windows. Windows also made the StartUp group icon, but didn't put anything in it.

A Program Put Them There

In most cases, when you install a Windows program, it will create a new group icon and place its own program icon inside that group. Some Windows programs come with more than one program you can run, so you might find more than one program icon inside the group.

I HATE WINDOWS!

I Can Put Them There?

At any time, you can add your own program icons to Program Manager. You also can delete program icons you don't use or want. And you can move program icons between program groups to better organize them to suit your tastes. Chapter 3 describes these tricks.

@☆#!
"I HATE THIS!"

Hey! I don't have icons for all my programs!!

Don't worry. Windows may not have created an icon for every program on your computer's hard disk. It only knows the most popular programs. There's nothing wrong with Windows if you don't see an icon for one of your programs. You can always add an icon for a program yourself (see Chapter 9).

Starting Programs

(With a click click here, and a click click there...)

You've got the icons. Now what? With those icons, you can start, run, launch, invoke, open, boot, tee off, or rev up a program (pick the term you like). If that program has an icon, read this section.

If that program doesn't have an icon, you can make one for it. Or you can tell Windows the name of the program and say, "Run this baby." Either way, this stuff is heavy duty, and I'm saving it for Chapter 9.

Is the icon right there in front of you? Probably not. It's nestled warmly inside one of those program group icons. You'll need to get at the program icon.

Start by double-clicking the program group that contains the program icon you want. (You can say "Open Sez Me" while you double-click,

though this isn't strictly required.) The program icon opens up into a window—a program group window—where you should see the program icon you want.

Zowie! I Do See the Program Icon I Want!

Then what are you waiting for? Double-click on the icon! The program will open in a window of its own. The name of the program will appear in the window's title bar.

Checklist

- The size of the program window may vary. Some programs open in a full, maximized, hog-the-screen window. Others open in a smaller window.
- To get out of the program, flip ahead to the section "Exiting a Program" in this chapter.
- Oops! Windows displayed an error message when you double-clicked on the program icon. Read the error message, click the OK button to make the message go away, then read Chapter 9 to find out what to do about it.

EXPERTS ONLY

Variety is the spice of Windows

If you don't like the click-click method, you can do either of the following to start a program: Click once on the program icon to select it, and then press the Enter key. Or click once on the program icon to select it; then click on the File menu and choose the Open command.

Sorry, I Don't See the Program Icon I Want

Okay, this happens sometimes. But just because you don't see the icon for the program doesn't mean that it isn't in the group window. It might be there, but hidden from view.

Does the program group window have a scroll bar on either the right side or the bottom? Windows will sprout scroll bars when there's more inside the window than it can show at once. Use the mouse to click on the arrows of the scroll bar to see the other icons in the window. You also can use the mouse to drag the "scroll box" within the scroll bar to scroll more quickly.

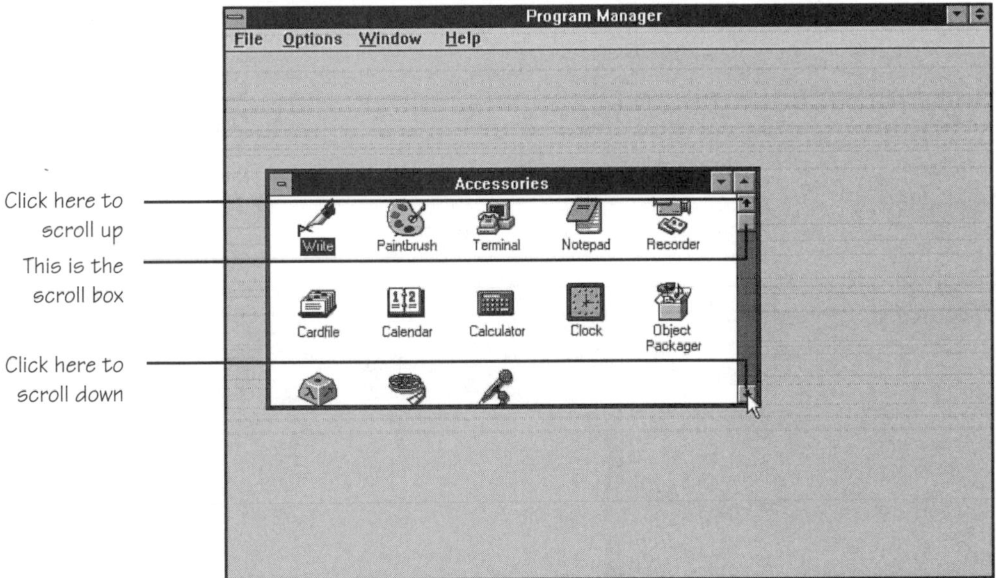

When you click on one of the arrows at either end of the scroll bar, the window scrolls in the direction of that arrow, letting you see more of the window's contents.

If there's no scroll bar, the group window is showing you all it's got, and it's got no more. So if you still don't see the program icon you want, close the window and try another group. To close the window, double-click on the Control menu box in the upper left corner. Then double-click on another group icon to see whether the program you want is inside it.

"I HATE THIS!"

No, no, no! Don't double-click on the Control menu box in the upper left corner of the big Program Manager window.

Doing that says you want to exit Program Manager, which will end Windows, which will put you back at the DOS prompt (don't pass Go and don't collect $200)! Each program group window you open has its own Control menu box, always shown as a short dash. That's what you want to double-click on.

TIP

If you know the name of the program group you want to open, here's a shortcut that might save you some time: Click on the Window menu; you'll see a list of program group windows. Click on the program group you want. Voilà! That window opens for you.

Tinkering with the Window Size

Some programs open in a maximized window—one that appears full screen. Others open in a smaller window. You can control the size of the window.

Big, Big, Big

To fill the screen with the window, find the up-arrow button in the upper right corner of the window (this is the *Maximize button*), and click on it.

Checklist

- ▼ When a window is "maximized," it is as big as it gets: you can't resize or move it.
- ▼ If the window is already maximized, you won't see an up-arrow button. It will be a button with a two-headed, up-and-down arrow on it. You can use this button to restore the window (coming up in "Somewhere In Between").
- ▼ Another clue that the window is already maximized is that there won't be any borders around the window.

Little, Little, Little

To reduce a window to an icon, find the down-arrow button in the upper right corner of the window (this is the *Minimize button*), and click on it.

Checklist

- ▼ Keep in mind that the program is still running. It's like putting the car in park, but not turning it off. You don't have to restart the car—or the program—to use it. If you do want to "turn off" (close) the program, read on.

continues

Checklist Continued

- Remember that if you want to return to a program you've minimized, you just double-click on its icon.
- When you minimize a program *group* window, it's closed. This icon doesn't really "do" much—that is, it doesn't start a program or anything—so basically you will just be opening it or closing it. It won't be running, like programs do.

Somewhere In Between

To make the window smaller than full-screen, find the double-arrow button in the upper right corner of the window (this is the *Restore button*), and click on it.

Checklist

- When a window is not full-screen, you can change its size. Monkeying with the size of windows is covered in Chapter 1. It's one the easiest things to do.
- When a program is maximized, you can't see anything else. Restore the window to a smaller size if you need to see the Program Manager or some other program in the background.

TIP

The windows on your on-screen desktop are like papers on your regular desk. A big piece of paper (a maximized window) might cover up everything else. To see what's beneath the paper (window), you have to move it or put it away (close it).

TIP

Sometimes you can see just parts of the papers on the desk. And sometimes you have to look around through lots of stuff to find what you need.

The Case of the Missing Program Manager

Keep in mind that the Program Manager is itself a program, so you can minimize its window, too. When you click the Minimize (down-arrow) button in the upper right corner of the Program Manager, its window shrinks to an icon, and the icon appears along the bottom of your screen. You can see the entire Program Manager again (make it a window) by double-clicking on this icon.

"I HATE THIS!"

Don't mess with the Program Manager

You can minimize the Program Manager and still have other programs running, but you cannot exit the Program Manager—that is, not without quitting Windows. You see, exiting the Program Manager is the same as exiting Windows.

Exiting a Program

(Let me out!)

You've learned how to get into a program, but how do you get out? Well, there are lots of ways.

The Program Has an Exit Command

Many Windows programs have a File menu, and one of the command items in this menu is called Exit (usually near the bottom of the File menu). To leave the program, click on the File menu; then click on Exit.

In some programs you might write text, or draw a picture, or do something else that you want to keep. If you try to leave the program without first saving your work, Windows will ask whether you want to save your effort. This confirmation appears in a dialog box, which typically has three buttons. Click the button that does what you want:

- Click Yes to save your work in a file. You'll need to type the name of the file (you get to choose the name), and press Enter when you're done. After your work is saved, the program ends.
- Click No if you don't want save your work. The program ends, and the stuff you were working on is lost forever. Choose this option with care.
- Click Cancel if you want to think about it some more. The program doesn't save your work, and your request to leave the program is ignored. You're back where you started.

When the program ends, Windows puts you back in the Program Manager.

TIP

If you want to know even more about saving files, you should check out Chapter 10.

BUZZWORDS

FILE

You computer doesn't just scatter data on the hard disk drive. Instead, it puts the data into "files." A program is one kind of file. Documents—such as letters and spreadsheets—that you create with applications are another kind of file. When you save your work, it's put in a file, and the file is given a name so you can use it later. For more info on the fascinating subject of files, see Chapter 6.

The Program Doesn't Have an Exit Command

If your program doesn't have an Exit command, you're still in luck: every well-made Windows program has a Control menu box, and every Control menu has a Close command.

First, click once on the program's Control menu box (it's in the upper left corner, beside the title bar). Then click on the Close command. As a shortcut, you can simply double-click on the Control menu box.

TIP

You might see two or more Control menu boxes in some programs. One Control menu box is for the program itself and is always located to the left of the program's title bar. Any other Control menu boxes are for windows you've opened from within the program. To leave the program, you want to use the top Control menu box—the one with the long bar, not the short dash.

When you use the Exit command, some programs ask for confirmation first. Click the Yes, No, or Cancel button.

There's No Exit Command and No Control Menu Box!

Ah ha! Sounds like you're using a DOS program, in which case there is no "standard" way to leave the program. If you don't know the magic incantations of how to get out, you'll need to consult the instruction manual for the program or ask someone who knows.

For your convenience, and to help you get out of the jam you've gotten yourself into, here are "get me outta here" instructions for a handful of popular DOS programs. These instructions don't include saving the work you've done with that program, so if you want to do that, you'll need some extra help.

If you're using	Then press these keys
WordPerfect for DOS	F7, N, Y
Microsoft Word for DOS	Alt, F, X
WordStar for DOS	Ctrl+K, X
Lotus 1-2-3 for DOS	/ (slash), Q, Y
Quattro Pro for DOS	/ (slash), F, X, Y
Quicken for DOS	Esc, E
MS-DOS Editor	Alt, F, X
MS-DOS Shell	Alt, F, X

If the keys in this table are separated with a comma, press them one after the other. If separated with a plus sign (+), press and hold the first key and then press the second key.

Getting a Program Out of the Way Instead of Ending It

You don't have to leave a program before you can do something else in Windows. Just put the program on "standby" by shrinking its window (minimizing it) into an icon. To get a program temporarily out of the way, minimize its window by clicking on the down-arrow button in the upper right corner of the window.

When you minimize the window, it shrinks into an icon—effectively tucked away until you want to use it again. This icon is placed along the very bottom of your screen. The program is still running, and you can return to it whenever you want. To go back to using the program, just double-click on the icon; the window will expand back out again.

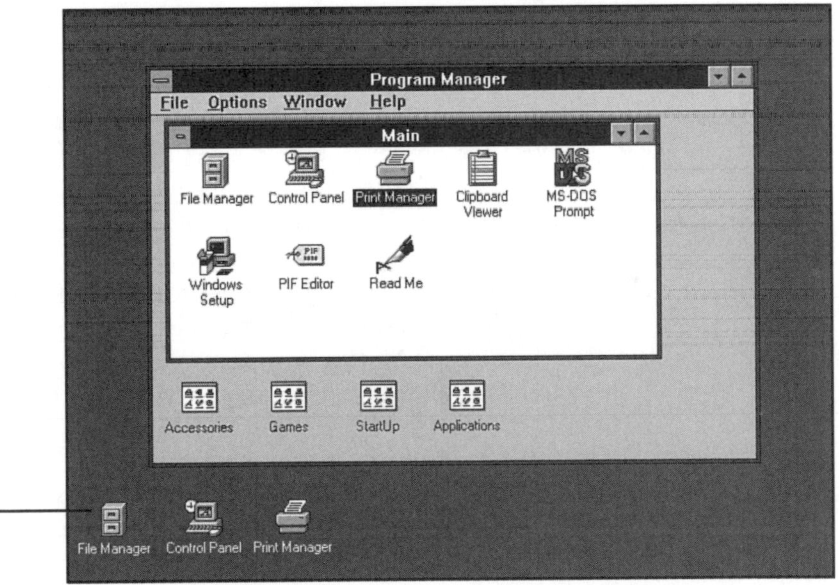

Minimized programs (still running)

"I HATE THIS!"

I can't see the icon!

Uh oh! You minimized your program window, but there's no icon for it at the bottom of your screen? In that case, the Program Manager window or another window is filling up the entire screen. To see the icon, click the Restore button (the double arrow) in the upper right corner of the window. This restores the Program Manager window to less than full-screen. You should now be able to see your program icon.

Running Two (or More) Programs

With Windows, you can run more than one program at once. Why would you want to?

- Because perhaps you never like to finish anything. You want to be able to start one program, do some work, change your mind, and go on to something else (promising to get right back to that first task).
- Or maybe you like to have everything close at hand. You don't want to look at a report without being able to look at some financial figures too. And while you're at it, you just might want to keep a window open for drawing, in case you want to doodle.
- Another possibility is that you might want to run a work-related program and a fun game at the same time. (Switching between them is easy, as described next in "Program Hopping.")
- Or it's entirely possible that you just like to run more than one program simply because you can. Who says you need to have a reason?!

To run the first program, start it the normal way: double-click on the program group icon, then double-click on the program icon.

The program will start, and it'll be contained in a window. Now to start the second program. Keep reading.

I Can Still See a Bit of the Program Manager on My Screen

If you can still see part of the Program Manager (because your program window doesn't fill the entire screen), start the second program by doing the same thing: First, click on the Program Manager window so that you can see all of it. Next, double-click on the program group icon, and then double-click on the icon of the second program.

Alas! The Program Manager Is Gone! Now What?

No, the Program Manager is not gone; it's just hidden by your program window. If you can't see the Program Manager, press Alt+Esc (hold down the Alt key and then press Esc), and the Program Manager will appear. Click anywhere on the Program Manager window. For the second program you want to run, double-click on the program group icon and then on the program icon.

Checklist

- ▼ Each program you open will appear in a separate window. The name of the program is shown in the title bar at the top of the window.

continues

Checklist Continued

- You may not be able to see the windows for both programs at the same time, but you can still move between programs—something you learn in the next section.
- If you can see both windows on-screen, the window on top denotes the active window. And the active window represents the active program.

BUZZWORDS

ACTIVE WINDOW

Windows allows only one program to be active at a time. Any other program that is running is put into a Sleeping Beauty–type slumber and is not awakened until you "kiss" it by clicking on it with the mouse or by using one of the methods detailed in "Program Hopping," next. The window for the active program is the one on top. That window also has a colored title bar (it's shaded if you have a single-color monitor). Windows for inactive programs appear underneath, and their title bars are grayed out (or white).

Program Hopping

If you have more than one program running at the same time, you can easily move from one to the next. To switch to a different program, just click on the window you want. Or you can pick the program from a Task List.

The Program I Want Is Visible

If the program you want to use is visible in a window on-screen, click on that window. That program becomes active.

The Program I Want Isn't Visible

If the program window you want is not visible, minimize one or more of the windows that are in the way. You minimize a window by clicking on its minimize button, the down-arrow button in the upper right corner of the window.

Or you can close the other windows completely, if you're done with them. To close a window, double-click on its Control menu box (located at the top left corner). When you close a program window, you leave the program!

Another Method: Switching with the Task List

You can also switch to the program you want by using a nifty built-in feature of the Program Manager; it's called the *Task List* ("task" is another name for a program that's running). The Task List displays all the programs currently chugging along in Windows.

First, display the Task List. One way is to press Ctrl+Esc (hold down the Ctrl key and then press Esc). Another way is to click once on the Control menu box for the active program, and then click on Switch To.

The Task List

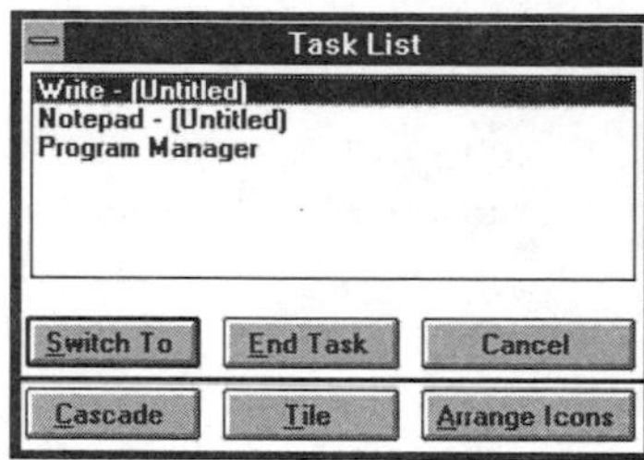

TIP

If none of your windows fills the whole screen, there is a third way to display the Task List: double-click anywhere on the screen "background," behind the Program Manager. But if the Program Manager or some other program window does fill the screen, you first have to make the window smaller by clicking its Restore button—the double-arrow button in the upper right corner.

No matter which way you summon it, the Task List appears with a list of all the programs you can switch to. Double-click on the program you want, and the Program Manager zips you right to its window.

Using Keyboard Shortcuts to Switch Programs

You can also use keyboard shortcuts to cycle through the running programs.

Press Alt+Esc. All program windows (including the one for the Program Manager) appear on your screen, one-by-one, each time you press Alt+Esc. Keep pressing Alt+Esc until you see the program or icon you want. When the program you want is on-screen, stop. If it's an icon, stop and then double-click on the icon.

I HATE WINDOWS!

Press Alt+Tab, but keep the Alt key pressed down. In the middle of the screen, the name of a currently running program appears. Release the Alt key if the program displayed is the one you want. If not, press Tab until you see the name of the program you want (remember, don't let go of the Alt key until you get to the right program).

"I HATE THIS!"

What gives? Alt+Tab doesn't do a thing for me!

If you press Alt+Tab but the Program Manager doesn't display the name of a currently running program, the "Fast Alt+Tab Switching" option is not turned on. (That's what the option is called, really.) Take a look at Chapter 17 to find out how to turn on this option—something you definitely should do, because it's a really neat, time-saving gimmick.

CHAPTER 3

Arranging Your Programs (A Place for Everything and Everything in Its Place)

IN A NUTSHELL

- How to keep the Program Manager neat and tidy
- Making your very own program groups
- Moving program icons between groups
- Copying program icons
- Changing program icon titles
- Changing program group titles
- Getting rid of icons you don't need

Once you've used the Program Manager for a while, you'll want to rearrange and organize things to better suit your tastes and way of working. You might want to put all your work programs in one group and your fun stuff in another. Or, if you aren't the only one who uses the computer, you can set up workgroups for yourself, your spouse, the kids, your grandmother, the dog, and so on.

In this chapter you'll learn all about keeping the Program Manager windows tidy and clean. And you'll learn how to change the text that appears under group and program icons.

Felix Unger's Program Manager

(All neat and tidy)

The Program Manager can become quite messy with all those windows and icons everywhere. If you're the Felix Unger type (he was the clean one in "The Odd Couple"), you'll want to arrange your Program Manager windows and icons from time to time to keep things tidy. The Program Manager doesn't do this for you, though it has some built-in tools to make the job a little easier.

Here are some ways to keep the place straightened, in case company drops by unexpectedly.

All Right, Who Left the Window Open?

The first thing you should do to get rid of window clutter is close all the windows you don't need. Keep windows open only if you use them quite a bit. Open a group window when you need to access something inside;

otherwise, keep group windows closed. To close a group window, double-click on its Control menu box.

Cascade or Tile (Shipshape windows)

You can also have the Program Manager quickly arrange the windows in a neat and orderly fashion, with at least a portion of each open window visible.

Choose the Tile command from the Window menu if you want the Program Manager to place all the open windows side-by-side. The Program Manager will shrink the size of the windows so that they all fit.

These windows are tiled

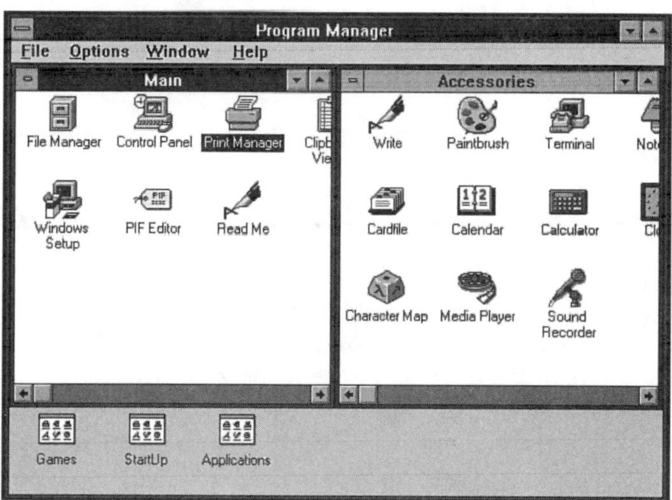

Choose the Cascade command from the Window menu if you want the Program Manager to give all the open windows a tasteful "waterfall"

effect. The Program Manager stacks the windows on top of one another, but leaves each title bar visible so that you can choose the window you want by clicking on it.

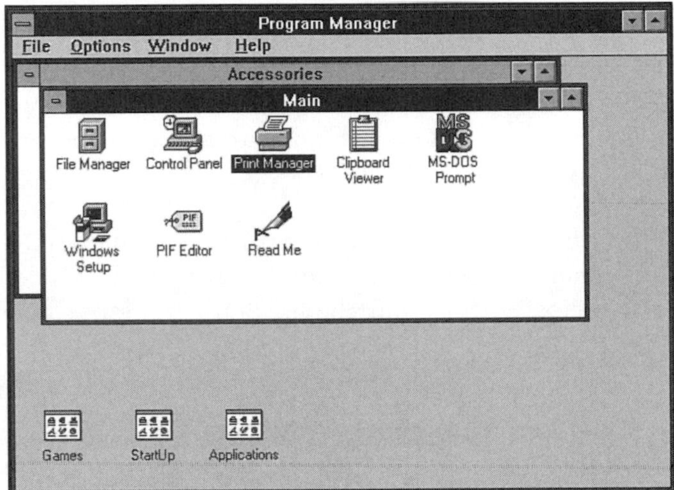

These windows are cascaded

Straighten Those Icons (All your icons in a row)

When all your group windows are closed, you may find that your program group icons are all over the Program Manager screen. To straighten them, click on the Window menu, and click the Arrange Icons command. This puts all the icons in neat little rows.

You can do the same thing to arrange the icons in your group windows. Open the window you want to straighten. Then click the Window menu, and click the Arrange Icons command. The icons in the currently active group window quickly snap to attention, all in a row.

TIP

If scroll bars appear on the bottom or right side of the window, it means that the window has more icons than it can show you at once. You may want to adjust the size of the window to accommodate all the icons. Change the size of the window by dragging any side or corner of the window. The art of moving and resizing windows is detailed in Chapter 1.

TIP

If you want to give your icons more room so that they don't line up so closely, change the icon spacing. This tidbit is covered in the next chapter.

Using Auto Arrange (Let the maid do it)

If you find yourself getting sick and tired of constantly fudging with the icons in group windows, just to keep them neat and orderly, you might appreciate this little trick: open the Options menu and choose the Auto Arrange command.

When Auto Arrange is on, the Program Manager will automatically adjust the position of the icons when you alter the size of the group window.

Checklist

- When Auto Arrange is turned on, a check mark appears next to the command. This tells you that Auto Arrange is active.
- Choose the command again to turn it off. The check mark goes away.

The Program Manager automatically saves your window and icon settings each time you leave Windows. That way, the next time you see Windows, it will look the same as it did the last time you saw it. Nuf said?

EXPERTS ONLY

Don't want to save?

If you don't want to save your "look," open the Options menu. You should see a check mark beside the Save Settings on Exit command, which means that it's on. Choose this command to turn off the feature and remove the check mark. When you exit Windows, it will forget how your windows and icons look.

Now suppose that you are exiting Windows but want to save the way your screen looks, just this once. Even though the Save Settings on Exit feature is turned off, you can record a "snapshot" of your icons and windows so that the Program Manager remembers them the next time you start Windows. Here's how: press and hold the Shift key, click on the File menu, and then click on the Exit Windows command. This records the window and icon settings; it DOES NOT exit the Program Manager (which would end Windows and return you to DOS).

Because the Save Settings on Exit feature is turned off, you have to go through this "Shift-Exit Windows" technique manually each time you want the Program Manager to take a new snapshot. My advice? Just leave the Save Settings on Exit feature on.

Creating Your Own Program Groups

Program groups are designed to help you classify your program icons. How you classify them is up to you (personally, I like to classify mine as animal, vegetable, or mineral).

TIP

> If you have a lot of programs, it's probably not a good idea to have a program group for each program you have. You'll constantly be opening and closing and opening group windows to find what you need. Plus, the Program Manager will get all cluttered with group icons. Instead, create a few key groups and keep your program icons within those groups.

To create a new group, follow these steps:

1. Click on the Program Manager window to make it active.
2. Click on the File menu and click on the New command.

   The New Program Object dialog box opens up.

3. In this box click Program Group as the kind of icon you want to create, and click OK.

The Program Group Properties dialog box opens

Program Group Properties

Description:

Group File:

OK

Cancel

Help

4. Click inside the Description entry blank (text box) and type the name of your new group, such as *Word Processors* or *Graphics Stuff* or *The Ronettes*—whatever suits your fancy. Leave the other entry blank, Group File, empty.

5. Click OK to tell the Program Manager that you're ready for it to make a new program group icon.

   A new, blank program group is created. This new window opens.

Checklist

- ▼ The new group window is empty; it contains no program icons. You have to put them there. The next section tells you how to shuffle icons around.
- ▼ You might get a creative burst later and want to use a better name for the group. You can change the name. This trick is covered later in this chapter, in "Changing the Name of a Program Group Icon."

Moving Program Icons

(The icon shuffle)

Windows doesn't force you to keep your program icons in the same group window. You can move them back and forth whenever you like. In fact, you might want to do this from time to time to organize your Program Manager "desktop."

To move icons from one group window to another, you first have to open the program group that contains the icon you want to move. Then, of course, you open the program group to which you want to move the program icon. Got that? You should have two windows open and should be able to see part of both. (If you can't see at least part of both windows, move or resize them.)

Point to the icon you want to move. Hold down the mouse button and drag the icon into the new window. Release the mouse button to put the icon into its new home.

"I HATE THIS!"

It's giving me the universal "NO" sign.

The Program Manager allows you to put program icons only into a group window. You can't place a program icon outside a group window. If you try to dump the program icon onto the desktop, the Program Manager let's you know that what you are doing is taboo by displaying the slash-and-circle symbol.

TIP

Here's a timesaver when moving icons from one group to another: Leave the "destination" group icon closed (don't open it into a window). Drag the program icon you want to move directly over the destination group icon. The Program Manager will "drop" the program icon into the group!

Copying Program Icons

(Double duty)

Instead of just moving program icons from one group to another, you can copy them. You'll end up with an original and a copy. For example, you might want to put a copy of the game Tetris in every program group.

To copy an icon, press and hold down the Ctrl key. Now use the mouse to drag the icon where you want it. Don't release the Ctrl key until you have dragged the icon to the right place. Except for holding down the Ctrl key, the procedure for copying program icons is exactly the same as it is for moving them.

Checklist

- ▼ A program icon isn't the program itself, but a "pointer" to the program file on your hard disk drive.
- ▼ Because you aren't actually copying the program itself, copying program icons doesn't waste any hard disk space by duplicating program files.

Changing the Name of a Program Group Icon

(The name game)

Unlike changing your name to Fred or Sue, which involves filling out all sorts of long forms and maybe even having a sex-change operation, it's pretty easy to alter the title that appears below a program group icon.

- ▼ You might want to make the title shorter. Short titles fit under the icons better and don't clutter up the screen as much. The less the clutter, the easier it is to find things.
- ▼ You might want to make the title more meaningful to you. Like what about that group called "Main"? If this group is such a "main"

one, why do we rarely use it? My favorite title for the Main group is "Random Stuff." It seems more appropriate.

- You might want the title to better reflect the contents of the group. If you get into the habit of moving program icons from one group to another, after a while the group titles may no longer represent what's inside them.

To change the title of a program group, click once (don't double-click) on the icon. Open the File menu and then choose the Properties command. A dialog box named Program Group Properties opens.

TIP

As a shortcut to opening the Program Group Properties dialog box, press and hold down the Alt key. Now double-click on the title of the group icon you want to change. Be sure that you double-click on the icon's title, not the icon itself; otherwise, the program group window will open. If this happens, close the window and try again.

In the dialog box find the entry blank labeled *Description*; it contains the name of the program group and is what you want to change. Notice that this text is highlighted (shown with a dark background), which means that the text is selected and that Windows is waiting for you to indicate what you want done with the text.

Press the Del key to erase all of the text. After deleting the text, you will see the flashing insertion point (also called a *cursor*) at the beginning of the Description entry blank.

Now type the new title for the program group. When you're done, click the OK button. The new title appears below the group icon.

Checklist

- You can use the space bar and all other keys, but you're limited to 30 characters for the name.
- Keep your names short and descriptive.

Changing the Title of a Program Icon

(An icon by any other name)

You can change the title of your program icons, just as you can with group icons. To change the program icon title, click once (don't double-click) on the icon. Open the File menu and choose the Properties command. The Program Item Properties dialog box appears.

TIP

> You can use a nifty shortcut to get to the Program Item Properties dialog: Press and hold down the Alt key. Now double-click on the icon (either the title or the icon—it doesn't matter with a program icon). Be sure to keep the Alt key pressed down as you double-click or you'll start the program. If this happens, exit the program and try again.

Press Del to erase the text that's currently in the Description entry box. This text is the old icon title. Type the new icon title (up to 30 characters). When you're done, click the OK button. The new title appears below the program icon.

TIP

If the name of an icon is really long, you can wrap it to two lines. This trick is unveiled in the next chapter.

Deleting Program Icons

(Out icon!)

Program icons only *represent* programs that are on your computer's hard disk drive; they aren't the programs themselves. If you delete the icon, you aren't deleting the program.

If you no longer use an icon, you can delete it. Or if you do delete the program from your hard disk, you'll want to delete the icon for it as well. This keeps you from accidentally trying to use the icon at some later date.

To delete a program icon, click on it once to select it. Open the File menu and choose the Delete command (or, as a shortcut, just press the Del key).

The Program Manager won't believe you at first; it double-checks to make sure that you really want to delete such a beautiful icon. Yes you do, so click the Yes button in the dialog box message that appears.

Be really, really, REALLY sure that you want to delete that program icon! Go slowly and triple-check that you've put the right icon on death row. Then, and only then, hit the Del key. Once the icon is gone, it's history. Sure, you can always create a new icon for the program—and you'll learn about this in Chapter 9—but the job is a bit complex if you're new to Windows.

Deleting a Program Group Icon

Let's suppose that you're feeling really adventurous and want to wipe out an entire program group. Well, the first thing you have to do is make sure that no icons are in it. You'd better open the program group (double-click on its icon), just to be sure.

If there are icons inside and you want to keep them, move them to a new group.

Minimize the window by clicking on the Minimize button—the down-arrow button in the upper right corner of the window.

Next, click on the program group icon once (don't double-click). A little pop-up menu will open, showing commands for what to do next. Click on the Close command in the pop-up menu, or press the Esc key. The pop-up menu disappears, and the group icon becomes selected. The icon is now active, which means that whatever you do next will affect it.

Delete the icon by pressing the Del key. To let the Program Manager know that you really, really want to get rid of the icon, click the Yes button in the dialog box message that appears.

CHAPTER 4

Making Windows Pretty (ooooh! aaahhhh!)

IN A NUTSHELL

- Changing the colors of Windows
- Painting a new desktop
- Picking out a desktop pattern
- Hanging wallpaper on your desktop
- Giving your icons more space
- Turning the sizing grid on and off
- Making the cursor blink faster or slower

Here's your chance to be an interior decorator of Windows. Windows is yours. You own it, and you can do what you want with it. There are no laws that say you must use Windows the way it came out of the box.

Don't like the color of the desktop? Don't like the way the mouse blinks? Change it! With DOS you are stuck with the ugly old black screen. With Windows you can use any color combination you want. This chapter is your key to Windows decorating.

Warning! Changing colors or the pattern or the wallpaper in Windows won't make you get more work done. It's just a high-tech way of tinkering around so that Windows looks cool. If you are interested only in productivity, skip this chapter.

Make It Pink! No, Make It Blue!

Your first step in making Windows oh-so-you is to change its colors. Windows lets you change the shade and hue of just about everything you see, including the title bar at the top of windows, window borders, backgrounds, text, menu bars...you name it.

The Windows Paint Department

To change the colors, first double-click on the Main program group icon to open it into a window. Find the Control Panel icon in the Main window and double-click on it to open the Control Panel. Inside are a bunch more icons. These icons represent "mini-programs" that let you control the way Windows works—hence the name Control Panel.

Look for a program icon called Color and double-click on it. The mini-program starts and the Color dialog box appears. Notice that in the middle of this dialog box is a picture—a representation of all the major parts of a window. Let's call this the "Example Picture."

What you see is only half of the Color dialog box. Click that big button named Color Palette to see the rest of the box. Poof! The Color dialog box doubles in size. Your painting tools are ready.

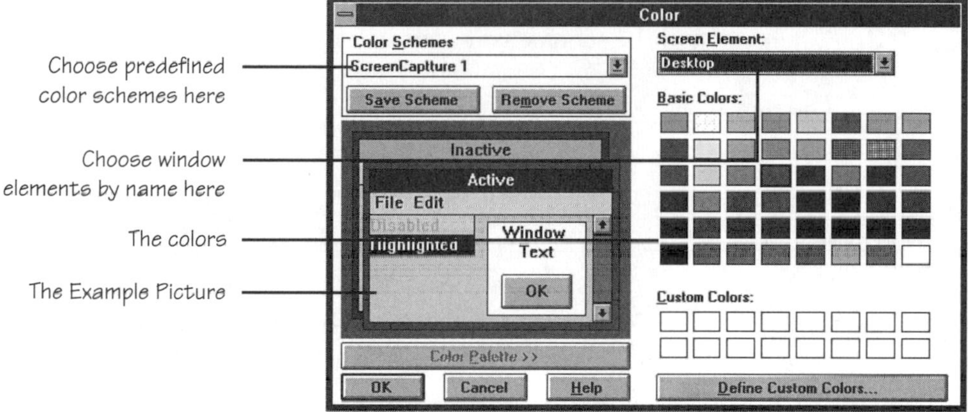

Using Premixed Colors

If you don't want to sit there picking out a different color for each window element in an attempt to make your choice of colors blend together in that "perfect" color scheme, you can choose a predefined color scheme. Windows comes with some pretty snazzy-looking (okay, unique) combinations, such as Black Leather Jacket, Hotdog Stand, and The Blues.

To use a predefined scheme, follow these steps:

1. Click on the down arrow beside the box labeled Color Schemes.

Color Schemes is at the top left part of the dialog box. A drop-down list appears.

2. Click on the color scheme you want.

   Each time you click on a color scheme, the Example Picture changes to show you the new colors. You can scroll through the list by clicking on the up or down scroll arrows at the right side of the list.

3. When you find the scheme you want, click on the OK button.

   The new scheme goes into effect.

"I HATE THIS!"

What's the deal with that fake OK button?

There are two OK buttons in the Color dialog box: one is in the bottom left corner (the real OK button), the other is in the Example Picture (the fake OK button). After you have picked a color scheme and are ready to repaint your desktop with it, you're supposed to click on the real OK button. The fake OK button is for something else, which you'll learn about in the next section.

Picking Your Own Colors

You might not like the choices Windows offers you for color schemes. If you are truly creative, you'll want to pick your own color combination. You can do that too.

To change a particular element of the Windows display, click on that part in the Example Picture. For instance, say you want to change the color of the active title bar (remember, this is the title bar of the

currently active window). To change the color of this bar, click on the part of the Example Picture that says "Active." The name of the element you clicked on appears in the box labeled Screen Element (in this case, the full name of the thing you clicked on is Active Title Bar).

Now click on the color you want for it—say hot pink. The new color is shown in the Example Picture.

Make additional color changes the same way. Click on a window element in the Example Picture (like maybe the fake OK button); then click on the color you want to change it to.

When you are done making changes, click on the OK button in the bottom left corner (the real OK button). The Color dialog box disappears, and any color changes you made take effect.

Checklist

- If you want to forget all those changes you've made and keep the current color settings, click on the Cancel button. When you click on Cancel, the Color dialog box disappears and Windows' colors stay the same.
- You don't have to click on a screen element in the Example Picture to change it. You also can select a screen element by name. Click on the down arrow beside the box labeled Screen Element. A drop-down list appears. Click the up or down arrows in the scroll bar beside this list to find the element you want. When you spot the right element, click on it. Then click on the color you want the element to be.
- Any changes you make in the Color dialog box stay in effect until you specifically change them again.

EXPERTS ONLY

A color for each of your moods

You can make color schemes of your own and save them for later (that way you can go back and forth between two or more color schemes, depending on your mood). In the Color dialog box, choose the colors you want, and then click on the Save Scheme button. In the dialog box that appears, give your color scheme a name (limit: 32 characters per customer); then click the OK button. You can include spaces in the name of your color scheme.

Once you have saved a color scheme, you can use the Color Schemes drop-down list to switch from that scheme to another one and back again whenever you want, as you learned in "Using Premixed Colors," earlier in this chapter.

Refinishing Your Desktop

Behind the Program Manager and all its windows is not the great beyond, but the great desktop. The "stock" desktop color is basic gray, which is fine for early autumn suits, but boring for Windows.

BUZZWORDS

DESKTOP

The desktop is the imaginary table where Windows places program windows and icons. Whether you can see this desktop or not, it's always there.

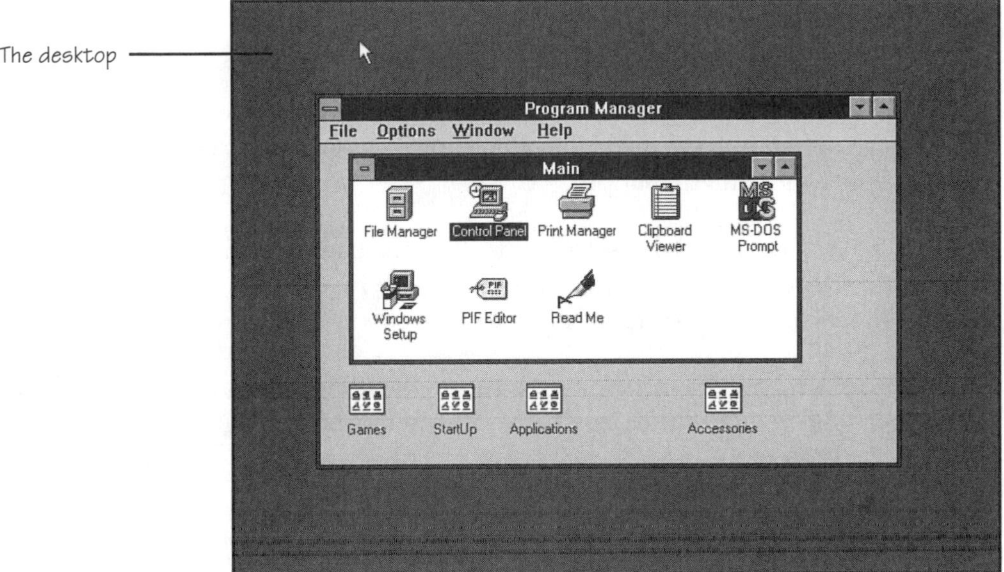

I can't find the desktop!

If the Program Manager or another program is maximized (fills the entire screen), you won't see the desktop. (It's like having gobs of papers all over your desk. Where's the desk?) To see the desktop, you have to minimize all the windows or make them smaller.

Windows lets you liven things up by staining your desktop with a different color or painting it in an unusual pattern. You can even lay down a brightly colored mural and use Windows against a panoply of stars, sunsets, or daisies.

Colorizing the Desktop

The desktop is one of the screen elements you can color in the Color dialog box. Open the Color dialog box as detailed earlier in this chapter. Then expand the Color dialog box to its full width by clicking on the Color Palette button.

To change the desktop color, click the background of the Example Picture, that narrow area surrounding the Inactive and Active sample windows. You should see the word *Desktop* in the Screen Element box.

Now, click on the color you want for the Windows desktop. Seafoam green is a nice choice. Or maybe candy-apple red, if you're feeling adventurous. Ah, the heck with it! Throw caution to the wind! How about that lovely hot pink?!!

Click on the OK button to leave the Color dialog box. Windows paints the desktop with the color you choose, no matter how hideous.

"I HATE THIS!"

You lied! Nothing changes!

If you choose a new desktop color but don't see a change, your desktop is probably covered up, and you can't see it. If there are windows maximized to full-screen, make them smaller or minimize them to icons. Do the same for the Program Manager window if it fills up the entire screen.

Selecting a Prefab Desktop Pattern

You're not limited to a solid-colored desktop. Windows lets you define a background pattern for your desktop. It even comes with a small selection of patterns to start you off, patterns like Scottie, Critters, and Tulip.

To change the desktop pattern, double-click on the Control Panel icon to open it, if it's not already open. Find the icon named Desktop (yes, desktop is both an element of the screen and a "mini-program"). Double-click on it to start the Desktop mini-program.

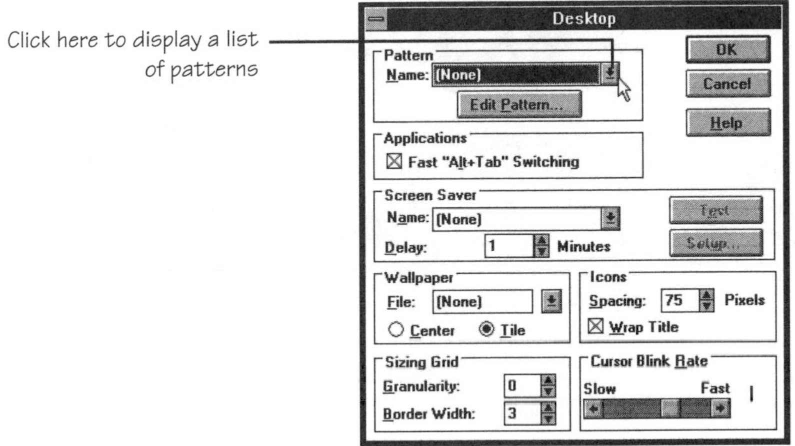

Click on the down arrow beside the box labeled Pattern Name. A drop-down list appears, showing you the names of the available patterns. When you find the desktop pattern you think you'll like, click on it (you'll have to try it out to see whether it's *you*). Then click on the OK button in the Desktop dialog box. Windows changes the desktop pattern.

Drawing Your Own Desktop Pattern (da Vinci!)

If you don't like any of the prefab patterns, you can create your own. Click on the Edit Pattern button in the Desktop dialog box to see the pattern. The Desktop Edit Pattern dialog box appears.

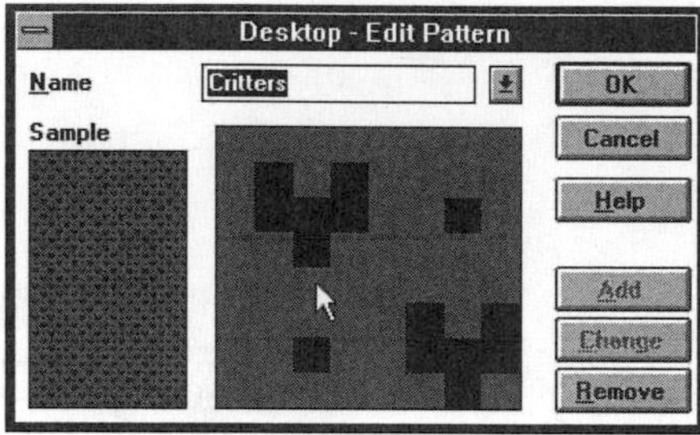

The Desktop - Edit Pattern dialog box

On the left side of this box is a sample of how the pattern will look when applied to your desktop. You can use the sample to see whether you like the way the pattern looks.

On the right is the design of the pattern. This picture is eight squares high by eight squares wide (these squares look like tiny dots when displayed on-screen), and it's repeated over and over again to create the whole pattern. Use the mouse to click on the pattern design to remove or add squares (do nothing if you like the pattern the way it is). Tinker around with the square-to-square combination until you get something you like.

Click on the OK button to leave the dialog box when you're done designing your pattern. Then click on the OK button in the Desktop dialog box to apply the new pattern.

Changing the Desktop Wallpaper

Changing the desktop color is like painting. Changing the pattern is like painting stencils all over the walls. If you can't decide on a color or pattern for your Windows desktop, slap up some wallpaper instead.

To select a wallpaper design, double-click on the Control Panel icon in the Main program group, and then double-click on the Desktop icon. You should see the Desktop dialog box.

Click on the down arrow beside the box marked Wallpaper File. You should see the names of several wallpaper designs. Scroll through the list by clicking on the up and down scroll arrows or by pressing the up- and down-arrow keys. When you find the wallpaper you like, click on its name.

Windows won't hang up your wallpaper until you click the OK button in the Desktop dialog box. So do that now.

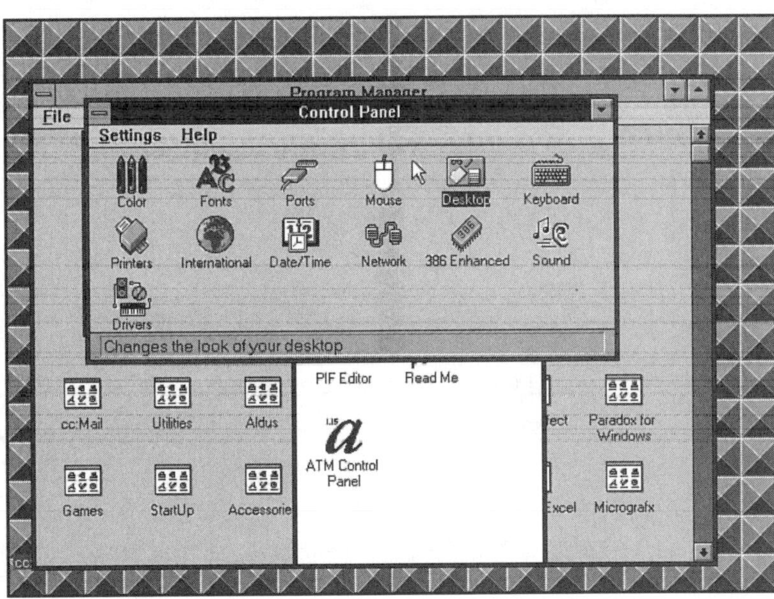

This is what your desktop looks like if you choose the wallpaper file called PYRAMID.BMP

"I HATE THIS!"

I don't see anything!

If you choose a wallpaper but don't see a change, your desktop is probably just covered up by windows. If any of your windows are maximized, make them smaller or minimize them to icons.

Maybe you still don't see the wallpaper. Look in the center of your screen. If you see a postage stamp-sized image of your wallpaper in the middle of your screen, you need to go back into the Desktop dialog box and choose Tile instead of Center. Most of the wallpaper selections included with Windows are the "tile" variety, which means that the picture is actually very small. If you choose Tile, Windows repeats this small picture as many times as necessary to fill the entire desktop; however, if Center is selected, the image appears only once, right in the middle of your screen.

TIP

If you start to run out of room on your hard disk drive, consider erasing any wallpaper files you don't use. Wallpaper files end with a .BMP file extension and are kept in the WINDOWS directory on your computer's hard disk drive.

Checklist

- Desktop wallpaper is really just a colorful drawing that Windows can use for its desktop. You can use the Windows Paintbrush program to create your own. Chapter 10 gives you the basics about Paintbrush.

- If you don't see any files in the Wallpaper File list, it means that whoever installed your copy of Windows elected not to include the wallpaper designs.
- If you get tired of wallpaper, choose None from the Wallpaper File list and click on the OK button. Windows removes the wallpaper.
- If you choose a tiled wallpaper, you can't also choose a color and pattern for the desktop. The pattern and color choices will be ignored.

EXPERTS ONLY

Wallpaper outlets

If you don't like the selection of wallpaper that Windows provides, there are plenty of other alternatives you can choose from.

Wallpaper art is available commercially from a number of software companies. You get a whole collection of wallpaper, with all sorts of eye-catching designs.

If you want freebie wallpaper, check with computer user's groups, over-the-phone computer bulletin board systems, and of course your coworkers. The selection runs from "Here's a picture of my two-month-old puppy being house-trained" to a snapshot of Cindy Crawford.

You also can draw your own art. Wallpaper is nothing more than a picture file you can create by using the Windows Paintbrush program. Create and save the drawing and then select it. Take a look at Chapter 10 if you want to learn how to use Paintbrush to do this.

More Windows Desktop Remodeling

As you personalize Windows according to your own tastes, changing the desktop colors may not be enough for you. Well guess what? There are even more options you can fiddle with to change the appearance of Windows.

To get to these options, you have to open the Desktop dialog box. Remember how? Double-click on the Main program group icon, then double-click on the Control Panel icon, and finally, double-click on the Desktop icon.

Changing the Icon Spacing (More elbow room)

Are your group icons crammed too close together? You can space them out by increasing the value in the Icons Spacing entry blank in the Desktop dialog box.

Double-click on the Icons Spacing entry blank and then type a number. (Or you can click on the little up or down arrow to the right of the box; each click respectively increases or decreases the number in the box by 1.)

The value in the Icons Spacing box is in "pixels." The standard setting is 75 pixels. I wouldn't go any lower than 50 or 60 pixels.

BUZZWORDS

PIXEL

Pixel is short for "picture element"—a.k.a. a dot. The Windows screen is really made up of a series of teeny-weeny dots, most commonly 640 dots (pixels) wide by 480 dots high. Your system might have more dots; then again, it might have less. It all depends on what kind of monitor you're using.

When you're done setting the icon spacing, click on the OK button to leave the Desktop dialog box.

You won't notice an immediate effect when you change the icon spacing. The reason: the Program Manager leaves the icons well enough alone until you specifically ask that they be rearranged. To do this, open the Window menu and choose the Arrange Icons command. Now watch as Windows respaces all the icons in the active window.

Crammed icons

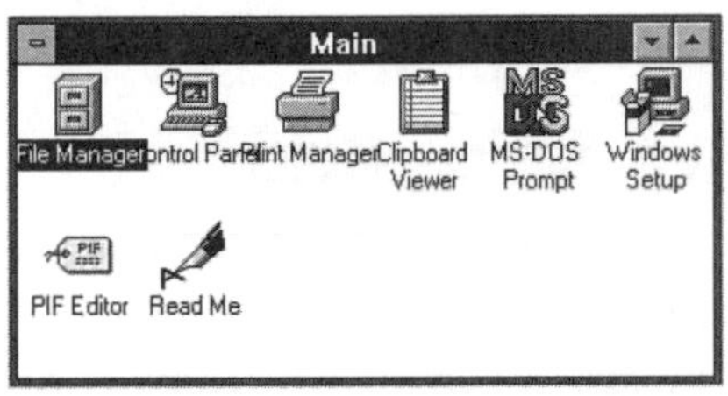

Icons spaced at 75 pixels

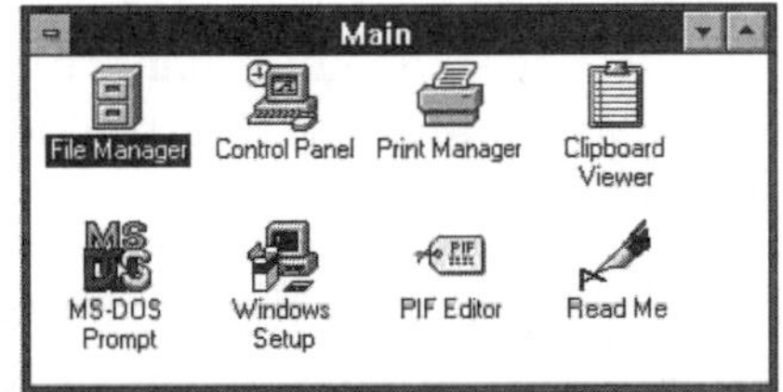

Those Long Icon Names

Long icon names (group icons and program icons) will run into one another, especially if the icons are spaced close together. To keep those long titles from touching, you can tell Windows to "wrap" them, so that the text spans two or more lines instead of one long one.

To wrap icon titles, click on the Wrap Title option in the Desktop dialog box. An X should appear in the box, indicating that you have turned on the Wrap Title feature. If the X isn't there, you just turned it off.

Click on it again to put the X back in the box. Click the OK button to close the Desktop dialog box and make the titles wrap.

Wrap Title turned off

Wrap Title turned on

The Elusive Sizing Grid

A seldom-used adjustment you can make in Windows is setting something called the "sizing grid." You can't see the sizing grid, but it's there nonetheless. Whenever you resize or move a window, the window's border will automatically jump to the nearest line in the invisible grid.

The usual setting (called the Granularity) for the sizing grid is zero, and you should keep it there. When the grid is set to zero, the grid essentially is turned off; you can create windows of any size, and place them anywhere.

If you change the setting, any windows you resize or move will "jump" into position, rather than glide there smoothly like before. Having your windows jump around unexpectedly while you size and move them is startling, to say the least.

Fatten Up Those Window Borders

A more useful setting is the Border Width option. The normal setting is 3, which means that the borders around windows are 3 pixels wide. If you have trouble using the mouse to grab borders when you are resizing windows, increase the Border Width setting, say to 5 or 6.

To change the border width, double-click on the Border Width entry blank in the Desktop dialog box and type a new number. (Or you can click on the little up or down arrow beside the entry blank to increase or decrease the value by 1, respectively.)

The smaller the number, the thinner the border. The smallest value is 1, which turns borders into thin lines. Not recommended. If you want a reasonably thick border, try a value of 5 or 6.

When you're done setting the border width, click on the OK button to leave the Desktop dialog box.

EXPERTS ONLY

Wanna make your coworkers boiling mad?

If you're feeling mischievous, stay at the office during lunch and change the Border Width option for all your coworkers! Set it to 1 (the smallest amount), so that the window border is just an ugly, hairline crack. It'll take them 20 minutes to figure out what's gone wrong and, with luck, will never finger you for the job.

A note of caution: if you try this little trick on the company bookkeeper, be sure that you've already gotten your paycheck.

Cursor Blink Rate (blink, blink, blink)

No doubt you've encountered the Windows cursor before: it's the little flashing line you see in entry boxes and in text-writing programs like Windows Notepad and Windows Write. The cursor is also known as the insertion point, because it's the point where text is inserted when you type.

Normally this little cursor thingie blinks once per second. That's fast enough for most folks, but it's too slow for others; for example, a slow-motion cursor is too hard to find if you're using a laptop computer with a liquid crystal display.

Windows lets you adjust the rate of the cursor, from a sprightly flash-flash-flash (about three times per second) to a poky f - l - a - s - h (roughly once every two seconds).

You set the rate of the cursor blink in the Desktop dialog box. Set the rate by sliding the Cursor Blink Rate scroll box to the left or right with the mouse. An example cursor flashes beside the scroll bar, letting you see whether you like the new setting.

When you're done setting the blink rate, click on the OK button to leave the Desktop dialog box.

TIP

If you're curious about those "Screen Saver" options in the Desktop dialog box, flip ahead to Chapter 11.

CHAPTER 5

For Keyboard Lovers Only

IN A NUTSHELL

- ▼ Why every command has an underlined letter
- ▼ What the Enter and Esc keys do
- ▼ How to use keyboard shortcuts to get around the Program Manager

There's no doubt about it—Windows is made for the mouse. But sometimes the mouse gets in the way and slows you down. Fortunately just about every major function in Windows has a keyboard shortcut. That way, you can use the mouse or the keyboard, whichever suits you. If you're used to using the keyboard to work your computer, you may find the keyboard shortcuts in the Program Manager to your liking.

Doing the Menu Thing

With a keyboard shortcut, you don't have to use the mouse to choose a command from a menu. Instead, you can let your fingers do the typing.

Have you noticed that in the menu bar, one letter is underlined in each menu name? The underline lets you know that you can press that key to get to the menu. To open (pull down) a menu, first press the Alt key and hold it down. Now press the key that corresponds to the underlined letter of the menu you want. Suppose that you want to open the File menu, which has an underlined *F* in its file name. You would press and hold down the Alt key and then press F.

Also notice that each command on the File menu has one underlined letter. Choosing a command is even simpler than choosing a menu because you don't have to deal with the Alt key. You just press the key that corresponds to the underlined letter of the command you want to choose, such as *P* for Properties. Pressing P is the same thing as clicking on the Properties command with the mouse.

"I HATE THIS!"

The Alt key. Hold it down or let it up?

You don't really have to hold down the Alt key. Windows lets you press it once and then let it go. You can then press the letter key that corresponds to the menu shortcut you want. But since Windows uses so many key combinations that *do* require you to hold down two or more keys at a time, I think it's a good idea to get into the habit of keeping the Alt key pressed down when you select a keyboard menu shortcut. Why bother trying to remember whether you have to hold it or not?

The Two Most Commonly Used Keys in Windows

Even if you stick with the mouse, you should memorize these two important keys: Esc and Enter.

The Esc key is the universal "Get me outta here" key in Windows. Press Esc when you want to cancel a dialog box without making any changes. And press it when you want to close a menu that's open.

Conversely, the Enter key is the universal "Just do it" key in Windows. Press Enter whenever you want Windows to carry out a command—for instance, when you want Windows to apply the changes you made in a dialog box. In most cases, pressing Enter after you select something is the same as double-clicking on it; clicking once on an icon, for example, and then pressing the Enter key is the same as double-clicking on that icon. Pressing Enter is also the same as clicking on the OK button.

Try Out These Keyboard Shortcuts for Size

Here are some more ways to use the keyboard in the Program Manager. With a couple of these shortcuts, you have to use the function keys—the keys labeled F1, F2, F3, and so on up to F10 or F12 (depending on the type of keyboard you have). These keys appear along the top or left side of your keyboard. Or both. Look around.

Notice that some of the keyboard shortcuts in this section are shown with a plus sign (+). The plus sign means that you have to hold down the first key and then press the second one. Then release both keys. You might as well know now that a lot of these keyboard shortcuts are also used in most Windows programs. Yahoo! If you learn these, you already know that much more about a bunch of Windows programs.

Press	To
Up, Down, Right, or Left arrow	Select the next icon in the active window
Enter	Open an icon into a window, or run a program
Alt+Space bar	Pull down the Control menu for a program
Ctrl+F6	Make the next window active
Ctrl+F4	Close the active window
Alt+F4	Close the active program
F10 or Alt	Activate the menu bar (doesn't open a menu)

Press	To
Left or Right arrow	Select the next menu name (after you activate the menu bar with F10 or Alt)
Down arrow	Pull open the active menu
Down or Up arrow	Choose a command in an open menu
Esc	Close an open menu (menu bar remains active)
Esc, Esc	Close an open menu and forget everything (press Esc twice)

Checklist

▼ Windows tries to give you a lot of hints as you go along. You'll often find keyboard shortcuts listed right next to the menu commands they duplicate! For instance, the "Enter" shortcut is shown beside the Open command in the File menu. This tells you that pressing Enter is the same as clicking on the Open command.

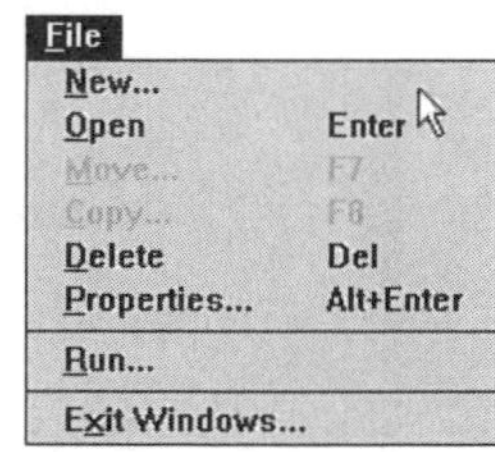

The File menu

continues

Checklist Continued

- ▼ You don't need to memorize the keyboard shortcuts all at once. I personally remember only a couple of keyboard shortcuts for the Program Manager, and maybe a few more for other programs. You shouldn't feel compelled to use the keyboard shortcuts just because they are there, no matter what the computer geeks in your office say.

PART II

Managing Files

Includes:

6: Fun with Files

7: File Manager Is My Friend

8: Taking Control of Files

CHAPTER 6

Fun with Files

IN A NUTSHELL

- ▼ File basics are DOS basics
- ▼ How the files got on your computer's hard drive
- ▼ Why files are put in directories
- ▼ The root directory and why it's important
- ▼ Do's and don'ts about directory and file names

"Files sound awful DOS-like," you might say. "I have Windows. Therefore, I don't have to worry about files."

Wrong.

Anything constructive you do with Windows revolves around using files. To use files, you must know how your computer deals with them. You need to know how files are named and where they are placed on your computer's hard disk drive.

This chapter is dedicated to files and where they go on your computer's hard disk drive.

Files, Files, Everywhere

Windows doesn't live alone. It shares an apartment with DOS, the disk operating system that makes your computer whir and click when you start it. Your computer can't run without DOS, and neither can Windows.

Windows uses DOS for managing files. DOS records the files and remembers where it put them so they can be fetched later.

BUZZWORDS

FILE

A file is a collection of related stuff, like a database of chicken recipes or a program. There are two kinds of files: program files and data files.

Program files contain the instructions that make programs work; they're created by the people who make the software. Data files contain your work; they are created by you.

Files are everywhere on your computer's hard disk drive. They got there because they came with DOS, Windows, or another program—or because you made them.

Program Files

Program files are copied onto your hard disk when you install a program. If you didn't install the programs that are on your computer, somebody else did—the person who sold you the computer, a coworker, your niece.

Checklist

- DOS is really just a fur-ball of files, several dozen in fact. The DOS files were the first ones your computer ever met: they were placed onto the hard disk drive of your computer when it was brand new.
- Like DOS, Windows is just a collection of files (well over a hundred). Each file does a particular job. Fortunately, to use Windows you don't need to know anything about its files or what they do.
- Every program has at least one file; that file is the program itself. In truth, most programs are composed of many files. Each file contributes to the program in some way.

CAUTION

Don't delete any program files in the program directory. Usually there's a main program file with a recognizable name that ends in .EXE, such as WP.EXE for WordPerfect and EXCEL.EXE for Excel. You might mistakenly think that this file is the only one you need. Wrong. Programs often have other "helper" files that are necessary for its operation. Don't delete any of these key files.

Data Files (I made it myself!)

As you use Windows and its programs, you'll make plenty of your own files. These files won't contain programs, but some type of data, like a letter or a drawing or a budget for your company.

Checklist

- When you create a file, you must save it to a disk. Saving the file enables you to open and work on the file again.
- Depending on the program you are using, you will follow different procedures to save the file and then open it again later.
- When you save a file, you assign it a name and a location.
- All files follow a rather crude but workable file name system, and it goes like this:

  name.extension

  The *name* can be from one to eight characters. The *extension* is purely optional, though most files have it. If you use an extension, it can be from one to three characters. The **.** (period) separates the name from the extension.
- As a general rule, you should only use numbers and letters in a file name.

TIP

Use file extensions to show how files are related. For instance, all .DOC files are document files, all .WKS files are worksheet files.

EXPERTS ONLY

File name rules

DOS is picky when it comes to file names. Either you can use only numbers and letters and forget the following rules, or you can memorize the rules:

- You can't use a space in file or directory names. But you can fake it by typing an underscore instead of a space (MY_FILE.DOC).
- You can't use these characters:

  ? * , + = / \ [ ] " ; : < > ¦

TIP

You're better off using just letters and numbers. Avoid characters like these:

$ # & @ ! ( ) - { } ' _ ~ `

Although these characters are "legal," they are harder to type and make directory and file names look like hieroglyphics.

Keeping Track of Your Files

Imagine that each of your files is a separate piece of paper and that your hard disk drive is a file cabinet, capable of storing thousands and thousands of files. Now suppose that every day you jam papers into the file cabinet with no regard for order whatsoever. What you end up with is a certifiable mess. Just try to find a particular piece of paper in the cabinet! You won't know where that paper is. What's the solution?

A Place for My Files, and Every File in Its Place

Fortunately the hard drive in your computer isn't just a big, open file cabinet, where you stuff files in haphazard fashion. Instead, your computer's hard drive is divided into *directories*. A directory is very much like a folder in a file cabinet. You put the pieces of paper that go together in one folder, then put the folder in the cabinet. Directories are an organizational tool; they help you keep track of your files.

When you want to find a piece of paper, you first go to the folder, then find the right piece inside it. Simple as that.

The Root or "Big Daddy" Directory

Every hard disk has at least one directory. This directory is the *root*, where you can put files and more directories. (These additional directories are sometimes called "subdirectories," but for simplicity we'll just call them all "directories.")

BUZZWORDS

ROOT

The first directory in a hard disk is called the "root" because it serves as the foundation for all other directories, just like the root of a tree serves as the foundation for its limbs and branches.

Checklist

- ▼ The root directory has a special name: \. That's right. Just a single character—the backslash.
- ▼ All other directories on your hard drive are directories of the root.

Directory Assistance

If you piled all your files into the root directory, you wouldn't solve your problem of how to find files. Instead, you should divide the hard disk into other directories.

Directories are most commonly created whenever some new program is added to the hard drive. Once the directory is made, the files for the program are placed inside it. The installation process of the program might have suggested a name for the new directory. You (or the person installing the program) have the choice of keeping the name or choosing another.

You won't have to wait around for some program to make a new directory for you on your computer's hard disk drive. You can create your own directory whenever you get the urge, then stuff it with whatever files you want. Windows makes it easy to create new directories, as you'll see in Chapter 8.

Checklist

- Directories have names so that you can refer to them. If a directory were nameless, there would be no way to get inside it.
- Directory names range from one to eight characters in length and usually contain only letters and numbers. You cannot include a space. Directory rules follow the same naming conventions as files do (see the previous "Experts Only" note on file name rules, back a few pages).
- Your computer lets you put directories into other directories. This is called "putting directories into other directories" (or *nesting*).

continues

Checklist Continued

- When you have a string of directories (directories within directories), you use a backslash to separate the directory names.
- It's unusual to nest directories more than three deep. Things get confusing when you have to go through five or six directories to get to the one you want.

The BUDGET directory is inside REPORTS, and the REPORTS and LETTERS directories are inside the root directory.

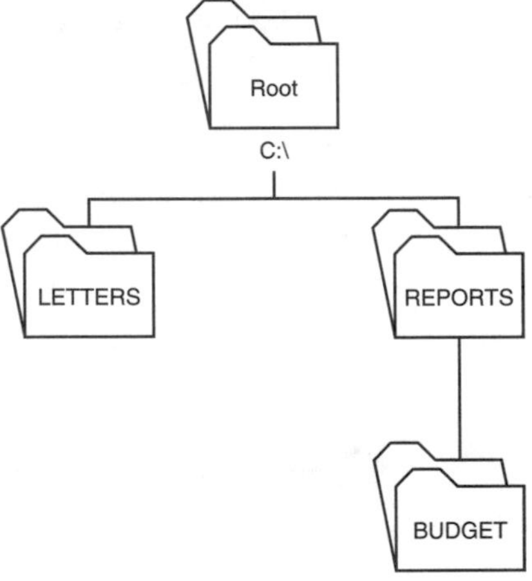

TIP

When you are installing a program, it's always a good idea to use the directory name that the program suggests. Typically the program's instruction manual assumes that you're using the suggested name and uses that name in the examples. When the names of the directories on your hard disk drive are different from the names in your manual, it can be quite confusing.

"I HATE THIS!"

I hate it when a directory looks like a file!

Directory names can have extensions too, like WINDOWS.DIR. Although DOS acts as if this kind of thing is perfectly acceptable, it's considered bad practice. Directory names with extensions are harder to type, and therefore you're more likely to make mistakes with them.

Some programs add extensions when creating directory names, but these programs are rare (and most often these directories are only "temporary"; they are automatically deleted when the program ends). For your own directories, avoid adding extensions.

EXPERTS ONLY

If you use a network at work (you lucky dog!) ...

Things are a little different for you. Many of the files you use aren't on a hard disk drive in your computer, but on a "file server" someplace else in the building. This file server is shared by other people in your office. Most file servers work differently than standard DOS disk drives and directories, so you have to follow a different procedure to get to your files. Accessing files on a network is a specialty subject, so hound your network guru at work for help.

The File Path

(Follow the yellow brick road)

Your computer can't find a file unless it knows which directories to look in. It's similar to your friends not being able to find your street if you don't give them directions (with some friends, this is not a bad idea). The directions to the file are called the *path*.

PATH

A path is a set of directions that tells your computer where to find a file.

Let's say the file you want is REPORT.DOC, which is inside the WINWORD\REPORTS directory.

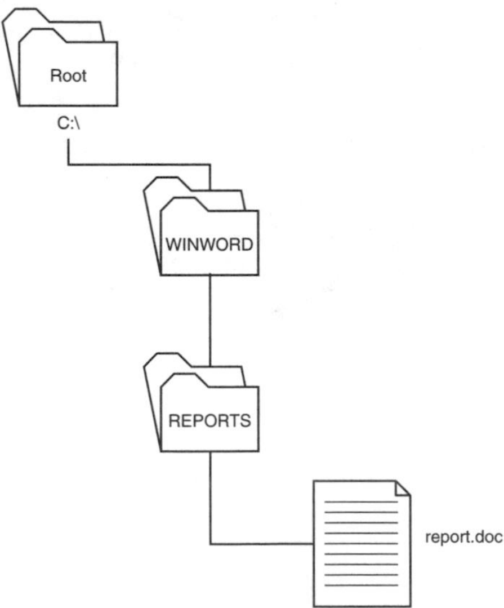

To make sure that your computer can locate this specific file, you include both the directory name and the file name, as in

C:\WINWORD\REPORTS\REPORT.DOC

This statement is the path.

Checklist

- **C:** indicates the drive. (You also have a drive A and maybe a drive B. To refer to files on these drives, you'd specify **A:** or **B:**).
- \ indicates the root directory.
- **WINWORD** is the first directory.
- **REPORTS** is the directory within WINWORD.
- **REPORT.DOC** is the file name.

The Do's and Don'ts of Picking Out a Name

Parents are always naming their kids after themselves. That's okay until someone calls and asks for Bob. "Do you want Big Bob? Bob Junior? Little Bob? Bob the Cat?" This is one naming problem you want to avoid when naming files and directories. Here are some others:

Checklist

- You can't have a file with the same name in the same directory. For instance, you can't have two files named BOB.TXT in a directory, because when you try to use the file, your computer will see that there are two and will break down sobbing. To avoid such an embarrassment, your computer won't let you put two files with the same name in a directory. If you try to give a file the same name as one that already exists, an error message appears and tells you to try another name. If you insist on using the same name, your file will wipe out the older file that has the same name.

- You can have two files with the same name if they are in different directories, but this might lead to confusion. Do you want the BOB file in the FRIEND directory or the BOB file in the ENEMY directory?

- As with file names, you can't have two directories with the same name—that is, unless the duplicates are not in the same directory. For example, you can have a directory named BUDGET in the root directory and another directory named BUDGET in the REPORTS directory, but you can't have two BUDGET directories in the root directory. It just wouldn't be kosher. Why have two directories with the same name? Will the *real* BUDGET directory please stand up?

- Don't give a file and a directory the same name. Even though DOS and your computer allow this sort of thing, some programs don't like it and may display an error message.

- The bottom line is this: it's a good idea to give your files and directories unique, descriptive names.

CHAPTER 7

File Manager Is My Friend (Say It Ten Times and You Might Believe It)

IN A NUTSHELL

- Starting the File Manager
- Changing disk drives
- Opening a new directory
- Finding files
- Opening a second drive window
- Copying and moving files
- Renaming and deleting a file
- Leaving the File Manager

There will come a time when you'll want to get a file from here to there. Here to there might be from your hard disk to a floppy disk so that you can give the file to someone else. Here to there might be from a floppy disk someone gave you to your hard disk. Here to there might be from one directory to another.

This is the "here to there" chapter. You learn how to copy, move, rename, and delete files using the File Manager. Just as the Program Manager helps you manage programs, the File Manager helps you manage files.

DOS vs. File Manager

The bad news: DOS handles all the file wheelings and dealings. If you are doing something with a file, DOS gets involved. The good news: the Windows File Manager insulates you from dealing with the grit and grime of DOS.

If you had nothing but DOS, you'd have to type long, arcane commands. For example, to copy a file from one directory to another, you'd have to type this:

```
COPY MYFILE.DOC C:\WINWORD\REPORTS\MYREPT.DOC
```

One little mistake and the command won't work. With Windows you don't have to deal with the brutal reality of DOS. You just "point and click" in the File Manager, and the job is done for you.

In fact, you don't need to know anything about DOS or the way it works, except for the very basics about files and directories. If you're new to files and directories, read Chapter 6 first, and then come back to this one.

Starting the File Manager

The File Manager is one of the programs that comes with Windows. The File Manager's icon is in the Main group. So, double-click on the Main program group icon to open it into a window. Find the File Manager program icon and double-click on it. After a moment, the File Manager program starts and the File Manager window appears. (Your File Manager window will have different directories and files than the one shown here. That's perfectly okay.)

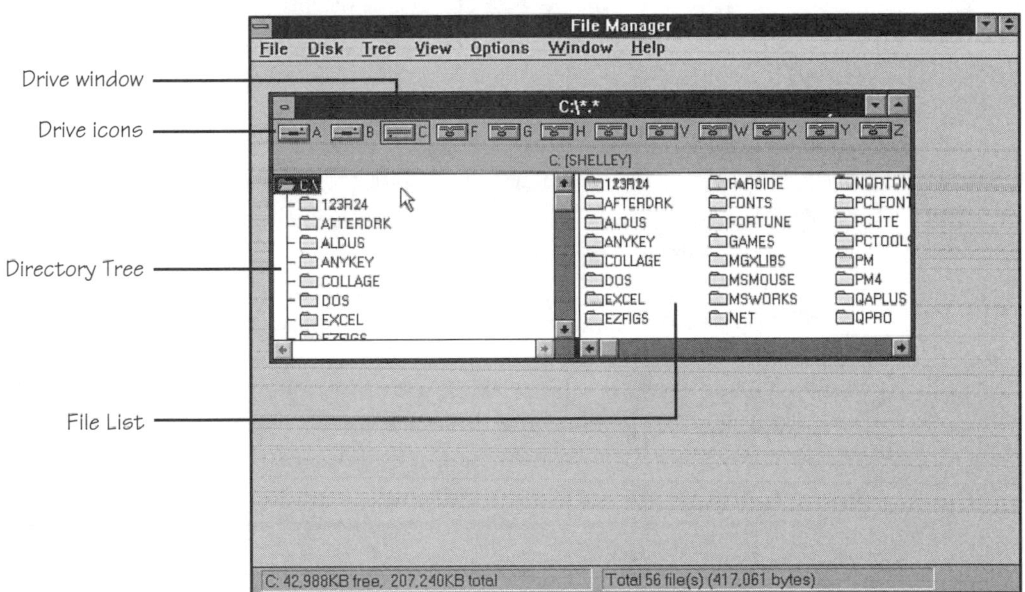

Checklist

- Inside the File Manager program window is the *drive window*. The drive window shows you the directories and files on your computer's hard disk drive.

continues

I HATE WINDOWS!

Checklist Continued

- The drive icons along the top of the drive window indicate the drives on your computer.
- The drive window is divided into two sections: the Directory Tree and the File List.
- The Directory Tree is on the left, and it contains a list of all the directories on your computer's hard disk drive. Windows shows each directory as a file folder. The root directory (C:\) appears at the top of the list. This is the open directory.
- The File List is on the right, and it contains a list of all the files (and other directories) inside the "open" directory in the Directory Tree.
- The drive window is just like any other window; you can change its size however you like.
- You can open more than one drive window at a time.
- Most often you'll be working with just one drive window in the File Manager, so expand the drive window to its full size (if it isn't already) by clicking on its Maximize button—the up-arrow button in the window's top right corner.

"I HATE THIS!"

I don't see a Directory Tree and a File List!

Someone has changed the File Manager window display on your computer. Don't panic. To get it back to normal, click on the View menu, and then click on the Tree and Directory command. This command divides the drive window into two parts, the Directory Tree and the File List.

TIP

When viewing both the Directory Tree and the File List, the drive window is split about evenly down the middle. You can change the split by placing the mouse pointer directly over the dividing line. The pointer turns into a double-sided arrow. Drag the mouse right or left to change the split. If you drag the dividing line to the left, you can display more files in the File List.

Changing Disk Drives

The File Manager always displays files on the drive you worked with the last time you used File Manager. If you want to look at files on a floppy disk, insert the disk in a drive. Then click on that drive icon. For example, to see the directories and files on the floppy disk in drive A, click on the icon labeled A. The drive window changes and displays the directories and files on the selected disk drive.

"I HATE THIS!"

I forgot to insert the disk!

If you don't insert a disk before clicking a drive icon, the File Manager displays this error message: `There is no disk in drive x` (but the x will be an *A* for drive A, or a *B* for drive B, and so forth). Put the disk into the drive and click on the Retry button.

Checklist

- ▼ The A icon is for your computer's floppy disk drive. If there's a B icon, it's for a second floppy disk drive.
- ▼ The C icon is for your computer's hard disk drive. Some computers have more than one hard disk drive, so you might see icons for drives C and D (and possibly more).
- ▼ Most likely, drive C will contain the files for Windows and DOS, and will be the one you'll use the most.
- ▼ If you're on a computer network, you might see a gaggle of drive icons (E, F, G…). Each icon represents a different drive you can access on the network. Working with networks is beyond the scope of this book, so if your computer is tethered to a network, you'll need to ask a knowledgeable person for extra assistance on how to use the File Manager with the network.

Opening a New Directory

The File Manager also always opens (displays files in) the directory you worked with the last time you used it. If the opened directory isn't the one you want to work with now, you must open another one.

The Directory Tree lists the directories in alphabetical order, starting with the root directory at the top. To open a different directory, click once on the directory folder you want. If the directory you want isn't visible, click the up- or down-arrow buttons in the scroll bar beside the Directory Tree.

If the directory you want to see is inside another directory, you have to *expand* the directory listing first. Double-click on the directory that contains the directory you want to see. The File Manager lists all the directories contained in the directory you double-clicked. If you double-click on a directory that doesn't contain other directories, nothing happens in the Directory Tree window.

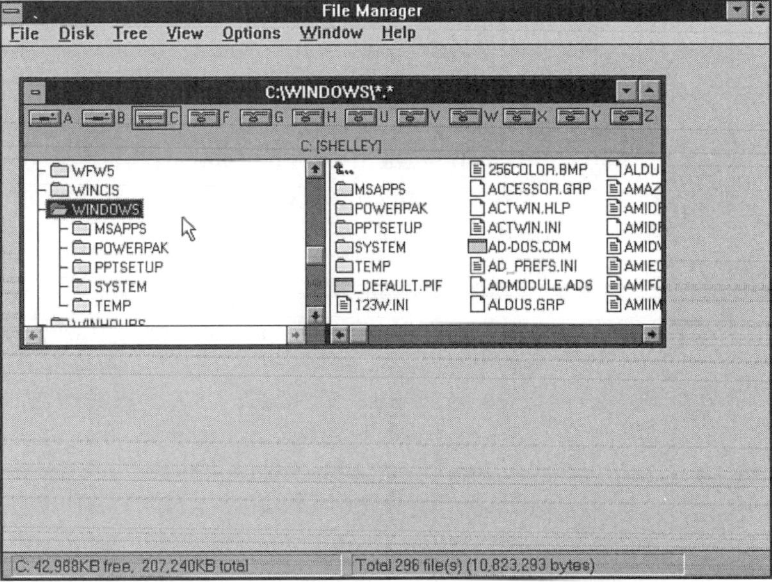

Double-clicking on the WINDOWS directory displays the directories that are inside it

To *collapse* a directory (show only the "container" directory), double-click on its folder.

"I HATE THIS!"

Help! All I see is the root (C:\)!

If all you see is C:\ at the top of the listing, you might wonder where, oh where, have all my directories gone? Relax. The directories are still there, but the listing is collapsed. You can tell File Manager to show you the other directories by double-clicking on the root directory folder.

Finding a File

Now that you've opened the directory you want to work with, you can locate any file that's inside it. You have to find a file before you can copy it, delete it, move it, and so on.

Checklist

- ▼ The File Manager displays the files in the File List in a sorted order. This chapter assumes that the files are sorted by name. To be sure that the files in the File Manager are sorted by name in alphabetical order, open the View menu and choose the Sort by Name command.
- ▼ The File Manager lets you display files in a single column or in multiple columns. When displaying files in a single column, the File Manager also displays various technical junk about the file, such as its size. You don't need to bother with the nitty-gritty of files and how big they are, so if the File Manager is showing file information, tell it not to. Open the View menu and choose the Name command. The files in the File List are shown with just their names, in three or four columns across.
- ▼ Look through the File List until you find the name of the file you want. If you don't see the file, use the arrows in the scroll bars to see more of the File List contents.
- ▼ When you find the file you want, click on it (don't double-click).

File Icons and What They Mean

Beside each file in the File List is a small icon. This icon tells you what kind of file it is. There are three kinds of file icons:

This file is a program.

This file is a document for a program. For example, it might be a letter for the Windows Write word processing program.

The File Manager is not sure about this one. It's not a program, and it's not a document file for a program Windows is familiar with. Most of your files will be this kind.

In addition to different file icons, you might see directory icons, which look like folders. These icons indicate the other directories that are inside the current directory.

Selecting a File

To select a file, click on it. This action tells Windows: "Hey, I want this file!" The file is shown highlighted, with a dark background. If you are feeling particularly adventurous, you can select lots of files at once. The next chapter unveils this trick.

"I HATE THIS!"

I hate it when a program starts or I get an error message!

When you click twice instead of once on a file name, Windows thinks you want to run that file. If it knows what program created the file, Windows will start that program. If it doesn't know, it may guess or give you an error message. Exit the program and next time, click just once!

Copying a File

Now that you know your way around the territory, you can put that knowledge to work. You'll do lots of stuff with the File Manager, but one of the most common tasks is copying files. You might want to copy a file to a floppy disk so that you can take the file with you. Or you might want to have a copy of a file in two directories.

To copy a file, first open the directory that has the file you want by clicking on it. Make sure that the directory you want to copy the file to (let's call this the "destination directory") is visible in the Directory Tree. If it's not, turn to "Two! Two! Two Windows in One!" later in this chapter.

Next, find the file you want to copy in the File List. Point to it with the mouse pointer. Hold down the Ctrl key, and then drag the file from the File List to the folder of the directory you want to move the file to. (To drag the file, click on the name or icon of the file, and hold the mouse button down. Continue to hold the mouse button while you move the mouse.)

While dragging the file, the mouse pointer turns into the shape of an arrow that has a document icon at its tip.

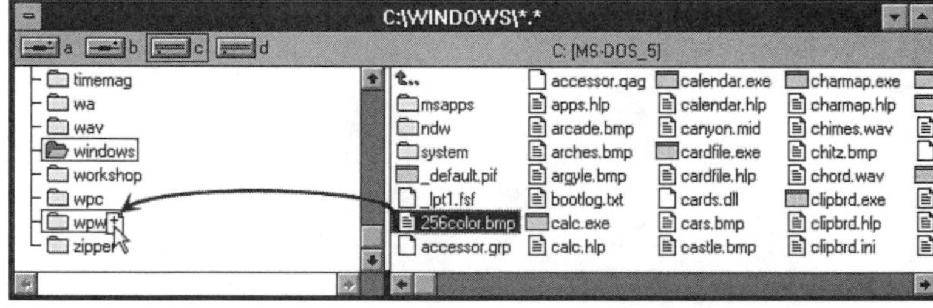

Copying a file

Inside the document icon is a + (plus) sign, telling you that the File Manager is copying the file. IF THE + SIGN IS NOT THERE, IT MEANS YOU'RE MOVING THE FILE INSTEAD OF COPYING IT! Drag the file back into the File List and release the mouse button. Try copying again, and be sure to press the Ctrl key while dragging the file.

When the file is where you want it, release the mouse button and the Ctrl key. Whew! File Manager displays a message box, asking whether you want to copy the file to the destination directory. Click Yes if you do, or No if you don't. Clicking No cancels the operation.

If you click Yes, you'll have two copies of the file: the original in the File List and a new clone in the destination directory. The two files are identical, and they have the same name.

If you try to copy a file into a directory that already has a file with the same name, the File Manager displays a Confirm File Replace message box to warn you. Be extremely careful how you answer this message. If you click the Yes button in the Confirm File Replace message box, *you will permanently erase the old file* and replace it with the new one. If you want to keep the old file, click on the No or Cancel button (each button does the same thing).

Moving a File

You move a file from one directory to another in almost the same way you copy a file. Say you want to move your BOB file from the FRIENDS

I HATE WINDOWS!

directory to the ENEMIES directory. Here's the difference: *don't* hold down the Ctrl key while you drag the file with the mouse.

When moving a file, the mouse pointer turns into the shape of an arrow that has a document icon at its tip.

After you drag the file, the File Manager displays a message box asking whether you're sure that you want to move the file. Click on the Yes button to move it; click on the No button to cancel the move.

Moving a file copies the file to the destination directory and then deletes the original.

"I HATE THIS!"

Arrrggh! I moved instead of copied!!

Perhaps the biggest mistake people make in the File Manager is to move a file when they mean to copy it instead. Remember, moving a file takes it away from the original directory. Be absolutely sure that's what you want to do, or you can really mess things up.

If you moved a file instead of copied it, you can easily correct the situation. Find the file in the directory you moved it to. Now copy it back to its old directory. When copying a file, always press and hold the Ctrl key. This key tells the File Manager that you want to copy the file instead of move it.

Two! Two! Two Windows in One!

What happens when you want to copy or move a file from one directory to another, but the destination directory is out of view in the Directory Tree? Or what if you want to copy a file to another drive?

The File Manager provides a couple of ways around this dilemma, but here's the easiest solution: Open a second drive window showing your computer's hard disk drive. Then copy or move the file between the windows.

To open a second drive window, open the Window menu and choose the New Window command. Or double-click on the drive C icon (above the Directory Tree).

A second drive window appears. Both drive windows show the same directories and files on your computer's hard drive. The windows are probably stacked on top of each other, so you may not be able to see them both. And if your first window is maximized, you won't see the second window at all.

To make it easier to see both windows, arrange them side by side by opening the Window menu and choosing the Tile command. The File Manager stacks the two drive windows one over the other.

To change what you see in a window, click on the window you want to change. Then click on the drive or directory you want to view, as described in "Changing Disk Drives" and "Opening a New Directory," earlier in this chapter.

Copying Files

To copy files between directories, display in the first window the file you want to copy. In the second window, display the spot where you want to put the file. Press and hold down the Ctrl key. Then drag the file from the first window to the second window.

When you copy files from one disk drive to another, you don't need to hold down the Ctrl key. The File Manager knows that you want to copy the file, not move it.

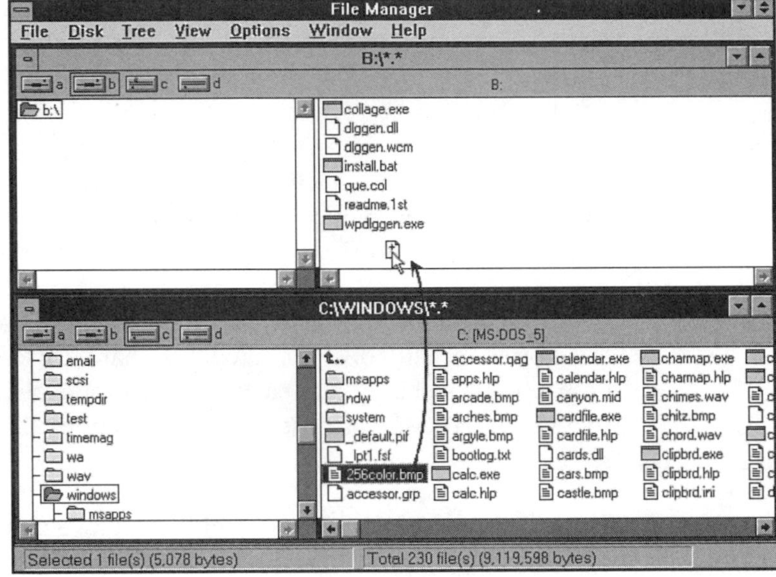

Copying a file to another drive

Moving Files (Move 'em up! Head 'em out!)

To move files between directories, start by opening two windows. In the first window, display the file you want to move. In the second window, display the spot where you want to put the file. Then drag the file from the first window to the second window. If you are moving a file to a different drive, press Shift as you drag.

The sections "Changing Disk Drives" and "Opening a New Directory" (earlier in this chapter) explain how to find the file you want, but here are some reminders:

- Click on the drive icon to display the files in another drive.
- Click on a directory folder to display files in another directory.

Copying a File to the Same Directory

Sometimes you don't want to copy a file to a different directory on your computer's hard disk drive, but you want to make a duplicate of a file in the same directory. There's nothing stopping you from making a copy of a file in the same directory, but the original and copy can't have the same name. So you need to use a different approach to copy files within the same directory:

1. Select the file you want to copy by clicking on the directory folder that holds the file and then clicking on the file in the File List.
2. Open the File menu and choose the Copy command. The Copy dialog box appears.
3. Click inside the entry blank labeled To. The flashing cursor appears there.
4. Type the name of the new file. Be sure to use only allowable characters in the file name, as described in Chapter 6.
5. Click on the OK button. The File Manager copies the file to the same directory and gives the copy the name you provided.

"I HATE THIS!"

Eeek! An error message!

You clicked OK and the File Manager displayed a big fat error message. The title of the message box reads "Error Copying File," and the text of the message is more confusing than the most obscure Egyptian hieroglyphics. What the File Manager is trying to tell you is that you didn't provide a valid file name. Either the name contains too many characters or has "illegal" characters, like spaces and asterisks and such. Click OK to make the error message go away, and then use a valid file name.

"I HATE THIS!"

Double eeek! A different error message!

You clicked OK and the File Manager displayed a message box that says `Confirm File Replace`. Whoa on this one!! The name you provided in the Copy dialog box is already in use by another file in the directory. If you want to proceed with the copy, click the Yes button in the Confirm File Replace message box. But remember that if you do, *you will permanently erase the old file!* If you want to keep the old file, click No or Cancel (they do the same thing). Then try the copy again, this time with a different name for the file.

Renaming a File

Okay. Suppose that you didn't read Chapter 6 on file names and you have hundreds of files named BOB. Or worse, you have files with such descriptive names as FILE01, FILE02, FILE03, etc. You've come to the conclusion that it would be much easier to find the file you want if the files had more recognizable names (you genius, you). Are you stuck with the "bad" names? No. If you want to give a file a new name, for whatever reason, you can.

First, click on the file in the File List. Open the File menu and choose the Rename command. When the Rename dialog box appears, type the new name in the entry blank labeled To. Be sure to use only allowable characters in the file name, as described in Chapter 6. Click on the OK button; the file is renamed.

Checklist

- When renaming a file, if you try to use a file name that already exists in the directory, the File Manager displays the Confirm File Replace message box. Click Yes if you want the renamed file to replace the existing file of the same name. Or click No (or Cancel) if you don't want the renamed file to replace the existing file.
- Rename *only* those files you made. Trouble is a-brewing if you rename a file that a program needs. If the file can't be found (because it has been renamed), the program may complain with an error message. Or worse, your whole computer could stop working.

Deleting a File

When you no longer need a file, you can delete it from your computer's hard disk drive. Only delete files you're sure you don't want anymore.

Although it is possible to "resurrect" a deleted file, the technique is complex and doesn't always work. If your computer uses MS-DOS version 5 or later, it comes with a program, called UNDELETE, that helps you "undelete" a previously erased file. If you accidentally delete a file you need, *don't do anything else with your computer.* Read *I Hate DOS* to learn how to use the UNDELETE program, or get the help of a knowledgeable person.

To delete a file, click on the file in the File List. Open the File menu and choose the Delete command.

The File Manager displays the Delete dialog box. Inside the dialog box is the name of the file you want to delete. Click on OK to delete the file; click on Cancel if you change your mind.

TIP

As a shortcut, you can delete a file by clicking on it and then pressing the Del key, which causes the Delete dialog box to appear.

Depending on the "confirmation options" set in your File Manager (the next chapter deals with these options), the File Manager may or may not display a warning message that you are about to delete a file. If the warning message appears, click on Yes to delete the file or on No (or Cancel) if you changed your mind.

Closing Drive Windows

If you have more than one drive window open, you can close any windows you don't need. To close a drive window, double-click on its Control menu box (in the upper left corner).

- Be sure to double-click on the Control menu box for the drive window, not the main File Manager window. When you double-click on it in the File Manager window, you're telling Windows you want to leave the File Manager!
- No matter how hard you try, the File Manager insists that at least one drive window remains open at all times.

Leaving the File Manager

(Hasta la vista, baby)

You're done messing around with files and you're ready to leave the File Manager. Open the File menu and click on the Exit command. The File Manager window disappears, and you are returned to the Program Manager.

Shoe®
By Jeff MacNelly
TOMORROW IS THE START OF A WHOLE NEW WEEK.

I BETTER GET MY EXCUSES ORGANIZED.

WELL, NO, I DIDN'T GET TO IT BECAUSE THE COPIER WENT DOWN YESTERDAY.

NOPE. DIDN'T GET THE MESSAGE... THERE'S SOMETHING WRONG WITH MY MACHINE.

SORRY... I MEANT TO GET IT TO YOU YESTERDAY...

BUT MY FAX IS ON THE BLINK.

I TRIED TO CALL IN FROM THE ROAD, BUT MY CAR PHONE'S IN THE SHOP.

© 1991 Tribune Media Services, Inc.
All Rights Reserved
I WOULD HAVE FINISHED IT YESTERDAY, BUT THE COMPUTER WENT DOWN...

WELL, THIS MORNING THE LASER PRINTER CRASHED,...

AND I COULDN'T GET MY MODEM ON LINE.

THAT'S THE GREATEST THING ABOUT ALL THIS HIGH-TECH EQUIPMENT:

3-12

HIGH-TECH EXCUSES.
MacNelly

CHAPTER 8

Taking Control of Files (You're In Charge!)

IN A NUTSHELL

- Working with multiple files
- Creating a new directory
- Throwing out a directory
- Formatting a new disk
- Running programs from the File Manager
- Starting a program and opening a document at the same time
- Personalizing the File Manager

Pretty soon you may become enamored with the whole file process. You might want to become a regular file acrobat. Then they'll sing about how you delete and move files with the greatest of ease.

Chapter 7 introduced the File Manager and discussed its most important jobs. In this chapter you'll get even more. The information covered here will help you save time, avoid DOS at all costs, and keep your directories shipshape.

Fiddling with a Bunch of Files

Most of the time you'll copy, move, and delete just one file at a time. But the File Manager also lets you manage multiple files. For instance, you might want to delete a whole gaggle of files you no longer need, and you can delete them all at once, rather than one at a time.

The secret to working with multiple files is to select more than one at a time, before you do the copy, move, or delete.

In the File Manager, display the File List you want to work with. The preceding chapter covers how to find the file you want.

To select a series of files that are together (one right after the other) in the File List, you need to use both hands. With one hand, click on the first file in the series, using the mouse. With the other hand, press and hold down the Shift key. Then click on the last file in the series. Release the Shift key. All the files between the first and last files are selected, and they're shown highlighted.

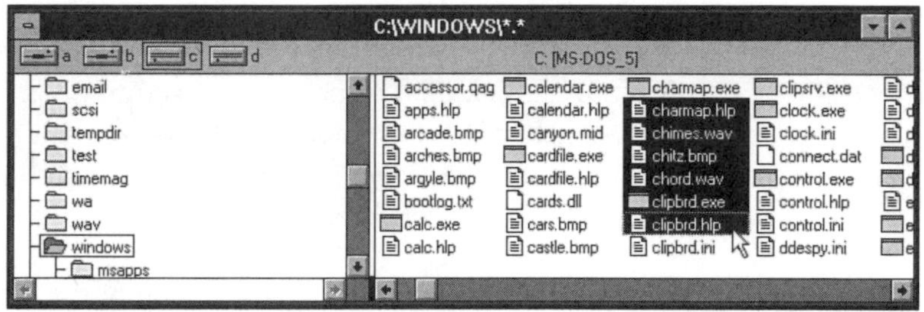

Shift-selecting files in the File List

To select a bunch of files that are not together in the File List, click on one of the files. Press and hold down the Ctrl key, and then click on each of the other files you want to select.

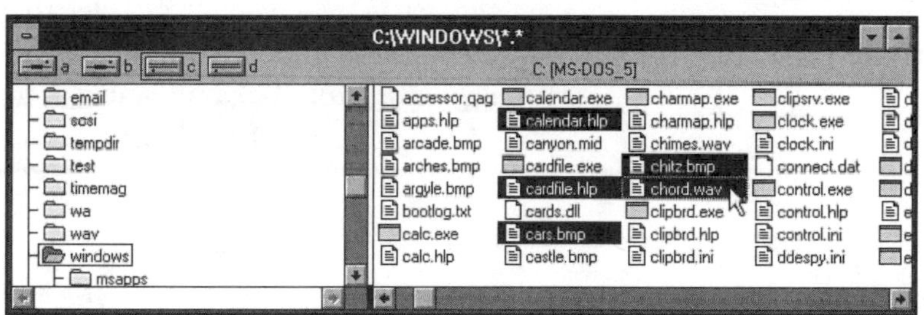

Ctrl-selecting files in the File List

To select all files, open the File menu. Then choose the Select Files command. You see the Select Files dialog box, with *.* in the text box. (If you don't see *.*, type it.) Click on the Select button and then on the Close button. All the files in the File List are now selected.

Checklist

- To deselect one file in a series of selected files in the File List, hold down the Ctrl key and click on the file.
- To copy the selected files, hold down the Ctrl key while dragging any one of the selected files to the folder in which you want to

continues

Checklist Continued

stick the duplicates. The pointer turns into an arrow that's holding onto a stack of itty-bitty documents. When you release the mouse button, the File Manager asks whether you really want to copy the selected files; click on Yes.

- To move the selected files, drag any one of the selected files to the folder where you want to move them. The File Manager asks whether you're sure you want to move the selected files; click on Yes.
- To delete the selected files, press the Del key. The File Manager displays a dialog box showing you all the files that will be deleted (you may not be able to see them all in the dialog box). Click on OK to continue deleting, or click on Cancel if you change your mind.

"I HATE THIS!"

Yes! I'm sure I want to delete those files!

When deleting files, the File Manager will ask your permission to delete each file, one by one. You'll see a dialog box that asks whether you're sure you want to delete the file.

Answer Yes to delete the file listed in the dialog box. The File Manager will delete the file, and the dialog box will reappear for the next file being deleted.

Answer Yes to All to delete all of the files.

Answer No if you change your mind and want to keep the file listed in the dialog box. The File Manager will not delete the file, and the dialog box will reappear for the next file being deleted.

Answer Cancel to stop deleting all files. Any files that have not been deleted yet are kept.

Remember!! Be careful when deleting files. Though it is possible to "undelete" deleted files, the process is complex and isn't always successful. If you accidentally delete a file you meant to keep, IMMEDIATELY STOP USING YOUR COMPUTER and ask for help from a knowledgeable person.

If you want to select a group of a certain kind of files, you can sort the files by type before you select them. Once they are grouped together, it is easier to select them.

Open the View menu and choose the Sort by Type command. The File Manager sorts the files by extension (last name) in alphabetical order. This sorting method groups similar files together, like all DOC document files or all TXT text files.

Creating a New Directory

(Getting organized)

The more you use your computer, the more files you make. And the more files you make, the more reason you'll have to create new directories for them to keep them organized. The File Manager makes creating a directory a simple process.

For instance, if you want to store all your Excel budget files in a separate directory, use the File Manager to create the directory. Then as you use Excel, that directory will be available for you to put files in.

Here's how you create your very own directory:

1. In the Directory Tree, click the directory folder that you want your new directory to appear under.

   If you want your new directory to be under the root directory, click on the C:\ folder at the top of the Directory Tree.

2. Open the File menu and choose the Create Directory command.

3. In the dialog box that appears, type the name of the new directory. Follow the directory name requirements detailed in Chapter 6. You'll do fine if you type a name from one to eight characters, using letters or numbers but nothing else (no spaces). No fair copping a directory name that's already in use.

4. Click on OK when you're done typing the name of the new directory.

Checklist

- If the File Manager doesn't like the new name, for whatever reason, it will display an error message in a message box. Click on OK to make the message go away, and try making the new directory again.

- After making the new directory, the File Manager just sits there, daydreaming. It doesn't open the new directory, and it doesn't display a banner that says "You did it!" The only way you can be sure that the new directory was indeed created is to find it in the Directory Tree.

Removing a Directory

(Pruning the Directory Tree)

If you no longer need a directory, delete it. You can delete directories just like you can delete files. Before deleting a directory, it's important to make sure that none of the files inside the directory are ones you want to keep. If you want to keep some files, move them to a different directory, because all the files left in the directory will be thrown out. Gone forever.

Click on the directory you want to remove. Then press the Del key.

The File Manager first displays the name of the directory in a dialog box, the Delete dialog box. Click OK to go on. Next, the File Manager asks whether you're sure you want to delete the directory. Click on Yes if you do or No (or Cancel) if you don't.

If the directory you're deleting contains files, the File Manager asks you to confirm that you want to delete each file in the directory. Click on Yes to All to delete all the files. Click on Yes to delete only the named file; Windows then goes through the files one by one. Click on Cancel to cancel the whole thing.

Formatting a New Disk

Another file-related task you can do easily with the File Manager is formatting disks. Brand-new disks usually aren't prepared for use in your computer. Before they can hold any data, you have to format them. You can't use a disk that hasn't been formatted.

BUZZWORDS

FORMAT

A disk that isn't formatted is like a parking lot with no lines painted on it. Without the lines, the cars don't know where to park. There's no order. Formatting "paints" lines on a disk so that your computer can store data on it in an orderly fashion.

A Short Lesson on Floppy Disks (Why all floppies aren't floppy)

Your computer has at least one floppy disk drive—drive A. But you might have two floppy drives, drive A and drive B.

Floppy disk drives look like mail slots on the front of your computer. And they kind of act like mail slots. To get information from the floppy disk to the hard disk, you use the floppy disk drive. The "mail" is the floppy disk.

Checklist

- Floppy disks come in two sizes: 31/2-inch and 51/4-inch. The 31/2-inch disk is encased in a hard plastic cover, but it is still a "floppy" disk. You match the disk size to the size of your drive: 31/2-inch disks go in 31/2-inch drives and 51/4-inch disks go in 51/4-inch drives.

- Floppy disks also come in two capacities for each size. The capacity is the maximum amount of data it can hold. A 31/2-inch disk can store 720K or 1.44M of information. A 51/4-inch disk can store 360K or 1.2M of information. Check out the next buzzword to find out what those Ks and Ms mean.

- The box that the disk came in will tell you its capacity. If you're not sure of the capacity, you might be able to tell by looking at it. Turn to Chapter 21 for more details; otherwise, ask a knowledgeable friend.

- Your computer probably also has a hard drive, called drive C. This drive is different from a floppy drive in these ways: the drive is inside the computer (you can't take it with you); you don't use a disk with this drive; the disk and drive are one; and the drive can hold a lot more information and is faster than a floppy drive.

BYTE, KILOBYTE, MEGABYTE

A byte is equal to about one typed character. K or KB stands for *kilobyte*; one kilobyte equals around 1,000 bytes (characters). M or MB stands for *megabyte*. One megabyte is equal to approximately 1,000,000 bytes.

Formatting the Disk

To format a disk, place it into drive A (or drive B, if your computer has one and it's the drive you want to use). Open the Disk menu and choose the Format Disk command. The Format Disk dialog box appears.

Click on the down arrow beside the Disk In box. Click on the drive you want to use, either A or B (pick the one your disk is in). Click on the down arrow beside the Capacity box. Then click on the capacity you want. Click OK to start formatting.

"I HATE THIS!"

Get that capacity right!!

Don't be careless about selecting the disk's capacity when formatting it. You can select the wrong capacity without realizing it, and your computer and the File Manager may not utter a peep in protest.

A disk that's been formatted at the wrong capacity is a time bomb. It may not reliably store the data you record on it. A file you thought was safely socked away on the diskette could suddenly disappear, because the disk was not correctly formatted. So choose that capacity carefully. And be like Santa: check it twice!

Run, Program! Run!

Most of the time you'll run programs by double-clicking on their icons in the Program Manager. But you can also run programs directly from the File Manager. Just double-click on a program file in the File List!

Suppose that you want to run the Windows Notepad program. First, open the WINDOWS directory by clicking on its folder in the Directory Tree. (That's where the file is stored.) Then find the NOTEPAD.EXE file in the File List, and double-click on it.

The File Manager uses little icons in the File List to show you what each file is for. Program files are shown with a program icon, which looks like a miniature window:

cardfile.exe

Types of program files

- Most of the programs you'll use in Windows will have the EXE extension. EXE stands for *executable*. (Why? Because another name for a program is "executable file.")
- Some small, simple programs use the COM extension—COM stands for *command*. Several of the programs you use with DOS use the COM extension.
- You may also see BAT files. No these are not secret Batman files from the Batcave. BAT files are little "scripts" used in DOS to automate commands. BAT stands for *batch*. Windows doesn't use BAT files much, so you can safely forget about them. When you do want to use one, just double-click on it, like you do with programs.
- PIF files help Windows know how to run your DOS programs. PIF stands for *program information file*. Inside this file is all sorts of juicy information that tells Windows what the DOS program likes and doesn't like. If you double-click on a PIF file, you start a DOS program.
- Treat BAT files and PIFs like unknown programs: don't use them unless you are sure that you know what they do and that you want to run one.

CAUTION

Don't go around double-clicking on every program you see, especially those in the DOS directory. Some DOS programs, like CHKDSK.COM and RECOVER.COM, should *never* be used in Windows. Treat unfamiliar programs just like stray dogs: be extra careful with them lest they bite!

EXPERTS ONLY

Where the PIF did these PIFs come from?

PIFs are made by Windows or your DOS programs or you. When you installed Windows, it searched through your computer's hard disk drive looking for popular DOS programs. If you decided to make icons for these programs, Windows made PIFs for them at the same time.

Many DOS programs create their own PIFs during installation. You can also make your own PIFs or, if your DOS program isn't behaving itself under Windows, change the information in existing PIFs.

PIFing isn't for sissies—even Einstein would have trouble with them. I'm sure you'll be disappointed when I tell you that you won't be learning about them in this book. If you do need help on using a PIF or DOS file, you'd best get the help of a really patient and kind computer geek.

Starting a Program and Opening a Document at the Same Time

(Program magic)

Here's a neat trick you can do with the File Manager: if you double-click on certain kinds of document files, the File Manager will start the program that created the file *and* open the document in that program at the

same time. This is a shortcut to starting a program and then manually opening a document file.

For example, double-clicking on a WRI (Write) document starts the Windows Write word processing program and automatically opens the file in the Write program; you can change it, or print it, or whatever.

The key to this trick is the file's extension. Windows automatically recognizes only certain extensions and knows which programs go with which documents (see table 8.1). Most Windows programs assign an extension by default, and it's a good idea to use that extension.

Table 8.1 Common Document File Associations

File Extension	Associated Windows Program
BMP	Paintbrush
CRD	Cardfile
DOC	Word for Windows
HLP	Windows Help
TRM	Terminal
TXT	Notepad
WRI	Windows Write
WK3	1-2-3 for Windows
XLS	Microsoft Excel

BUZZWORDS

ASSOCIATE

To "associate" a file with a program (that is, with the program you used to create the file) means that you establish a link between the program and the file's extension, such as TXT or WRI. This link tells the File Manager which program the file belongs to.

Setting Confirmations

(Are you sure? Are you doubly sure?)

The File Manager can become quite the nag: "Are you sure you want to…?" "Do you really want to…?" You can tell the File Manager to mind its own business by changing its confirmation options.

To change one or more File Manager confirmations, open the Options menu and choose the Confirmation command. The Confirmation dialog box opens up. This box contains five check box options.

If a box has an X in it, that option is turned on (enabled). The option is turned off (disabled) when there is no X in the box. You enable or disable an option by clicking in the box.

CAUTION

When it doubt, leave the confirmations on. The confirmations are there to help you avoid mistakes. You can turn off a confirmation, but remember that if you do, you have to be extra careful of what you do in the File Manager.

Let's assume that all the options have an X, so that confirmation is on for everything. Click on:

- File Delete to turn off confirmation when you delete a file. The File Manager will still display a dialog box with the name of the file you are deleting, but the "Confirm File Delete" message will not appear.

- Directory Delete to turn off confirmation when you delete a directory. As it does when deleting a file, the File Manager will still display a dialog box with the name of the directory you are deleting, but the "Confirm Directory Delete" message will not appear.

- File Replace to turn off confirmation when you replace a file with another one. Files are replaced when you give a file a name already in use, or when you copy (or move) a file from one directory to another, and the destination directory already contains a file with the same name.

- Mouse Action to turn off confirmation when you move or copy a file using the mouse.

- Disk Commands to turn off confirmation when you format or copy a disk.

PART III

Managing Programs

Includes:

CHAPTER 9

Making Icons and Running Programs

IN A NUTSHELL

- Making program icons
- What to do when a program icon won't work
- How to find programs on your hard disk drive
- Running a program without an icon

Running a program is easy enough to do if the program you want to run has an icon. But not all programs on your computer's hard disk drive have an icon. Does that mean you're out of luck, unable to run the program? Not at all.

The Program Manager lets you run any program on your computer. This chapter tells you how to do just that. It also tells you how to make icons for programs that don't have them and how to find programs.

The Art of Icon Making

Icons make it a lot easier to run programs. All it takes to start a program is a double-click on its icon. Without the icon, you'll have to use the crankshaft method to run a program, as described later in this chapter.

If there's a program you use a lot that doesn't have an icon, consider making one for it. Making an icon involves some up-front work, but that work will pay off later. To create a program icon, follow these steps:

1. Double-click on one of the group icons in the Program Manager to open the window where you want the icon to appear. For example, if you want to add the program icon to the Accessories group, double-click on the Accessories group icon to open the Accessories window.

2. Open the File menu and choose the New command. A dialog box appears, and the Program Manager asks what type of item you want to create: a Program Group or a Program Item. Program Item should be selected (a dot should appear inside the Program Item button). If it's not, click on the Program Item option to select it.

3. Click on the OK button. The Program Item Properties dialog box appears.

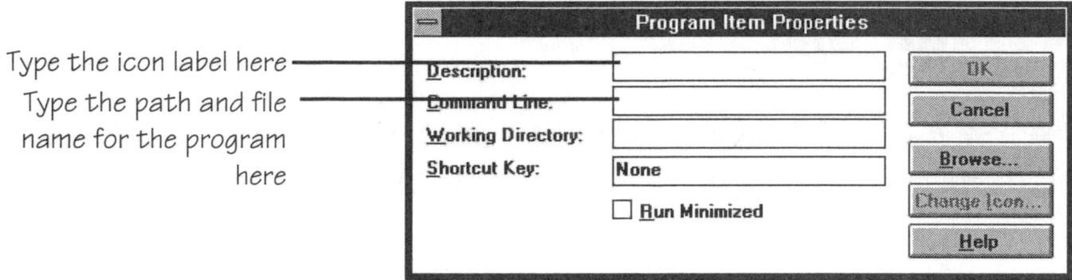

4. In the entry box labeled Description, type the text you want to show under the icon. Try to be descriptive. An icon labeled "Stuff" doesn't tell you a whole lot about the program it represents.

5. Click in the entry box labeled Command Line. Type the complete path to the program, including the program file name. For instance, you might type **C:\WP51\WP.EXE** for WordPerfect. If you don't know the file name of the program or where it is on your computer's hard disk drive, read "Treasure Hunt for Programs," later in this chapter.

PATH

A path is directions that tell Windows where to find a program. As part of the path, you also include the program file name. This tells Windows which program to run. Chapter 6 covers all the ground on paths.

6. Leave the other two entry blanks the way they are.

7. Click on the OK button to create the new icon for your program. The Program Item Properties dialog box disappears, and Windows makes the new icon.

To run the program, you just double-click on the icon. That's the payoff!

Error Message Blues

You've followed the directions above to a T, but after you click on OK, the Program Manager displays an error message that reads something like:

```
The path SPIFFY.EXE is invalid
```

The Program Manager balked at making an icon for the program because it couldn't locate the program on your computer's hard disk drive. (Note that you won't see the name SPIFFY.EXE, that's just my example. You'll see the name of the program you are trying to add.)

To get rid of the error message, click on the OK button. The error message goes away, and you are returned to the Program Manager.

CAUTION

Even though you got the error message, the Program Manager still makes the program icon for you. Don't try to double-click on the icon, because you'll just get another error message saying that the program could not be found. The icon is useless, so delete it.

Click on it once, press the Del key, and then click on Yes.

Typical reasons for the error message

- You typed the wrong name for the program. This problem is easy enough to fix. Try creating the icon again, but this time type the right name. Check the program manual for help on figuring out the right name, or take a look at the next section.
- You typed the wrong directory path—also easy to fix. Create the icon again, with the correct path.

- ▼ You didn't type a directory path, and the Program Manager couldn't find the program on your computer's hard disk drive. You must include the path of the program so that the Program Manager knows which directory to look in to find the program. Create the icon again, and type both the path and the program name.
- ▼ The program isn't anywhere on your computer's hard disk. You have to install the program first!

Treasure Hunt for Programs

The Command Line entry blank in the Program Item Properties dialog box is great if you already know the name of the program you want to run and exactly where it is. But what if you don't know or remember this stuff? It's not as if C:\HGRAPH\HG.EXE is right there on the tip of your tongue. Heck, you may not even be able to remember all the names of your coworkers, let alone all your files and where they are.

Instead of typing that convoluted path and file name, you can "browse" around. Browsing isn't as easy as it sounds. You still have to understand directories and paths to find the program. So if you're new to this stuff or need a refresher course, check out Chapter 6.

Browsing the Browse Dialog Box

Here's how to browse:

1. From the Program Item Properties dialog box, click inside the Command Line entry box. If you don't know how to get to this dialog box, see the steps on creating a program icon, back a few pages.

2. Click inside the Command Line entry box. Then click on the Browse button. The Browse dialog box appears.

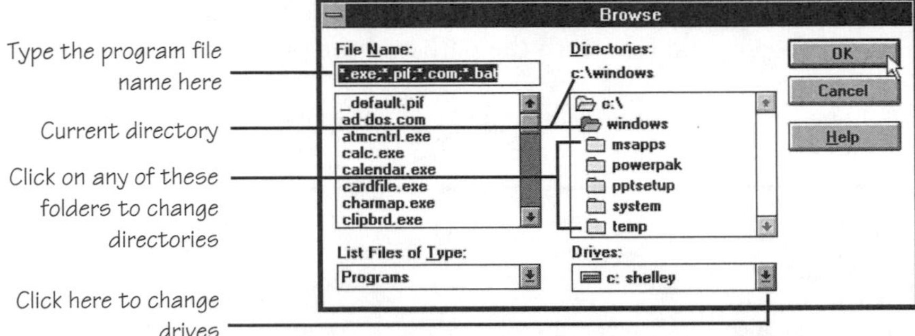

Checklist

- The *file list box* on the left shows all the program files in the current directory (probably the WINDOWS directory).
- Only those files with the extension .EXE, .COM, .PIF, or .BAT are listed. These are the types of programs that Windows can run. (Chapter 8 talks about what these file extensions mean.) The most common kind of program uses the .EXE extension.
- The *directory list box* on the right shows you the current directory and disk drive.
- In the list on the right, you see little folders. The top folder is named C:\ and indicates the root directory. This folder is always open.
- The current directory, probably WINDOWS, is listed next. This folder is also open. The current directory is always shown open.
- Below the current directory, you might see any additional directories that are inside the current directory (folders within that folder). These folders are closed.

I See the Program!

If you see the program file you want, click on it. You got off easy.

If there are more files than will fit in the file list box, a scroll bar appears on the right side of the box so that you can scan up and down the list to see more items. Use the mouse to click the up and down arrows in the scroll bar to see more files. If you see the program file as you scroll through the list, click on that file.

After you click on the program file you want, click on the OK button. The Program Manager takes you back to the Program Item Properties dialog box, and the program you selected is shown in the Command Line entry blank with appropriate path and file name. Click inside the Description entry blank and type the text you want to show below the icon. Click on OK to close the dialog box; the Program Manager creates the new icon.

I Don't See the Program!

If you don't see the program file, it means that the file is not in the current directory. You'll have to look through the other directories on your computer's hard disk drive to find the file by using the directory list box on the right.

BUZZWORDS

CURRENT DIRECTORY

The current directory is like a file drawer that's open. The open file drawer is the one that you go through to find something. Windows works the same way. The current directory is the one that Windows has open at the moment; the files contained within it are the ones shown in the file list box. The same logic applies to the current drive, which you'll read about next.

If the directory you want to look inside is shown in the directory list box, double-click on it. The directory folder opens (the inside of the folder turns gray), and the files in the file list box change to show you what's inside the directory.

If the directory you want to look inside is not shown in the directory list box, first double-click on the C:\ folder. Now you'll see all the directories that are in the root directory. Double-click on the folder you want to open. You might have to scroll through the list to find the folder you want.

Remember that folders can be inside other folders. You may have to slog through several folders to get to the one you want. If you get lost in a folder that's not familiar to you, you can always regain your bearings by clicking on the C:\ folder and starting over.

When you find the file you want, go back to the section "I See the Program!" to finish out the browse.

I *Still* Don't See the Program!

If the file isn't in any of the directories you've looked through, it may be on another drive. You can also look through files on another disk drive by clicking the down-arrow button on the right side of the Drives box.

CAUTION

If you select a floppy drive without a disk inside the floppy drive, Windows gets upset and tells you that there's a problem "reading" the drive.

A little list pops up into view, showing you the drives you can select from. Click on the drive you want. If the file you want appears in the file list box, click on it and return to "I See the Program!"

You should not select drive A or B, because these are floppy disk drives. Unlike your computer's hard disk drive, floppy disks can be removed from your computer. If you make an icon for a program that's located on a floppy disk, you must reinsert that disk into the computer every time you want to run the program. If the program you want to run is on a floppy disk, copy the program from the floppy disk to your computer's hard disk. See Chapter 7 for details on how to do this.

I Give Up

Can't find the program you want anywhere? Don't panic! Click on the Cancel button in the Browse dialog box to close it. You can either start all over again or say, "The heck with it!" and get somebody to help you locate that blasted program. Click on Cancel again to close the Program Item Properties dialog box.

Running Any Program, Any Time

(The crankshaft method)

The easiest way to run a program is to double-click on its icon. But if the program has no icon, and you don't want to bother making one for it, the Program Manager still lets you run it.

This alternate method is used most often to install a new program. The program disk most likely contains an installation program that automatically installs the program and creates the right program groups. To run this installation program, you have to use this alternate, "crankshaft" method. Most other times, however, you won't want to hassle with using this method to run a program.

To run any program, open the File menu and choose the Run command. The Run dialog box appears. This dialog box contains an entry blank where you can type in the name of the program you want to run.

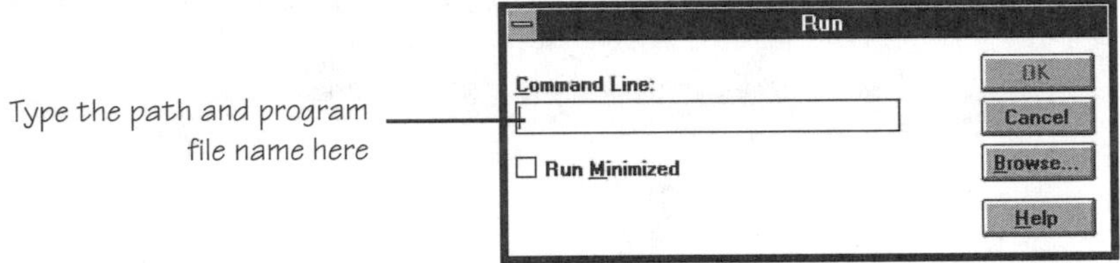

If you know the name of the program you want to run, just type it into the entry blank. For example, to run the Windows Notepad program, type **NOTEPAD.EXE** (upper- or lowercase, it doesn't matter). If the program is not in the current directory, be sure to type the path and the program file name.

Now click on the OK button. If all goes well, Windows cranks up your program and you're on your way. Consider treating yourself to a quart of chocolate marshmallow cookie dough ice cream.

Checklist

- ▼ If you want to run a program that isn't on your computer's hard disk drive, read the next section, "Running a Program That's on Another Drive."

▼ If you don't know the name of the program, you can browse around to find it. Turn the page and read the section called "Browsing for Files."

▼ If you see an error message, flip ahead to "Windows Couldn't Find the Program."

Running a Program That's on Another Drive

You can run a program on any disk drive connected to your computer. To run a program on another drive, type this command in the Run dialog box:

A:\SETUP.EXE

Decoded, this command indicates the drive letter (followed by a colon and a backslash) and the program name.

TIP

> You usually run a program from a different drive when you are installing a new program. Check the manual for what to type in the Run dialog box.

Checklist

▼ You might need to include a full path for the file so that the Program Manager can find the program on the other disk.

▼ You can type the path, if you know it, or have the Program Manager help you find the file on the disk by using the Browse dialog box. See "Browsing for Files," next.

Browsing for Files

Don't know the exact name of the program you want to run? Have the Program Manager help you find it. In the Run dialog box, click on the Browse button. The Browse dialog box appears, showing you the programs and directories you have on your computer's hard disk drive.

This Browse dialog box is exactly the same one you get when you make a new icon for a program. See the section, "Treasure Hunt for Programs," earlier in this chapter, for complete details on how to use the Browse dialog box. Here's a summary:

Checklist

- If you see the program file you want in the file list, click on it.
- If you don't see the program file you want, it might be in another directory on your computer's hard disk drive. Double-click on the folders in the directory list box to see the innards of other directories. Click on the file in the file list when you've spotted the one you want.

Windows Couldn't Find the Program

If, for whatever reason, the Program Manager was unable to run the program—perhaps it couldn't find a program with that name—you're told so, in no uncertain terms. Windows throws an error message at you:

```
Cannot find file BALONEY.EXE (or one of its components).
Check to ensure the path and filename are correct and
that all required libraries are available.
```

Let's figure out what the heck the Program Manager is trying to tell us here. BALONEY.EXE is the name of the program you want to run. (BALONEY.EXE is just an example name; you probably don't have a program with that name on your computer's hard disk drive!)

Click the OK button to zap away the error message. The Program Manager returns you to the Run dialog box. You can either click the Cancel button to forget running the program, or try figuring out and correcting the problem.

Reasons you might get an error message

- If the program file isn't on the hard disk at all, you can't run it, silly.
- If the program file is tucked away in a different directory than the Program Manager is looking in, you need to specify a different path. Read Chapter 6 for directions on providing the path. Or try browsing for the file, as covered earlier.
- You might have misspelled the name of the program file. Double-check your spelling. Look in the program manual for the program name. To correct a misspelling (either in the file name or the path), click inside the Command Line entry blank. Press the right or left arrow keys to place the flashing cursor to the right of the mistake. Press Backspace one or more times until the incorrect characters are rubbed out. Retype the correct characters.
- You also might have misspelled the path for the file. Be sure you type the entire path. Use backslashes to separate directory names within the path.

If you get the error message again, either Program Manager still can't find the program, or another file the program needs can't be found.

Double-check that the program file name and path are entered correctly, and if the program still won't run, get the help of your friendly local computer guru.

CHAPTER 10

Using Windows Mini-Programs

IN A NUTSHELL

- Using Windows' Open and Save dialog boxes
- Writing with Windows Write
- Making pictures with Paintbrush
- Using the other Windows mini-programs

One of the best things about Windows is that once you learn one program, you can easily learn another. Tasks such as opening and saving files work similarly in most Windows packages. This chapter starts by giving you the keys to the Open and Save dialog boxes that pop up in most Windows programs.

And who says you don't get anything for free? You do with Windows. It comes with a collection of programs for such things as writing letters, drawing pictures, or keeping track of your daily appointments. These programs don't have all the bells and whistles that a similar, expensive program might have, but they do quite well in a pinch. They are called "mini-programs," because they aren't fully loaded. This chapter talks about the mini-programs that come with Windows.

TIP

Experiment with these freebie Windows programs. Most of the stuff you learn while playing—er, experimenting—with these programs will apply to any Windows program you use.

Save and Open

(The keys to file access)

Windows tries to make it easy to open and save document files. It comes with "standard" dialog boxes, which most Windows programs use, for these tasks. These dialog boxes are considered "standard" because once you learn how to save or open a file in one program, you'll know how to do it in the others. Cool, huh?

This section will help you make sense of the dialog boxes in Write and Paintbrush, as well as in other Windows programs, such as Word, Excel, and so on.

Keep This File

If you create a document and want to keep it for later use, you must save it. Saving takes the information in the document and writes it to the disk in a file. While you are working on a file, it's stored in memory, but memory isn't permanent. If the computer is turned off or the power goes out, all that work is history, never to be seen again. Swear words, sobs to the company computer guru, or sacrifices to the electronic gods will not make your work reappear. The moral of the story is this: save your work or you will be severely bummed.

To save a document file, open the File menu and choose the Save As command. The first time you save a document, you have to give it a name. The Save As dialog box appears. The file list box on the left shows all the files in the current directory (the directory you used the last time you selected the command). The directory list box on the right shows you the current directory and disk drive.

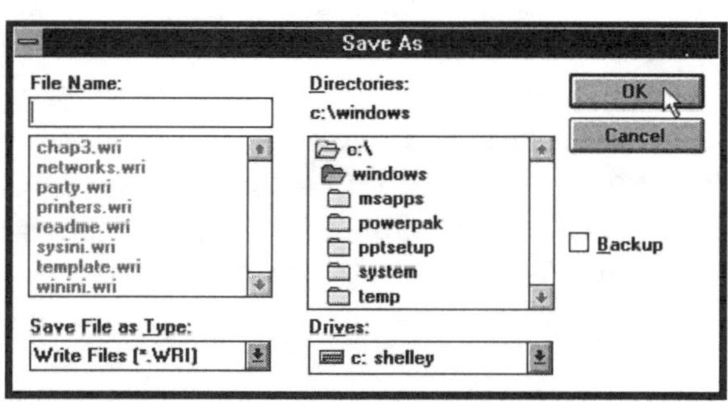

The Save As dialog box

Type a file name and click OK. If you're saving a document file, the file is recorded in the directory shown in the directory list box on the right. If this isn't the directory where you want to store the document file, choose another directory. You'll learn how to do that pretty soon, in "Changing to Another Directory."

Open This File

To open a document file, open the File menu and choose the Open command. The Open dialog box appears. The file list box on the left shows all the files in the current directory (the directory you used the last time you selected the command). The directory list box on the right shows you the current directory and disk drive.

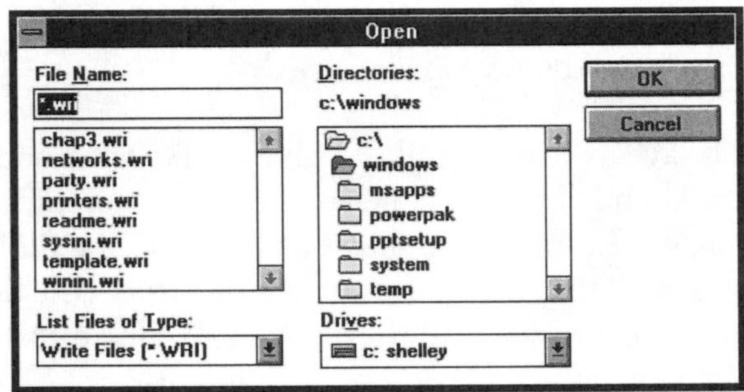

The Open dialog box

If you're opening a document file and see its name in the file list box, click on it (if necessary, use the scroll bars to see more files); then click on the OK button. You can double-click on the file name instead, if you want to. Either way, the file opens. If you don't see the file you want in the file list box, you might need to change the directory or the disk drive as described in the next section.

Changing to Another Directory

The file list box shows the files in the current directory. If you want to open or save a file in another directory, you must first make that directory current.

The directory list displays the names of directories, beside pictures of little folders. The top folder is named C:\ and is the root directory. This folder is always open. The current directory is listed next. This folder is also open. Below the current directory you may see any additional directories that are inside the current directory (folders within that folder). These folders are shown closed.

If the directory you want is shown in the directory list box, double-click on it. The directory folder opens (the inside of the folder turns gray), and the files in the file list box change to show you what's inside the directory.

If the directory you want is not shown in the directory list box, first double-click on the C:\ folder. Now you'll see all the directories that are in the root directory. Double-click on the one you want.

"I HATE THIS!"

Where is that darned directory?

Remember that directories can be inside other directories. You may have to open several directory folders to get to the one you want. If you get lost in a directory that's not familiar to you, you can always regain your bearings by clicking on the C:\ folder.

Changing to Another Disk Drive

Use the Drives box to change the current disk drive. When you change the disk drive, you can open a document file that's on that drive. And if you save a file, the file is saved onto that disk.

To change the drive, click the down-arrow button beside the Drives box. A little list pops up into view, showing you the drives you can select. Click on the drive you want.

CAUTION

Don't select a floppy drive unless there's a disk inside the floppy drive. If you do, Windows gets upset and tells you that it's having trouble "reading" the drive. If you get this message, click on Cancel to make the error message go away, and swear that you'll never do it again. Or make sure that the disk is properly positioned in the drive, and click on Retry.

Throw Out That Typewriter

(Heeeeeere's Windows Write!)

Use Windows Write to write letters, memos, and reports. You can print onto paper whatever you write. And you can save your written documents, in case you want to use them later.

BUZZWORDS

DOCUMENT

A document is a file you create with a program.

Windows Write (I'll just call it Write from now on) is a word processor, and a fairly simple one at that. The basic stuff in Write is the same in any Windows word processor, so what you learn about Write will help you if you move up to a bigger, fatter word processor.

Don't expect Write to be able to put together really complex documents for you. If you need to create a letter or a memo, Write is perfect for the job. If you need to create a dissertation for your Ph.D., you'll need to buy a more sophisticated word processor.

Starting Write (Write away!)

Start Write by double-clicking on the Accessories group icon and then double-clicking on the Write icon. Write starts and displays its window.

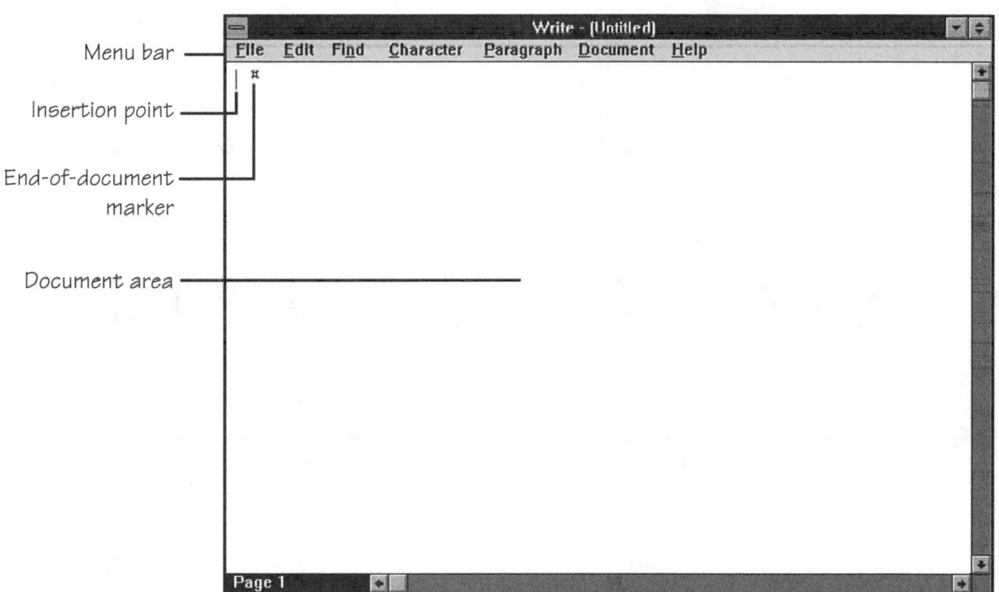

TIP

If the Write window appears less than full-screen, click on its Maximize button in the upper right corner, the button with a ▲ on it. It's easier to work with Write—and most Windows programs in general—when they are expanded to full screen.

Checklist

- ▼ The inside part of the Write window (the document area) is where the text you type will appear.
- ▼ The flashing vertical bar is the insertion point, sometimes called the *cursor*. The insertion point tells you where text will appear when you type on your computer's keyboard.
- ▼ The four-pointed doohickey is the "end of document" symbol. No text can appear after the doohickey.

Typing Text (Let your fingers do the typing)

To write with Write, just start typing on the keyboard. As you type, the characters appear to the left of the flashing insertion point.

Write doesn't work like a typewriter! You don't need to press the Enter key at the end of each line to start a new line. Write will do that for you. This nifty little feature, which all good computer word processors have, is called *word wrapping*. Press the Enter key when you specifically want to start a new line or when you want to begin a new paragraph.

Moving Around

The flashing insertion point always tells you where text will appear when you type. If you want to add text in the middle of something you've already written, you need to move the insertion point there first.

Press the up-, down-, right-, or left-arrow keys to move the insertion point around the document area. The insertion point will only go where you've written text.

Using the mouse, move the mouse pointer (the pointer becomes shaped like an I instead of an arrow when it's within text) to where you want to move the insertion point, and click.

Erasing Text (No eraser needed!)

Let's say you type "Faster than a speeding locomotive! More powerful than a bullet!!" Any Superman fan will tell you that you've got "locomotive" and "bullet" switched around. You need to erase the wrong parts and retype the phrase correctly.

To erase text, you first need to move the insertion point to the text you want to get rid of. Place the insertion point to the right of the text you want to delete. Then press the Backspace key for every character you want to rub out.

TIP

You can also use the Del key to eliminate unwanted text. The Del key gets rid of characters to the right of the insertion point.

With the incorrect text gone, type the correct version. If you're describing Superman, the correction reads: "Faster than a speeding bullet! More powerful than a locomotive!!" You can take it from there. (Here's a hint: "Able to leap tall buildings....")

Tinkering with Text

Spruce up your documents by using some of Write's more advanced features.

Checklist

- ▼ To select text, position the mouse pointer right before the first character of the text you want to delete. Then drag the mouse to select all the characters to the end of the text you want to delete (press and hold the mouse button while you move the mouse). Let go of the mouse button, and the dragged-over text is shown highlighted—that is, *selected.*
- ▼ To make text bold (look darker when printed), select it with the mouse. Then open the Character menu and choose the Bold command.
- ▼ To make text italic, select it, open the Character menu, and then choose the Italic command.
- ▼ To move some text, select it, open the Edit menu, and then choose the Cut command. This command moves the text to the Windows Clipboard (the Clipboard is a "hidden" feature of Windows). Click on the spot in the document where you want to move the text; the flashing insertion point appears at this spot. Open the Edit menu and choose the Paste command. The previously cut text is inserted where the flashing insertion point is located.

- To copy some text, repeat the preceding procedure, but choose the Copy command instead of the Cut command.
- If you make a mistake, like deleting a word you didn't mean to, open the Edit menu and choose the Undo command. The wording of the Undo command changes to reflect the thing you are about to undo, such as *Undo Typing* or *Undo Editing*.

Saving and Opening a Document

Careful! Write doesn't automatically save your work. You have to do that yourself. To save or open your document, see the section "Save and Open" at the beginning of this chapter.

Printing a File

After you create a document in Write, you probably want to print it out so that the whole world can read your words of wisdom. Be sure that your printer is on and ready. Then open the File menu and choose the Print command. The Print dialog box appears. Click on OK to start printing, or on Cancel if you change your mind. Your printer will spit out your document one page at a time.

Leaving Write (Exit Stage Write)

When you're done with Write, open the File menu and choose the Exit command. The Write program ends, and you're returned to the Program Manager.

If you haven't saved your work yet, Write asks whether you want to. Click on Yes to save or No to abandon your work. If you click on Yes, Write displays the Save As dialog box. Give the file a name and then do all the other junk, as explained in "Save and Open." If you click on No, the file is not saved, but is jettisoned into deep space where all unwanted Write documents go.

Bring Out the Picasso with Paintbrush

Windows Paintbrush lets you dabble in computer art. Paintbrush is a fun program if you just want to experiment with making colors and designs. You can use Paintbrush to create invitations, place cards, signs, letterheads...you name it. You might even discover a new artistic talent!

Starting Paintbrush (Get your brushes ready)

Start Paintbrush by double-clicking on the Accessories group icon and then double-clicking on the Paintbrush icon. Paintbrush starts and displays its window.

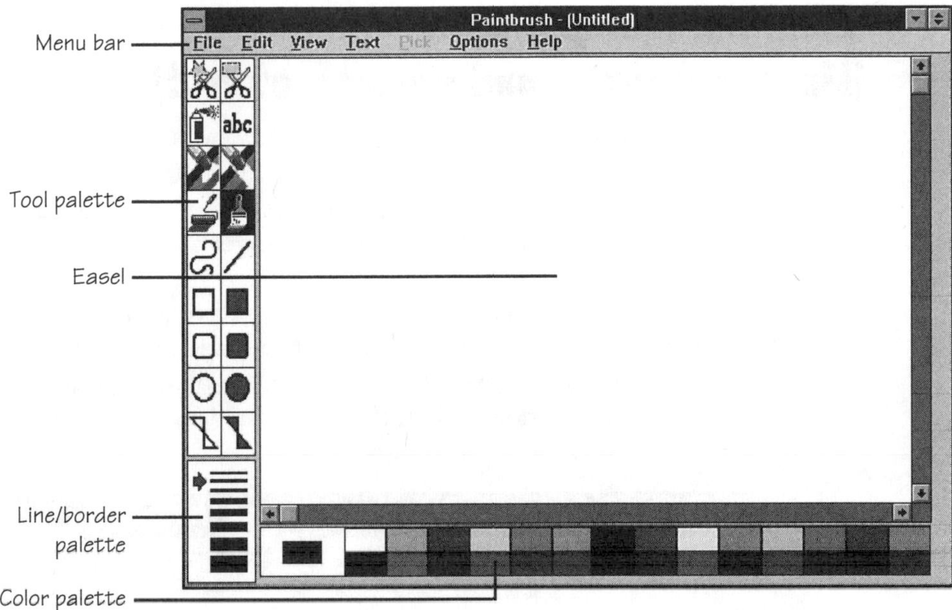

If the Paintbrush window appears less than full-screen, click on its Maximize button (the one with the ▲ on it) in the upper right corner.

Checklist

- ▼ The painting area (called the *easel*) is where you draw your picture.
- ▼ The painting tools appear along the left edge of the window. Click on a tool and use it to paint your picture.
- ▼ Use the line/border palette to change the thickness of lines and borders in your picture.
- ▼ Pick a color from the color palette.

Using the Drawing Tools (Lines and circles and squares, oh my!)

If you know how to draw a picture using a crayon, you know how to paint with Paintbrush. Click on a tool (see table 10.1), then place the mouse pointer in the easel. Press and hold the mouse button and move the mouse (remember, this is called "dragging") to draw.

For example, to draw a line, click on the Line tool in the tool palette (the Line tool is the one with a / on it). Move the mouse onto the easel. Press and hold the mouse button. As you move the mouse, a line appears. Let go of the mouse when the line is the length you want.

Table 10.1 Tools You Can Use to Draw Things

Icon	Name	Description
abc	Text	Types text in the drawing easel.
	Paintbrush	Paints color with the paintbrush tip of your choice.
	Curve	Draws a curvy line. After drawing a line, you can use the mouse to tug at the line to change its shape.
/	Line	Draws a straight line.
	Empty rectangle	Draws a square or rectangle, without color inside.
	Filled rectangle	Draws a square or rectangle, with color inside.

Icon	Name	Description
	Empty rounded rectangle	Draws a square or rectangle with rounded corners, but without color inside.
	Filled rounded rectangle	Draws a square or rectangle with rounded corners and with color inside.
	Empty oval	Draws a circle or oval, without color inside.
	Filled oval	Draws a circle or oval, with color inside.
	Empty polygon	Draws a multi-sided shape (polygon), without color inside.
	Filled polygon	Draws a multi-sided shape (polygon), with color inside.

TIP

When you get tired of painting in basic black, click on a new color in the color palette. Now what you draw is in the color you selected!

Here are some pointers to keep in mind while you doodle with Paintbrush:

Checklist

- Double-click on the Paintbrush tool to change the tip of the brush. In the dialog box that appears, click on a brush tip; then click OK. (The slanted lines are great for calligraphy!)
- To make the Paintbrush tip bigger, click on a thicker line in the line/border palette.
- To draw a perfectly straight horizontal or vertical line, hold down the Shift key while you draw with the Paintbrush tool.
- To draw straight vertical, horizontal, or 45-degree angle lines, hold down the Shift key while you draw with the Line tool.
- To clear all of the easel at once, double-click on the regular Eraser tool. Click on No in the dialog box that asks you whether you want to save your work.
- To change the color of a filled shape, such as an oval or rectangle, click on a color in the color palette with the right mouse button.
- To change the border of a filled or unfilled shape, click on a color in the color palette with the left mouse button.
- To edit a picture dot-by-dot, open the View menu and choose the Zoom In command. Use the mouse to position the Zoom In box where you want to edit; then click the mouse. To get out of zoom view, choose Zoom Out from the View menu.

Oops! I Don't Like That

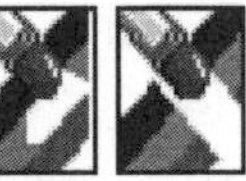

Paintbrush comes with two erasers: a regular eraser that erases everything (the one on the right) and a color eraser that erases just a particular color (the left eraser). The regular eraser is the one you'll use the most. To erase a portion of your picture, click on the regular eraser tool. Move the mouse onto the easel, and drag the mouse around to erase the part of the picture you don't want.

Starting Over

If you don't like what you've done so far, and you want to start all over, don't erase every little bit of your drawing. Instead, throw the old easel away and start with a new one! Open the File menu and choose the New command. Paintbrush asks whether you want to save the artwork you've already done. Click on No if you don't want to keep your work. Once you click on No, there's no turning back. Your Mona Lisa-in-progress is lost forever. Click on Cancel if you change your mind and want to go back to doodling some more with the same picture.

Saving and Opening a Picture

If you want to keep your picture, you'll need to save it in a document file before leaving Paintbrush. Otherwise, your painting will be forever lost. See "Save and Open" at the beginning of this chapter for the scoop on saving and opening files.

Printing a Picture

Print your Paintbrush picture by opening the File menu and choosing the Print command. The Print dialog box appears. Click on OK to start printing or on Cancel if you change your mind. Your masterpiece is recorded on paper. If your printer prints only in black and white, any colors you've used in your picture turn into various shades of gray.

Exiting Paintbrush (Cleaning up)

When you're done with Paintbrush, open the File menu and choose the Exit command. The Paintbrush program ends, and you're returned to the Program Manager.

If you haven't yet saved your work, Paintbrush asks you whether you want to. Click on Yes to save the work or No to abandon it. If you click on Yes, Paintbrush displays the Save As dialog box. Give the file a name and do all the other stuff you learned in "Save and Open," earlier in this chapter. If you click on No, the file is not saved.

...and the Rest of the Gang

Write and Paintbrush are the stars of the Windows mini-programs, but there are a number of supporting cast members worthy of note. Here's a brief review. (To open any of these mini-programs, double-click on the program icon you want in the Accessories group window.)

Notepad

Notepad is a simplified version of Windows Write. Notepad really isn't word processor; it's a text editor. It lets you write and edit text, but has none of the more advanced features of Write.

Terminal

Terminal is a telecommunications program. If your computer has a modem, you can use it to connect with other computers over the phone. Terminal is used to make or receive calls and pass data back and forth.

Cardfile

Cardfile is an electronic version of a 3-by-5-inch card file. You fill in a card with whatever information you want to keep, and Cardfile remembers it for you. You can use Cardfile to keep track of phone numbers, birthdays, recipes...just about anything.

Calendar

Calendar helps you keep your schedule straight. Click on a day of the month, and you can write your schedule so you don't forget it. You can even ask the Calendar to beep out an alarm from your computer's speaker to remind you of an important meeting or phone call.

Clock

This mini-program displays a window that gives you the current time.

Calculator

Use the Windows Calculator when your $5.99 pocket calculator has been swiped off your desk again.

TIP

Windows actually comes with two calculators. There's the standard four-function calculator for everyday calculations. Then there's a confusing-looking "scientific" calculator with all sorts of buttons and stuff for figuring out logarithms, exponents, tangents, and other things most people have never even heard of. You can switch between them with a click of the mouse. If you're using the standard calculator and want to get to the scientific calculator, open the View menu and choose the Scientific command.

If you want to learn about the mini-programs called Sound Recorder and Media Player, read the next chapter.

CHAPTER 11

Fun Stuff

(Making Windows the Life of the Party)

IN A NUTSHELL

- Using a screen saver
- Making sounds with Windows
- Recording your own sounds
- Playing songs with Windows
- Playing Solitaire
- Playing Minesweeper

Windows isn't this stuffed shirt that's only good for business, business, business. It has its fun side, too. In this chapter, you'll find out how to make Windows play movies, how to hear sounds and songs, and how to get started with the games that come with Windows.

Using a Screen Saver

(It's show time)

Personal computers used to have single-color (monochrome) monitors. The "color" was usually white or sometimes a Seasick Green or a Jaundice Yellow. The background was always black.

In all monitors, the colors are created by a special kind of paint that glows when it's hit by teeny-tiny beams shot from the back of the picture tube. The paint used in monochrome monitors had a problem: over time the paint wouldn't "unglow" completely. The result was that an image left on the screen a long time could "burn" into the paint and remain there forever.

To avoid this problem, computer pioneers (they're called "nerds" today) came up with programs that temporarily shut off the picture so that an image wouldn't etch itself into the monitor screen. These programs became known as *screen savers*. Screen savers worked automatically—if you didn't use your computer for a while, the screen went blank. When you pressed a key, the screen would magically reappear.

Life in Modern Times

Most of today's computers use full-color monitors, and the paint (technically called "phosphor") used in these monitors isn't nearly as susceptible to the old burn-in problem.

People still use screen savers, but not so much for saving the screen. Instead, screen savers are used as entertainment and as a security device to keep others from using your computer when they aren't supposed to.

Windows comes with a screen saver. If you want to use it, you need to turn it on and tell Windows which screen saver "movie" you want to show. I say "movie" because it's a continually moving picture that displays on-screen. After you do these things, whenever there is a period of inactivity at your computer (the standard time delay is two minutes) the screen saver takes over and plays the movie.

Turning on the Screen Saver

To turn on the screen saver, double-click on the Main group icon and then double-click on the Control Panel icon. Within the Control Panel window, double-click on the Desktop icon. The Desktop window opens.

Click the down arrow beside the Screen Saver Name box. A list of the screen saver movies appears. Your list might show more choices than usual if you have additional screen saver programs, such as After Dark. Click on one of the screen saver names.

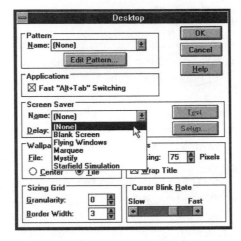

Screen saver choices

Click on the OK button to close the Desktop window. You've just turned on screen saving. Double-click on the Control menu box in the upper left corner of the Control Panel window to close it, and you're ready to go back to work.

Checklist

- By default, the screen saver activates if you don't use your computer for two minutes. After two minutes, the screen saver takes over.

- You can make the time delay as short as a minute or as long as 99 minutes. In the Desktop window, click inside the Delay box. To delete the old entry, press the Backspace or Del key, depending on where you clicked in the box; then type a new delay time (whole numbers only, from 1 to 99).

- When the screen saver movie appears, you can reactivate your computer and display the regular Windows screen by pressing a key or clicking or moving the mouse.

- ▼ You can preview any screen saver movie before buying a ticket for it. To preview a movie, select it in the Screen Saver Name box (in the Desktop window), and then click on the Test button. The movie starts (bring your own popcorn). To stop the preview, move the mouse or press any key.
- ▼ If you decide that you don't want to use the screen saver anymore, choose None in the Screen Saver Name box.
- ▼ In addition to using the movies that come with Windows, you can also buy additional movies for your screen. One popular screen saver package is After Dark.

A Critic's Guide to Screen Saver Movies

Here's a brief review of each of the "movies" provided with Windows.

Movie	Critique
Blank Screen	A really boring tale about a screen that goes blank. No pictures, nothing. Might be interesting to Bergman fans, but nobody else. Discerning audiences will just say no to this one.
Flying Windows	An exhilarating story about a bunch of Windows icons that flap their wings and move around the screen. Fun for the whole family.

continues

Movie	Critique
Marquee	Don't be fooled by the opening movie, where the words "Windows 3.1" crawl across your screen like a slug creeping along the sidewalk. Who would want to watch that? You can be the director of your own creatively distasteful messages and have them zip (or creep) across the screen, in whatever colors, type size, or typeface you want.
Mystify	More brightly colored lines than *Home Alone*. More random zigzag patterns than *Pretty Woman*. Two thumbs up!
Starfield Simulation	In the tradition of *Star Wars*, *Star Trek*, and *The Martians Kidnap Santa Claus*, this screen saver brings swashbuckling outer-space adventure to the home computer screen. (Watch for the cameo by Jack Palance as The Mutant.)

Setting the Password

The screen saver movie, by itself, is a fun diversion. To make screen saving really useful, you can tell Windows to require a password before stopping the screen saver movie. This feature might be handy if you don't want anyone else to see what you're working on when you leave for lunch.

To set the password, open the Desktop window and choose a screen saver movie (other than None or Blank Screen). Then follow these steps:

1. Click on the Setup button. The setup window for the selected screen saver opens. Each screen saver has its own setup window.

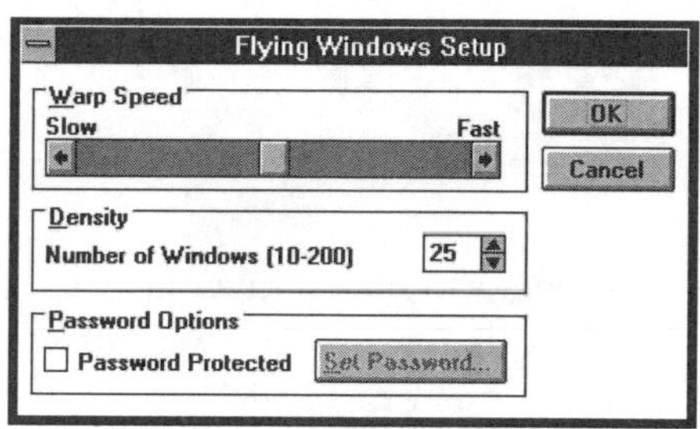

You get this setup window if you selected the Flying Windows screen saver

2. Click inside the Password Protected box.

3. Click on the Set Password button. The Change Password dialog box appears.

4. Click inside the New Password entry blank if it's not already selected, and type the password you want to use.

5. Click inside the Retype New Password entry blank and type the same password again. Be sure to spell it the same (upper- and lowercase variations don't matter).

6. Click on OK three times.

Choose a password you'll never forget. You'll be pretty embarrassed if you forget your password and can't get back to Windows (but if this happens, be sure to read Chapter 17). By the same token, don't choose a password someone else can

CAUTION

easily guess. Things like your first name or the name of your pet canary are out. A good password might be your middle (or maiden) name, but spelled backward. Or your favorite color. Or your favorite movie star. You might want to jot down the password and tuck it away someplace. But don't write "This is the password for my Windows screen saver." That way, someone rummaging through your desk will never know what the notation "Mel Gibson" means.

Now, whenever the screen saver appears, you must type in the password to reactivate Windows. Windows warns you whenever you make a mistake typing the password. Click on OK and try again.

Making Embarrassing Sounds with Windows

Clank! Chunk! Vroooom! Burp!! Ordinarily, when your computer makes strange and unusual sounds, something's broken. But not always! With Windows, your computer can make all sorts of sounds—from cute little baby cootchy-coos to revolting, earth-trembling belches.

"I HATE THIS!"

This fun might not be available on your system

If you don't have a sound board (described next) or a special driver (a program that can work with sound), you won't be able to try out any of the fun in this section. Get a sound board or skip this section.

Sound Boards

Windows comes ready to make sounds, but your computer might not have the right equipment for it. Though your computer is equipped with a little transistor radio speaker, Windows doesn't use it to make sounds. Instead, your computer needs what's known as a *sound board* to make sounds. The sound board, also called a *sound card,* is connected to one or two speakers so you can hear the sounds.

Checklist

- Sound boards are an accessory you can add to your computer. Most computers don't come with a sound board, so it has to be added by the dealer, you, or someone else. If your computer doesn't already have a sound board, you'll need to add one before you can have Windows make cool sounds.

- There are lots of brands of sound boards for personal computers. Popular models are the Sound Blaster, the Thundercard, and the Microsoft Sound System.

- Sound boards plug inside your computer, which means that computer wimps should never attempt to add one without getting expert help. Adding the sound board requires you to open your computer and fiddle around with its guts. This is spooky stuff if you've never done it before. You're better off paying someone a bribe to do the work for you than risking blowing up your computer.

- Though all these sound boards make the same sounds, they don't work the same way. You have to tell Windows which sound board is plugged into your computer. This job isn't easy; it requires you to know some pretty technical things about your computer, including gibberish like "addresses" and "IRQs." Unless you know this stuff already, you'll want to get the help of a knowledgeable friend.

For the remainder of this chapter, I'm assuming that a sound board is already plugged into your computer, and that Windows has been told which board you're using and how it's installed.

Using the Sound Recorder (The Windows tape deck)

To play a Windows sound, you must first run the Sound Recorder program. Double-click on the Accessories group icon, and then double-click on the Sound Recorder icon. The Sound Recorder program window appears.

To tell the Sound Recorder what to play, open the File menu and choose the Open command. The Open dialog box appears. The File Name list box shows the four Windows files (and maybe some others). All the files have the extension .WAV.

Checklist

- Windows comes with four sounds. Each sound is contained in a separate file. Windows sound files always have the extension .WAV (for sound wave).

- Here are the four Windows sounds: CHIMES.WAV plays a short medley of bells, like strumming an electronic harp. CHORD.WAV strikes a single musical chord. DING.WAV gives you a "ding," like running over the dinger hose at a gas station. TADA.WAV plays two chords together; sounds like "ta da!"
- You aren't limited to just these sounds. You can purchase additional "WAV files" and play them with the Sound Recorder. You can purchase sounds such as the whoosh made by the doors in Star Trek, or James Brown's yell, or a toilet flushing.
- If no sound files are listed, read the next section.
- If you see the sound files but they are in light gray, it means you don't have a sound board or driver. You can't use the Sound Recorder. Sorry.
- If you see the sound files, you're ready to play one of them. Skip ahead to the section called, "I See the Sound Files."

I Don't See the Sound Files

Just because you don't see any WAV sound files in the Open dialog box doesn't mean they aren't on your hard disk drive. They're probably in some other directory on your computer's hard disk drive.

The WAV sound files are normally kept in the WINDOWS directory. If that's not the directory you see in the Directories list box, click on the C:\ folder, then find the WINDOWS folder. Click on it to show the files that are inside the WINDOWS directory.

TIP

New to the Open dialog box? It works the same as the Open dialog box in the Windows Write and Paintbrush programs, which are discussed in Chapter 10. Check out that chapter for the straight dope on how to use the Open dialog box.

If you're already looking at the WINDOWS directory and the files aren't there, someone must have moved them. You could fish around all the directories on your hard disk to find out where they are, but an easier way is to pin down the joker that moved the files, and demand—under penalty of torture—that he or she tell you where the WAV sound files are.

TIP

If you've added extra sound files to your system, they probably won't be stored in the WINDOWS directory. You'll have to switch to the directory where you put the files. You do remember where you put those files, don't you?

I See the Sound Files

If you do see the sound files in the Open dialog box, click on the WAV sound file you want to hear (say, TADA.WAV). Then click on the OK button. The Open dialog box goes away, and Windows loads the sound file into the Sound Recorder program. You're now ready to play it back. Click on the play button to play the sound.

Checklist

- ▼ Click on the stop button to stop the sound playback before it gets to the end of the recording.

- Click on the rewind button to start the sound over again.
- Click on the forward button to go to the end of the sound.
- To play another sound, open the File menu and choose the Open command. Then click on the next sound you want to play.
- When you're ready to leave the Sound Recorder program, open the File menu and choose the Exit command.

Linking Sounds to Windows "Events"

If you want to have a lot of fun, you can link a WAV sound file to some event in Windows, such as when Windows starts, or ends, or displays one of those life-or-death error messages. For instance, you can have the computer bark (if you have a bark sound) every time you start Windows.

To link a sound to a Windows event, follow these steps:

1. Double-click on the Main group icon, and then double-click on the Control Panel program icon. The Control Panel opens.
2. Double-click on the Sound icon in the Control Panel. The Sound dialog box appears.

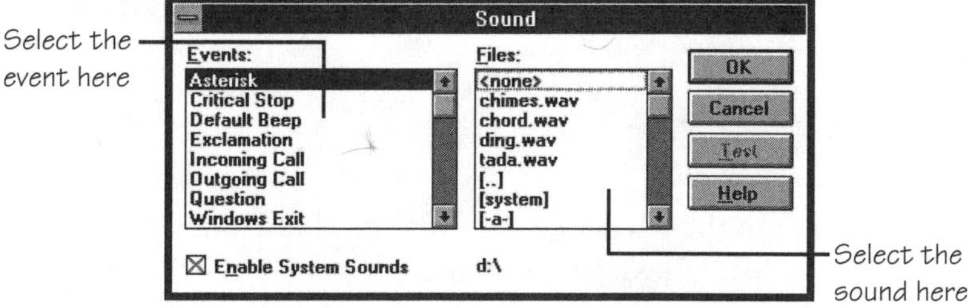

The list box on the left contains the Windows events you can use, like Windows Start and Windows Exit. The list box on the right shows you which WAV sound files you have.

3. To link a sound to an event, click on the event in the left box, and then click on the sound in the right box.

   To hear the sound, click on it and then click the Test button.

4. Click OK when you're done. The Sound dialog box disappears.

5. Double-click on the Control menu box of the Control Panel window to close the window.

Jamming with Windows

The WAV files are short sound files. For longer melodies, most sound boards can play a different kind of sound file, called MID (the MID stands for *MIDI*, a standard used in connecting professional-level electronic musical instruments to a computer). MID files contain information on the notes to play, how long to play them, and which electronic instrument is supposed to play them. (WAV files are the actual recording.)

"I HATE THIS!"

This fun is for sound board owners only

If you don't have a sound board, you can't play MID files. Sorry!

You use the Media Player program that comes with Windows to play back MID files. Windows includes one MID file called CANYON.MID,

a sort of jazzy instrumental. The song plays for a little over two minutes. You can also purchase additional MID files.

To play a MID song on your sound board, you must run the Media Player program. Double-click on the Accessories group icon, and then double-click on the Media Player icon. The Media Player program window appears.

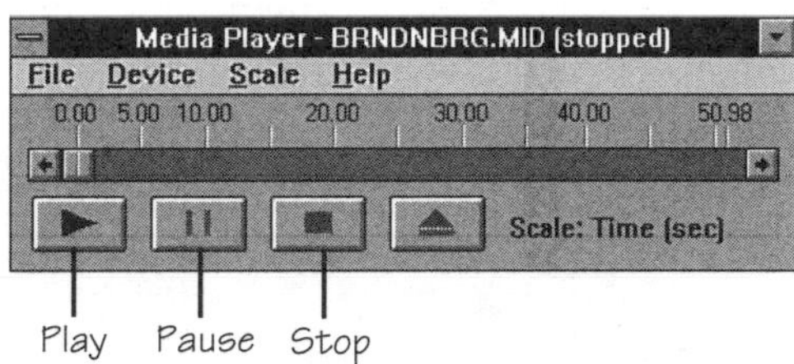

Inside the Media Player program, open the Device menu and choose the MIDI Sequencer command. The Open dialog box appears, showing you the MID song files you can play. Click on a file (try CANYON.MID) and then click OK.

Click on the Play button to play the song file you've selected.

Checklist

- If you don't see any MID files or you don't find the one you want, you could be looking in the wrong directory. Fish through the other directories in the Directories list box until you find the MID file you're looking for. The Open dialog box in Media Player works the same way as the Open dialog boxes for Windows Write and Paintbrush. Go back and read the beginning of Chapter 10 if you want more information on how to use this dialog box.

- Click on the Stop button to stop the song before it reaches the end.

continues

Checklist Continued

▼ Click on the Pause button to temporarily pause the song. Click Play again when you're ready to restart it.

▼ Drag the scroll box left or right in the scroll bar to move backward or forward, respectively, through the song.

▼ When you're ready to leave the Media Player program, open the File menu and choose the Exit command.

"I HATE THIS!"

It sounds like my Aunt Mil singing!

Windows isn't exactly the best musician you'll ever hear. If you play a MID song file and it sounds out of key, Windows probably isn't using your sound board right. You might need to reinstall it or change the way the instruments—the guitars, the pianos, and so forth—are "mapped" in the board.

You can read more about mapping instruments in the user's guide that came with Windows. Or better yet, ask someone else to do it for you.

Windows Likes to Play Games, Too

Tired of the daily rut? Looking for a little diversion to help you make it through the day? Windows comes with two addictive game programs: Solitaire and Minesweeper. Run the programs when you don't have anything else to do. Heck, run them when you *do* have something else to do!

Solitaire

The Solitaire game simulates the time-honored solitaire card game. This variation of solitaire is similar to Klondike, where you start with eight stacks of cards. The object is to restack the cards in order by suit in four piles at the top.

TIP

Windows makes it virtually impossible to cheat at Solitaire (though it is possible, as you'll see in "Quick & Dirty Dozens" at the back of this book). If you like an unclean card game, this one's not for you.

To play Solitaire, double-click on the Games group icon, and then double-click on the Solitaire program icon. The Solitaire window opens, and the cards are automatically dealt for you.

Solitaire window

Checklist

- Drag the cards from one stack to another. To deal out a card from the deck (the top left card), click once on the deck. An O appears on the play board when all the cards in the deck have been dealt out. Double-click on the O to turn the deck back over and keep drawing cards. For more information, use the on-line help.
- To put a card in one of the four stacks along the top of the window, just double-click on it. Solitaire puts the card in the right stack.
- To change the design of the deck of cards, open the Game menu and choose the Deck command. You see a selection of card backs. Click on the one you want. Then click on OK.
- Watch for Windows tricks with some of the cards, such as the hands holding the cards and the palm tree with the sun. (Hint: Watch the sun. It pops on shades every now and then, and it smiles. And watch the cards in the hand.)
- To undo the last move you made, open the Game menu and choose the Undo command.
- To leave the Solitaire game, open the Game menu and choose the Exit command.

Minesweeper

To play the Minesweeper game, double-click on the Games group icon, and then double-click on the Minesweeper program icon. The Minesweeper window appears. Inside the window is a mine field. The object is to click on one square at a time in the mine field until you have cleared all the mines. Winning at the Minesweeper game is part skill, part luck.

Minesweeper window just after a blow up

Checklist

- If you click on a square that has a bomb underneath it, you're blown up kablooey!
- If you see a number in the square, there are that many bombs around the square. You're supposed to use these numbers to deduce where the bomb is, so you can avoid it.
- If you don't see anything in the square, there are no bombs around that square. You know that you could be at least one square away from any potential bombs.
- Keep clicking squares until you either win the game or get blown up. If you think there's a bomb under a square, use the right mouse button to click on it. This places a flag on the square.
- You win the game when you clear all the squares that don't have a bomb.
- When you're done playing the Minesweeper game, open the Game menu and choose the Exit command.

CHAPTER 12

Doing the Cut-n-Paste Shuffle

IN A NUTSHELL

- Using "cut and paste" to move text
- Copying text
- Sharing text between documents
- Sharing text between programs

It's a lot easier to copy something than to do it all over again. You learned that in grammar school when you typed up a little something on Elvis Presley, copied it, and then taped a copy in every report due that month. Mrs. Ambrose got the scoop on Elvis for your history report on great Americans. Ms. O'Connor received the same information (with a different introduction) for your report on Civil War writers. And Mr. Flabersham got that same bit about Elvis in your report on classical music.

OK. So maybe that information on Elvis didn't work in *all* those reports, but as you work in Windows, you'll find information that you want to move elsewhere.

Windows lets you "cut" text from one place and move it to another—even to a different document or a different program. When you cut text, you remove it from the first location and put it in a new spot. If you're really fond of what you created, you can copy it to different places—you know, leave it where it's at and put it somewhere else too. You'll learn about cut, copy, and paste in this chapter.

Moving Text

(Put it here! No, put it there!)

Cutting and pasting is a great way to reorganize your writing. If you think your opening paragraph would make a better closing, just select it, cut it, and paste it someplace else.

Just about every Windows program that creates text documents—like the Windows Write word processor discussed in Chapter 10—lets you cut and paste text. And as an added benefit, most of the programs do it the same way. So once you learn how to cut and paste text in one program, you already know how to do it in the others.

To cut and paste text, just follow these four simple steps. These steps work in nearly all Windows programs that make text documents (if you'd like to follow along, you can use the Windows Write program).

1. *Select the text.* Use the mouse to select the text you want to cut. Drag the mouse (press and hold the mouse button while moving the mouse) from the beginning of the text you want to cut, to the end of it. All the text in between is selected and is shown highlighted.

2. *Cut the text.* Open the Edit menu and choose the Cut command. The text is removed from the document and is placed in a temporary holding tank called the "Clipboard."

3. *Click on the new spot for the text.* Find the place where you want to move the previously cut text, and click there. This sets the flashing insertion point (a flashing vertical bar) at that spot.

4. *Paste the text.* Open the Edit menu and choose the Paste command. The text is retrieved from the Clipboard and pasted into the document.

BUZZWORDS

CLIPBOARD

The Windows Clipboard temporarily stores data (like text and pictures) so that you can retrieve it later.

Checklist

- The Windows Clipboard holds just one clipping at a time. Each time you cut out a section of your document, it erases the stuff that was previously in the Clipboard. That means you must paste the text after you cut it, before you cut out something else.

continues

Checklist Continued

▼ When pasting, Windows doesn't remove the text from the Clipboard. It merely takes what's in the Clipboard and duplicates it in the document. You therefore can repaste the cut text as many times as you like. Just click on the new spot and choose the Paste command again (from the Edit menu).

Copying Text

(Say it again, Sam)

You don't have to remove the text in your document to paste it someplace else. Instead of cutting and pasting, you can copy and paste. Suppose that you want to make an important point in more than one place. You can copy the text and put it in as many places as you want.

TIP

Copying text also comes in handy when the text you have in one place is *about* the same thing you want to say in another. Copy and paste the text that's similar to the text you want elsewhere; then modify the copy. I did that with the previous and following sets of steps. The steps for moving are about the same for copying, so I copied the steps for moving and then modified them so that they work for copying.

Copying and pasting is nearly the same as cutting and pasting:

1. *Select the text.* Use the mouse to select the text you want to copy. Drag the mouse (press and hold the mouse button while moving the mouse) from the beginning of the text you want to copy, to the

end of it. All the text in between is selected and is shown highlighted.

2. *Copy the text.* Open the Edit menu and choose the Copy command. The text remains in the document and is also placed in the Clipboard.

3. *Click on the new spot for the text.* Find where you want to copy the text, and click there. This sets the flashing insertion point at that spot.

4. *Paste the text.* Open the Edit menu and choose the Paste command. The text is retrieved from the Clipboard and pasted into the document.

Sharing Text between Documents

(More of the same)

There's no law that says you can cut (or copy) and paste text only within the same document. Suppose that you want to copy some text in one document and then paste it in another. Maybe you like the way you worded a particular paragraph and want to use that paragraph again in a different document. Why retype it? Copy it.

To share text between documents, cut or copy the text in the first document. Then open the second document. Most Windows programs let you have more than one document window open at the same time. In the second document, paste the text.

If the program doesn't let you open more than one document, you'll need to cut (or copy) the text in the first document, then save and close that document. You'll then need to open or create the document you want to paste the text to. Then paste the text in that document.

Sharing Data between Programs

The information you create in one Windows program can be shared with other Windows programs. You can paste information (text, numbers, and pictures) into a similar program, such as from one word processing program to a different one, or you can paste the text into a different type program, such as from a spreadsheet to a word processing program. Sharing data lets you take all the kinds of things you can create—numbers, text, pictures—and show them off in one tell-all document.

"Sacré bleu, how is this possible?" you ask. Simple. The Windows Clipboard is shared between all Windows programs. If you put something in it from one program, you can paste it into any other program.

Here's how you perform this magic:

1. Start the first program and open the document that contains the information you want to copy or cut. The information can be text, a picture, or data from a spreadsheet.
2. Open the Edit menu and choose the Cut or Copy command to cut or copy the selected information, respectively. The information is now on the Clipboard.
3. Press Alt+Esc until you return to the Program Manager.
4. Start the other program and open the document in which you want to place the stuff you just cut or copied. Place the insertion point where you want the information to appear.
5. Open the Edit menu and choose the Paste command to paste the information.

Checklist

- There are lots of variations of this procedure. You can start both programs first and then hop from one to the other. Or you can start one program, cut or copy the text, exit the program, and then start the next one. For help on program hopping—moving from program to program—see Chapter 2.

- In some cases, you'll need to check the appropriate program manual when you are pasting data from one program type to another. For instance, when you paste numbers from a spreadsheet to a word processing document, what can you expect? (Most of the time, you'll get a table.)

- There are lots of fancy things you can do with pasted text. You can "link" the text so that when you change the text in one document, it is automatically updated in the other. This magic is beyond the scope of this book.

- The Windows Clipboard is multilingual. You can cut and paste graphics as well as text. That means you can cut and paste in programs like Windows Paintbrush that deal with graphics instead of text. Suppose that you have a company logo you created in Paintbrush. You want to use this logo in the letters you write with Windows Write. All you need to do is copy the logo in Paintbrush, switch to Write, and paste it in.

- Not all programs can accept data created in another program. Windows tells you so by displaying an error message. If you get the message, click the OK button to make the message go away.

Shoe
By Jeff MacNelly
THIS COMPUTER HAS CHANGED MY LIFE...

I FINALLY HAVE A SWIVEL CHAIR.

I BET THIS COMPUTER HAS REVOLUTIONIZED THE WAY YOU DO YOUR JOB.
NO, NOT REALLY.

WHAT?!
I NEVER USE IT.

BUT THE COMPUTER HAS TOTALLY CHANGED LIFE FOR MILLIONS...
RIGHT.

IS THERE SOMETHING WRONG WITH IT?
SHOULDN'T BE. IT'S BRAND-NEW.

THEN MAYBE IT'S THE SOFTWARE.

DO YOU HAVE TROUBLE WITH THE MEMORY FUNCTION?
ALL THE TIME.

YOU MEAN THE COMPUTER NEEDS MORE CAPACITY?
NO.
I MEAN I CAN'T REMEMBER HOW TO TURN IT ON.

CHAPTER 13

Printing with Windows

(Putting It Down on Paper)

IN A NUTSHELL

- How to select a printer
- How to print a document
- How to stop printing
- How to handle printing problems

I HATE WINDOWS!

Much of the work you do with your programs is stuff you'll want to share with others. How will your family be complete without reading your poem on leftovers? How can your coworkers survive without seeing your drawing of Mr. Pinchfinkle in accounting? The easiest way to show off what you've done on the computer is to print it. That's what we'll talk about in this chapter.

Printing your work requires that you have a printer connected to your computer. If you don't have that, there's no sense reading this chapter. Get a printer, hook it up, then come back.

Selecting a Printer

It isn't uncommon to have more than one printer connected to a computer. This is especially true in offices, where a bunch of people share printers. Windows lets you specify which printer you want to use. Once you've "selected" the printer you want, Windows remembers it for the next time you print. That way, if you use the same printer later, you don't have to select the printer all over again.

To select a printer, double-click on the Main group, and then double-click on the Control Panel icon. The Control Panel window opens. Find the Printers icon in the window and double-click on it. In the middle of the Printers dialog box that appears is a list showing you the installed printers; these are the printers that Windows knows about, and the ones you can use.

"I HATE THIS!"

I don't see any printers in the Printers dialog box!!

If you don't see any printers in the Printers dialog box, it means that when Windows was installed on your computer's hard disk drive, nobody told it about any of the printers you

"I HATE THIS!"

might want to use. You'll need to tell Windows about at least one printer before you can print with it, a process called "installing a printer." If you need to install a printer, collar the nearest Windows guru to do the work for you.

If you have to do it yourself, the user's guide that came with Windows talks about the various steps involved. You will need to know some technical things about your printer and your computer, so have those manuals nearby. And get out the original disks that came with Windows, because you'll need those, too.

Click on the printer you want, click on the Set as Default Printer button, and then click on Close. Double-click on the Control menu box in the Control Panel window to close it.

You are now ready to print with the printer you have selected.

TIP

Some programs have a command in their File menu called Print Setup, or something similar. You can use this command instead to select the printer you want to use.

Printing a Document

Let's say that you've written a memo with Windows Write. You've checked it over to make sure that you spelled the boss's name right this time. Are you ready to print? Not quite. First you have to check the preliminaries. Read on.

Making Sure You're *Really* Ready

Before you print, be sure that the printer is turned on and ready. Your printer will signal that it's ready by saying so, either by displaying the word READY or by illuminating a Ready or On-Line light (or both).

Okay…the printer is on and it says it's rarin' to go. Are you ready to print? Not quite. Hold your horses.

Next, make sure that there's paper in the printer. Laser printers have a paper tray; pull out the tray and fill it with paper if it's empty. Other kinds of printers may use continuous paper—sheets joined at the head and toe, and folded up in a neat stack. You'll have to weave it up and into the printer in some contorted fashion. If you don't know how, ask someone for help.

Now. Are you ready to print? You bet!

Let 'er Print!

To print, open the File menu and choose the Print command. Most programs, including Windows Write, display a Print dialog box. The dialog box tells you the name of the printer you're using to print the document, along with some other technical stuff, which you can ignore for the time being.

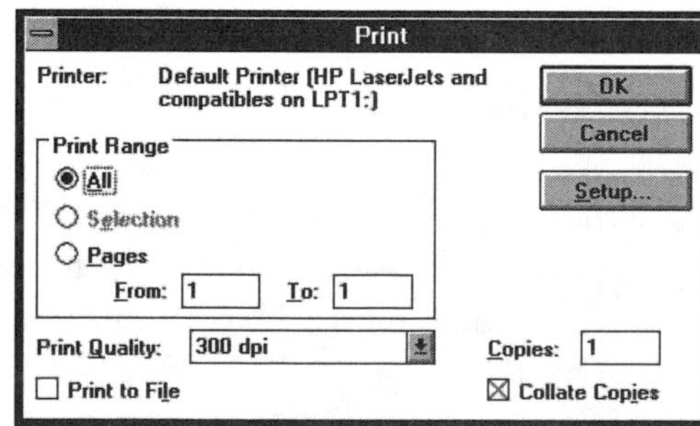

The Print dialog box in Microsoft Write

Click on the OK button to commence printing. Most programs—and this includes Write—pop up a little message that gives a printing status report. The status report tells you that printing hath begun. Within a few moments, the printer should spring to life. The printer won't stop until it prints your entire document or runs out of paper, whichever comes first.

"I HATE THIS!"

Hey! I never got a Print dialog box!

Write is a good example of how to print with Windows, because most other Windows programs work the same way. The notable exception is that some programs don't use a Print dialog box. Printing starts immediately after you choose the Print command from the File menu.

More on Printing

The Print dialog box, if the program you're using displays one, lets you control some aspects of printing. The innards of the Print dialog box differ from one program to another. For the most part, you don't need to change anything, but here are some common things you might want to tinker with:

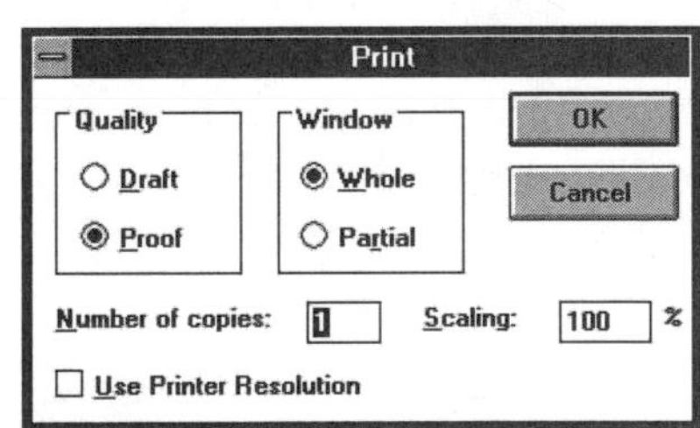

Example of a Print dialog box

Checklist

- Some Print dialog boxes let you pick the part of the document you want to print. You can print the entire document, a range of pages, or just the selected text. Click on the option you want.
- If you want more than one copy, some Print dialog boxes have a place to type the number of copies you want. Type the number and press Enter. (If you want to save wear and tear on your printer, just print one copy and use a copier to make duplicates.)
- Sometimes different print qualities are available. If you want just a quick printout, look for a Draft option.

Stopping a Print Job

(Stop the presses)

During printing, Windows will display a status message telling you, "I'm working, I'm working!!" In the same box with that message is a Cancel button.

Click on the Cancel button if you want to stop printing. If the status box goes away before you can click on the Cancel button, you're too late. Your printer has already been told to print the document, and printing has already started or is about to commence.

Uh-Oh! It Didn't Print

If the print gods are smiling on you, you'll actually get something from your printer when you ask Windows to print. But if they are frowning and you therefore end up empty-handed, here are some ways you can appease them so that your documents are printed.

Nothing Printed!

You clicked on the Print command in the File menu, but nothing happened. Nothing except that a couple of seconds later, Windows displayed a big, fat error message complaining that something is wrong with your printer.

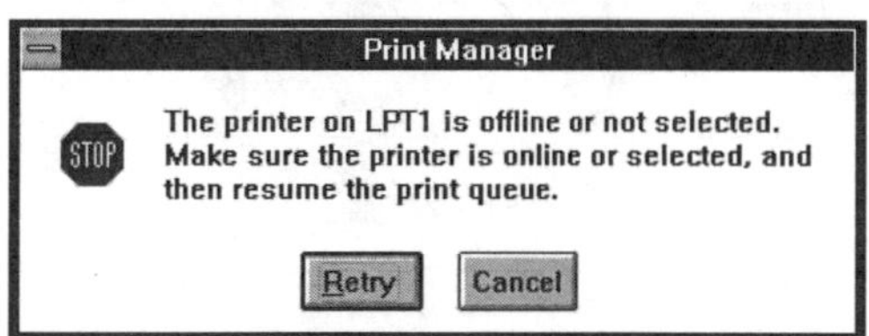

A print error message

You can use the message to help isolate the problem. For instance, the error might say that the printer is out of paper. If the printer is out of paper, put more paper in it, silly.

Some error messages might require some deductive reasoning on your part. If you get an error message saying that the printer is off-line or not connected, it could mean that

- The printer is turned off. Turn it on!
- The printer is not on-line. Press the On-Line button to put it on-line.

I HATE WINDOWS!

- The cable to the printer is loose. Check all the cables.
- The printer isn't properly connected to the computer. Get help from someone who knows how printers should be connected.

After reading the error message and fixing the problem, click on the Retry button to try to resume printing. If you want to cancel printing, click on the Cancel button.

If you fixed the problem, printing can proceed and the printer will process your document. If the trouble remains or another problem crops up, you'll see yet another error message.

"I HATE THIS!"

I get no printing and no error message!!

Windows doesn't always respond to all printing problems. It depends on your printer and the nature of the problem. For example, Windows might not tell you that the paper has jammed in your printer. You'll need to catch that kind of problem yourself.

The Print Command Looks Old and Gray

You opened the File menu and tried to click on the Print command, but noooooo! The Print command is all faded and grayed out. Clicking on Print does absolutely nothing.

When a command is grayed out in a menu, it means that the command isn't available. And when the Print command is not available, it means Windows is not yet set up for printing. Before you can print, you need to tell Windows what kind of printer you are using and how it is connected to your computer. These details are beyond the scope of this book. If you can't print with Windows, ask the office computer guru for help.

CHAPTER 14

Eighteen Super Cool Windows Programs (Count 'Em, 18!!)

IN A NUTSHELL

- Microsoft Word for Windows
- WordPerfect for Windows
- Ami Pro
- Microsoft Excel
- Lotus 1-2-3 for Windows
- Borland Quattro Pro for Windows
- Microsoft Works for Windows
- Norton Desktop for Windows
- CorelDRAW!
- Microsoft Publisher

- Freelance Graphics for Windows
- WinFAX
- Microsoft Entertainment Pack
- After Dark
- Far Side Calendar
- Wired for Sound/Pro
- SimCity, SimEarth, and SimAnt
- Visual Basic

Windows would be nothing if there weren't scores of programs you could use with it. This chapter proudly presents 18 of the biggest, brightest stars in the Windows universe.

How the stars were picked

The programs chosen for discussion in this chapter were nominated and voted on by a select panel of judges. Me. The results have been sealed in a Ziploc bag in my freezer until this moment. My mailman is responsible for any auditing of the awards.

Disclaimer: I'm not personally responsible if you don't like the programs I've picked.

In this chapter you'll find short descriptions of what the programs do, what you can expect of them, and who publishes them. You'll also see a picture of one or more sacks of money, to give you a rough idea of what each program costs. Each sack is equivalent to $50, so a program with eight sacks costs about $400.

Microsoft Word for Windows

Word processing is used by 85 percent of the computer-using public. It's one of the easiest programs to understand: it's an electronic version of a typewriter.

In the word processing category, Microsoft Word for Windows is a perennial favorite. With Word for Windows you can write documents as long as you want and as complex as you want. Yet Word for Windows is easy to use.

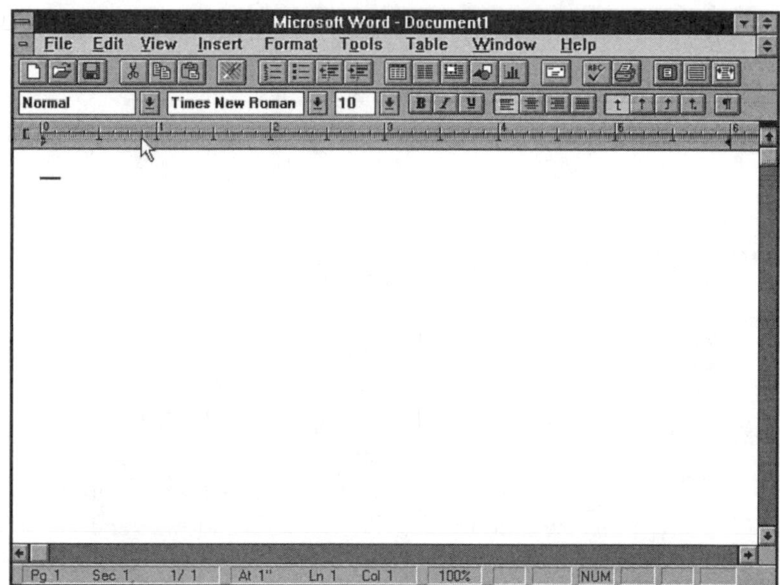

The Word for Windows screen

What's neat about Microsoft Word for Windows?

- You can combine pictures with your words.
- You can include tables with lots of numbers in neat little columns and rows.

continues

What's neat about Microsoft Word for Windows? Continued

- You can give your text a new look by using any of a number of fonts, and you can change the size of the text from itty-bitty things you need a magnifying glass to read, all the way to big poster-sized monsters several inches high.

- Word for Windows comes with a spelling checker that helps you correct misspellings and typographical errors. And it comes with a grammar checker to help you catch them improper use of words that can makes you sound like a ninny. You can even use the built-in thesaurus to find bigger and more impressive sounding words.

Microsoft Word for Windows, Version 2.0 $$$$$$$$
Microsoft Corporation

WordPerfect for Windows

If you were a DOS user before boarding the good ship U.S.S. Windows, there's a good chance you used the DOS version of the world's best-selling word processing software: WordPerfect.

WordPerfect for Windows is exactly what its name implies: WordPerfect for Windows. The DOS and Windows versions of WordPerfect offer pretty much the same features, though they don't work the same way.

Why WordPerfect?

- If you use the DOS version of WordPerfect and want to move to the Windows version, you'll probably be able to learn the Windows version pretty quickly.
- In the DOS version of WordPerfect, you have to memorize all sorts of special keys, and the writing screen only shows the text of your documents. In the Windows version, you command the program by clicking on menus and buttons, and you see text and graphics on the writing screen, exactly as they will appear when printed.
- The program's forte is big, complex documents, but simple letters and memos are no problem.
- After you're done writing, you can use the built-in spelling checker and grammar checker to make sure that you haven't committed any literary boo-boos. (Versions prior to 5.2 don't come with a grammar checker. Sorry.)

WordPerfect for Windows, Version 5.2 $$$$$$$$
WordPerfect Corporation

Ami Pro

The word *ami* is French for *friend*, and Ami Pro is a professional friend to anyone using the computer for word processing. Ami Pro has all the ingredients you'd expect in a Windows word processor, including a selection of fonts, a spelling checker, and a grammar checker.

What makes Ami Pro friendly?

- Ami Pro's claim to fame is that it's the most WYSIWYG of all the Windows word processors. (WYSIWYG? See the next buzzword.) The other word processors don't normally show extra stuff such as headers and footers (text that repeats at the top and bottom of each page) as you write. But Ami Pro shows you everything.
- Ami Pro is particularly well-suited to making documents that contain lots of pictures and other types of graphics. For example, Ami Pro makes it easy to write and arrange a document to create a slick-looking newsletter or brochure.

WYSIWYG

WYSIWYG is an acronym for "what you see is what you get." WYSIWYG (pronounced "wizzy-wig") refers to how closely the printed version of a document resembles the version you see on-screen.

Ami Pro, Version 3.0 $$$$$$$$
Lotus Development Corporation

Microsoft Excel

Microsoft Excel is an electronic spreadsheet program. If you've never seen an electronic spreadsheet program, you've probably seen a bookkeeper's ledger; they both do pretty much the same thing. In the electronic spreadsheet program, you put numbers into "cells." The cells are like the little rectangles in a bookkeeper's ledger sheet.

The value of an electronic spreadsheet program over an ordinary bookkeeper ledger is that the program does all the calculations for you. You can put away your calculator, because the electronic spreadsheet program does the addition, subtraction, multiplication, and division. The one thing it won't do is embezzle company funds (at least this hasn't happened so far).

Excel is considered one of the best electronic spreadsheet programs in the world, capable of everything from adding two numbers to complex calculations involving the finances of the biggest corporations.

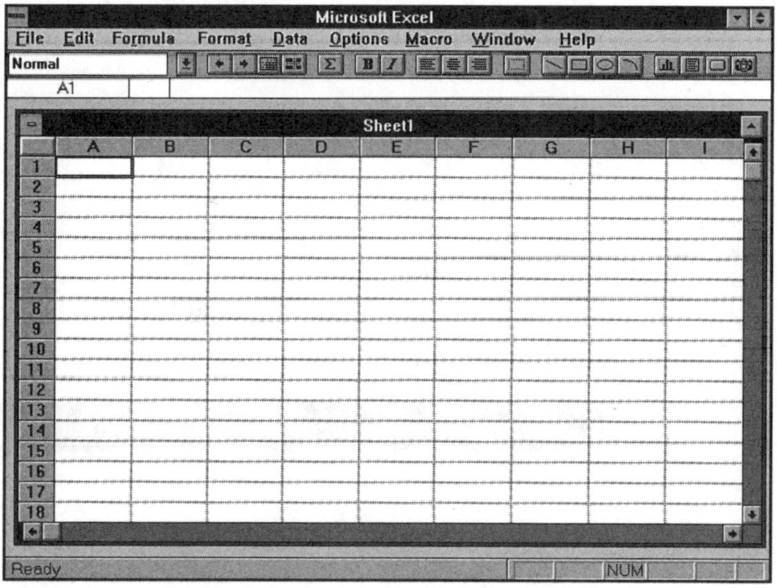

The Microsoft Excel screen

With Excel, you can play "what if." You type a number, and Excel shows you how this affects a set of other numbers. For example, you can punch

in numbers to show your boss that giving you that raise really won't affect the company's profits. Well, it's worth a shot anyway.

You also can create some pretty snazzy-looking charts with Excel.

Microsoft Excel, Version 4.0 $$$$$$$$
Microsoft Corporation

Lotus 1-2-3 for Windows

1-2-3 is a funny name for a program. But this one program did more for personal computers than any other program before it or since. In many respects, you have Lotus 1-2-3 (Lotus is the name of the company that makes 1-2-3) to thank for the computer on your desk. Er, come to think of it, maybe "thank" isn't the right word....

In any case, 1-2-3 is an electronic spreadsheet program. Lotus 1-2-3 for Windows is a version of 1-2-3 specifically designed for Windows.

The most common use of Lotus 1-2-3 is to add up a column of numbers, such as the amount of money spent by each of three departments in a company, like this:

Month	Dept. A	Dept. B	Dept. C
January	235.09	715.55	239.94
February	512.20	99.22	187.83
March	312.00	473.29	1.98
TOTAL	1059.29	1288.06	429.75

The results in the TOTAL line were calculated instantaneously by 1-2-3. If you make a change—say you realize that Dept. C really spent $198.00 in March, not $1.98—you can change just that number, and 1-2-3 will automatically recalculate everything all over again.

Sometimes numbers alone don't tell the whole story. A picture tells the story better. With 1-2-3 you can turn any set of numbers into a chart, like a pie chart or line chart. If your company is making more money this year than it did last year, the upward-pointing line in the chart gets the good news across in an instant. And it makes you an instant hero for pointing it out so clearly to everyone else.

Lotus 1-2-3 for Windows 1.1 $ $ $ $ $ $ $ $
Lotus Development Corporation

Borland Quattro Pro for Windows

Quattro Pro is another electronic spreadsheet program, like Microsoft Excel and Lotus 1-2-3. And like these programs, Quattro Pro lets you type a set of numbers and then calculates those numbers in just about any way you want. If you need to get your point across by using pictures, Quattro Pro lets you turn any group of numbers into a high-quality chart.

Of all the electronic spreadsheet programs for Windows, Quattro Pro has the most features to make your spreadsheet documents look their best. You can place charts anywhere and change the size and style of text. With a bit of fudging, you can turn your spreadsheets into classy overhead transparencies for stockholder's reports and for life-and-death meetings with the CEO.

Quattro Pro for Windows $ $ $ $ $ $ $ $
Borland International

Microsoft Works for Windows

Microsoft Works for Windows is an all-in-one program. It combines the most popular computer applications in one package. You get a word processor, an electronic spreadsheet, a data manager (to keep track of phone lists and that sort of thing), and a telecommunications program that lets you chat with other computers by telephone. (Your computer needs an accessory called a "modem" to connect to other computers over the phone.)

The Works programs all live under the same roof, which makes it easier to work with them, even at the same time. You can calculate some numbers in the spreadsheet portion of Works, then jump over to the word processor and plug those numbers into a memo. Windows alone makes this kind of program hopping and data sharing fairly easy, but Works for Windows makes it even easier.

Works for Windows is a "jack of all trades, master of nothing." None of the programs in the Works suite are heavyweights, so don't expect any of them to deliver knock-out punches. If you need a set of simple and straightforward programs to use in Windows, put Works to work on your computer.

Microsoft Works for Windows $ $ $ $
Microsoft Corporation

Norton Desktop for Windows

If you've been around computers for any amount of time, you've probably seen a picture of Peter Norton. He's this fellow who always stands around with his arms crossed. Peter is a writer and programmer, and he developed one of the most popular utility programs ever sold for the PC—Norton Utilities.

UTILITY

A utility is a special kind of computer program. Unlike an application program (like a word processor), a utility program doesn't help you create documents. Instead, it makes using your computer easier or better.

Norton Desktop for Windows is a replacement for the Windows Program Manager. The Norton Desktop does the same basic job as the Program Manager—it lets you run other programs—but it offers lots more. For instance, Norton Desktop combines both the Program Manager and the File Manager. You don't have to run the File Manager program to do things with files or disks.

Norton Desktop for Windows 2.0 $ $ $
Symantec

CorelDRAW!

Windows comes with a simple drawing program called Paintbrush. It lets you sprinkle colors on an electronic easel. The colors are applied as little dots; lots of dots together form the images you see in a Paintbrush picture.

There's another kind of drawing program for computers. This kind of program uses geometric shapes (like lines, circles, and squares) to create pictures. You combine these shapes to make complex drawings. CorelDRAW! is that kind of drawing program. If you need to sketch complex drawings—like a cut-away view of a V-8 car engine—CorelDRAW! is just the program to do it.

But most folks use CorelDRAW! for simpler tasks, like making bar and pie charts. And they use the built-in fonts to make all sorts of fancy signs, or things like menus for restaurants.

CorelDRAW!, Version 3.0 $$$$$$$$$$
Corel Systems

Microsoft Publisher

In the old days, if you wanted to publish a newsletter, you had to print out the text and use scissors and glue to paste it on a stiff board. If you needed to add pictures and headlines, why, that only meant more cutting and pasting.

Desktop publishing programs change all that. With a desktop publishing program, you can write and arrange text in neat little columns. Got a picture? Drag it onto the page with the mouse. You can change the size and style of the text whenever you like. The end result is a professional-looking typeset-quality document.

Microsoft Publisher is one such desktop publishing program. Unlike most other desktop publishing programs for the computer, Publisher isn't for professional graphics designers. It's for the person who needs to produce a newsletter, a brochure, or some other high-quality document every once in a while.

With Publisher, you assemble documents one page at a time, using your computer screen as a "layout board." When you want to add text, just drag it to the right place on the page. If the text is too long to fit in one column, Publisher breaks it up into two columns.

You place pictures, lines, boxes, and other pieces onto the page the same way, much as you'd do if you were pasting the document together with real glue. But with Publisher, you don't get your fingers all sticky.

Microsoft Publisher 1.0 $$$$
Microsoft Corporation

Freelance Graphics for Windows

Presentations have become all the rage in business these days. Flashy, colorful slides and overhead transparencies help sell ideas, especially when those ideas are difficult to express the old-fashioned way: talking.

Freelance Graphics for Windows is a presentation-maker program. You use it to create all sorts of images, such as charts that show a company's profit and loss, or like graphs that show how much money there is to be made selling bubble gum.

You can then turn these images into slides. Or you can print them on paper or overhead transparencies. You can even use the computer itself as the presenter. Just tell Freelance what images you want to show and how long of a delay you want between each one, and you have an automated multimedia presentation. And all this without saying a word.

Freelance Graphics for Windows, Version 2.0 $$$$$$$$
Lotus Development Corporation

WinFAX Pro

If your computer has a fax board in it (so that you can use your computer as a fax machine), WinFAX Pro lets you send and receive faxes while using Windows.

Suppose that you want to send a fax. First you create the fax document by using just about any popular Windows program, like Word for Windows. Then you fire up WinFAX Pro and tell it where you want the document sent. A "phonebook" feature in WinFAX Pro lets you select from among a bunch of frequent recipients. Click on the Send button, and you're done. WinFAX Pro can even create the fax cover sheet for you, making your job that much easier.

When receiving files, WinFAX Pro lurks around in the background, waiting for your phone to ring. One ringie-dingie, two ringie-dingie, and WinFAX Pro answers the phone to receive the incoming fax. You can view the received fax on-screen or print it out. As an added benefit, WinFAX Pro can even "read" the fax and convert it to text, which means that you can use your favorite word processor to edit it.

WinFAX Pro, Version 3.0 $$$$$$
Delrina Technology

Microsoft Entertainment Pack

Okay, so you win at Solitaire in 50 moves or less. And you've figured out the secret to Minesweeper, no longer a challenge to you. Microsoft offers three entertainment packs; each pack (sold separately) adds even more games you can use with Windows.

In Pack 1 you get a nifty Tetris game, a version of mah-jongg, and a solitaire game that must have been designed by the most sadistic programmer in the world (the name of this game is Cruel—and is it ever).

In Pack 2 you get a funny and entertaining game named PipeDream, where you must connect a series of plumbing fixtures before the ooze spills out of the pipe. There's another, more complex mah-jongg game, plus RattlerRace, where your rattler races another guy's rattler.

In Pack 3 you get a ski simulator (handy if you've broken a leg in a real ski accident) and WordZap, for those who like to think fast and prove they're smarter than a computer. Knowing most computers, that shouldn't be too hard.

Microsoft Entertainment Pack $ (per pack)
Microsoft Corporation

After Dark

If you leave your computer on all day, the image on your screen might etch itself onto your monitor over a period of months or years. Well, that was the way it used to be, before color monitors, which don't suffer nearly as much from burned-in images. In the old days, it was fashionable to equip your computer monitor to "blank out" if you didn't use your computer for a couple of minutes. A program that blanks the screen is called a *screen saver*.

After Dark is a screen saver program. And because it's meant to be used with Windows, which is typically run on computers with color monitors, After Dark isn't what you'd call a "gotta have it" program. But lots of people swear by it because of the other jobs it does.

First and foremost is that After Dark is entertaining. Instead of just blanking out the screen, After Dark displays all sorts of constantly moving, brightly colored images, like stars, fish, and flying toasters (yes, the toasters have wings).

On a more practical standpoint, After Dark can lock out unauthorized use of your computer while you're away from your desk. If you're at lunch, coworkers passing by your desk can see the animated graphics on your screen, but they can't see your work. They must enter a password (which you get to choose) before they can use your computer.

Windows has a built-in screen saver, and it's similar to After Dark in a lot of ways. But After Dark offers more variations in the animation screens.

After Dark, Version 2.0
Berkeley Systems

Far Side Daily Planner

There's good news for the millions of Far Side cartoon fans who want to brighten their days as they sit behind a computer monitor. *The Far Side*, created by Gary Larson, comes to PCs in the form of the Far Side Daily Planner.

This program combines a loony Far Side cartoon calendar with an appointment book. Rigged to automatically run when you run Windows, the Far Side program greets you with one of 365 cartoons—a different one each day.

Depending on your luck and the whims of the program, you might even be treated to a little "animated short"—like a painter erasing parts of your screen (don't worry; it's not permanent). Far Side fanatics will recognize their favorite cows, bugs, and cavemen. Even though the cartoons are ones that have already been published, a true Gary Larson fan won't mind.

Far Side Daily Planner 2.0 $ $
Amaze, Inc.

Wired for Sound/Pro

Clang! Booiing! Rinnnng! That's Microsoft Windows making those noises, with the help of a program called Wired for Sound/Pro. Wired for Sound/Pro creates all sorts of zany sound effects, using either the speaker that's built into your computer or a sound-making board that's plugged inside. Sound effects include a barking dog, a cartoon "boink," a cat's meow, a foghorn, and even James Brown saying "Uh!" Admit it. You've always wanted your computer to say "Uh!" In all, the Wired for Sound/Pro package includes over 50 sound effects.

These sounds can be triggered by certain things Windows does. For example, when you get an error message, your computer says "Uh!" (or it meows or barks or whatever). You determine the things that trigger the sounds. You might like to have your computer utter "whooppee" when you leave Windows, which is probably the smartest thing your computer will ever say.

Wired for Sound/Pro $ $
Aristosoft

SimCity, SimEarth, and SimAnt

Ever fancy yourself as a world leader? Or how about the mayor of your city? SimCity and SimEarth (two different programs, sold separately) let you build cities or complete earthbound societies—then decide their fate.

Just like in real life, as leader you have to deal with natural and unnatural catastrophes that are beyond your control, like tornadoes, giant human-eating reptiles, and radioactive fallout from nuclear explosions. The object of both SimCity and SimEarth is to design your colonies to survive these disasters. You win the game when your people come out alive (if you've ever tried to make a colony on Mars, you know how hard this really is).

Another Sim game (sold separately) is SimAnt, where you scrounge around in the dirt like an ant. Think the life of an ant is all fun and games and raiding picnics? Try killer lawn mowers, human stampedes, icky spiders, and cans of Raid. While avoiding these denizens, you also have to conquer the killer red ants. Hmmm...sounds like life in the office.

SimCity, SimEarth, SimAnt $ $ (per program)
Maxis

Visual Basic

If you're a computer programmer or have always wanted to learn programming, Visual Basic is one of the best ways to write your own Windows program.

Windows is a visual medium, where you directly interact with a program by clicking on menus, buttons, and other on-screen objects. Visual Basic

picks up on this idea and first requires you to design the way your program will look. You then write programming instructions to make it all fit together. This is unlike most other programming tools, where you write first, then worry about how it looks to the user.

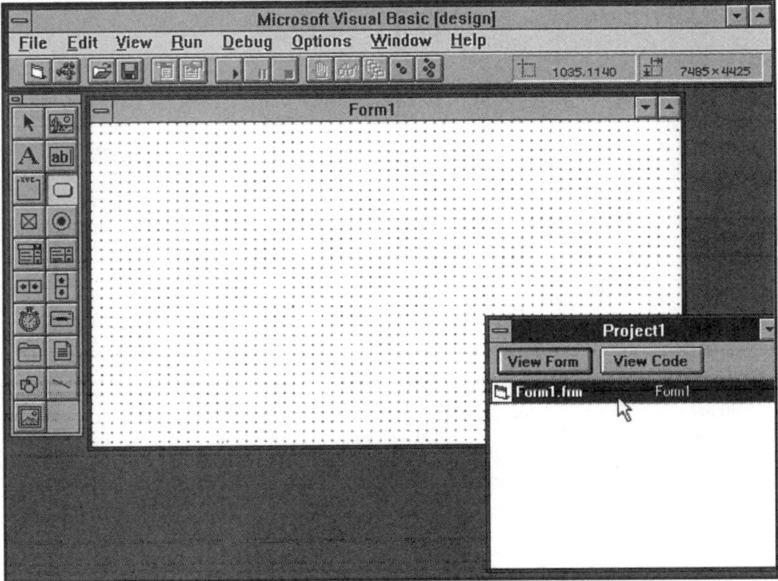

The Visual Basic screen

The "Basic" part of the name Visual Basic doesn't mean that the programs you make with it are basic and simplistic. "Basic" stands for the programming language used in Visual Basic. BASIC was one of the first all-purpose programming languages for the IBM Personal Computer, and Visual Basic is a version made just for Windows.

How experienced do you need to be to program with Visual Basic? You don't need prior programming experience, but you have to be pretty comfortable with both your computer and with Windows. If you've reached that point, you can take a stab at learning Visual Basic.

Visual Basic, Version 2.0 $ $ $ $
Microsoft Corporation

CHAPTER 15

Using Boring Old DOS Programs with Windows

IN A NUTSHELL

- ▼ Why use DOS programs with Windows?
- ▼ Starting a DOS program
- ▼ Making a window out of a DOS program
- ▼ Exiting a DOS program temporarlly
- ▼ Leaving a DOS program
- ▼ DOS programs that give you trouble
- ▼ Slipping out of Windows to use a DOS command

Windows can do all sorts of neat things. But beyond this soft and fuzzy paradise is a hard and prickly reality: not all programs are designed to take advantage of Windows. The horrible truth (are you sitting down?) is that programs are still being written for DOS, and you might need to use one of them.

Many DOS programs are well-behaved under Windows, so you don't need to worry about using them. This chapter tells you how to run DOS programs in Windows and get the most out of them. You'll also learn how to avoid trouble and how to understand what Windows is trying to tell you when trouble does rear its ugly head.

Why the Heck Run DOS Programs from Windows?

At first glance, it might seem that running a DOS program from within Windows is like flying from New York to Chicago via Los Angeles. It seems like the long way to go about things. Why mess with the middle man?

If you use Windows only occasionally and use your computer mostly from the DOS prompt, you might as well not use Windows to run your DOS programs. When you're done with your Windows business, leave Windows and go back to DOS.

On the other hand, if you use Windows most of the day, it would be inconvenient—not to mention a waste of time—to leave Windows just to run a DOS program. You can run DOS programs from the comfort of Windows. Read on.

Starting a DOS Program

Starting a DOS program from within Windows is the same as starting a regular Windows program. If there's an icon for the program, double-click on it. If there's no icon for the program, start it by using the Run command from the Program Manager's File menu; or make an icon for it. Both of these are described in Chapter 9.

Most DOS programs start without a hitch. The ones that fuss cause all the headaches. If your DOS program starts, read the next section. If your DOS program doesn't start, turn to "I Don't Wanna Run under Windows, and You Can't Make Me!" later in this chapter.

Showing the Program in a Windows Window

When you start a DOS program, it'll probably appear full-screen. This is the regular way for Windows to run DOS programs and is the most efficient. But if you're running Windows in something called *Enhanced Mode*, you can pop the program into a window and resize it or move it around the screen. That way you can see your "black sheep" DOS programs along with your respectable Windows programs.

EXPERTS ONLY

Windows a la mode: How do I tell which mode I'm in?

Windows operates under two different modes, depending on the technical aspects of your computer. *Enhanced Mode* (also called 386 Enhanced Mode) offers the most features and capability. The other mode is Standard Mode.

To check which operating mode you're in, open the Help menu from the Program Manager and choose the About Program Manager command. The About Program Manager dialog box appears. The third from the last line says either Standard Mode or 386 Enhanced Mode. Click OK to return to the Program Manager.

To place a DOS program in a window, press Alt+Enter from within that program. Notice that when the DOS program is in a window, the window appears with a title bar on top and borders around all the edges.

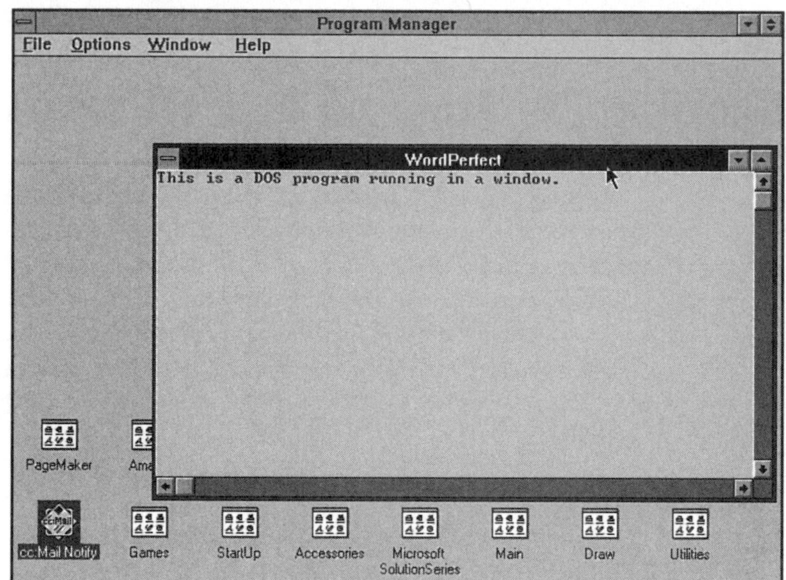

Running a DOS program (WordPerfect) in a window

Checklist

- You can control a DOS program window just the same as you can a regular Windows window—resize it, move it around the screen, or reduce it to an icon by clicking on its Minimize button (top right corner). However, you can't close a DOS program window and exit the program by double-clicking on its Control menu box. You must exit the program in the *program's* way.

- To return to full-screen and take the program out of the window, press Alt+Enter again.

- You can also use Alt+space bar to put your DOS program in a window. The Alt+space bar technique pops the DOS program into a window, makes the window as large as it can possibly be, and pulls down the window's Control menu. The window will likely fill only the top portion of the screen, because DOS programs don't fill up the screen the same way Windows programs do.

- If you minimize the program and the Program Manager isn't maximized to fill the entire screen, the icon for your DOS program is shown at the bottom of the screen. To return to your DOS program, double-click on its icon.

Putting the DOS Program Aside Temporarily

Miss your Windows programs? You can leave the DOS program for a while and switch to a different program that you need right now.

If you've put the DOS program in a window and you can see the Program Manager, click on the Program Manager window. Then start or switch to the program you want.

If you didn't put the DOS program in a window or if you can't see the Program Manager, press Ctrl+Esc (hold down Ctrl, press Esc, then release both keys) to display the Windows Task List. From this list, you can pick another program to switch to. To pick another program, click on the one you want in the list, and then click on Switch To.

Checklist

- Do *not* click on the program icon that's in the group window. Clicking on that icon starts another copy of the program.
- Take care when running other programs while a DOS program is idle and displayed as an icon. You might be able to run only one or two other programs while the DOS program is running. If Windows displays an error message and says there's not enough room to run a program, click on OK to make the message go away. You need to shut down one or more programs before you can start another.

Leaving the DOS Program

When you get done with your DOS program, you'll want to quit it. Unlike Windows programs, each of which follows the same general rules for letting you get out, there's no such common ground in DOS programs. How you get out of your DOS program is up to the program. Take a look at the following list for ways to exit some of the more popular DOS programs. If you still can't get out of the program, either look in the manual that came with it or holler for help.

If you're using	Press these keys
WordPerfect	F7, N, Y
Microsoft Word	Alt, F, X
WordStar	Ctrl+K, X
Lotus 1-2-3	/ (slash), Q, Y
Quattro Pro	/ (slash), F, X, Y
Quicken	Esc, E

I'm Stuck in a DOS Program and I Can't Get Out

If a DOS program becomes obstinate and fails to respond to your commands, you're stuck. How can you get out? Before you press the Reset button, try this procedure. Put the program in a window. Then click on the Control menu box in the upper left corner of the DOS program window to display the Control menu. Choose the Settings command. You see the Settings dialog box.

For now, you can ignore most of the options in this dialog box; the important thing is the ominous-sounding Terminate button. The Terminate button is the Arnold Schwarzenegger of Windows buttons. Click on this button to exit the program.

You get a message warning you to use this option only as last resort. Click on OK to terminate, or Cancel to stop. If you click on OK, you are returned to Windows. Be sure to say "Hasta la vista, baby!" when you

click it. (Okay, saying "Hasta la vista, baby!" doesn't do anything, but with an Austrian accent, it sounds pretty cool.)

CAUTION

If you're *sure* you are stuck, press the Reset button on the front of your computer or press Ctrl+Alt+Del. (Hold down Ctrl, then hold down Alt, and press Del. Then release them.) This method is the very last resort. And you'll lose any data you haven't saved.

"I Don't Wanna Run under Windows, and You Can't Make Me!"

From time to time, you might run into an obstinate DOS program that refuses to cooperate with Windows. It just won't start, no matter how much you beg or curse. You might even get an error message like the one shown in the following figure. If you get such a message, read it and then click on the OK button to make it go away.

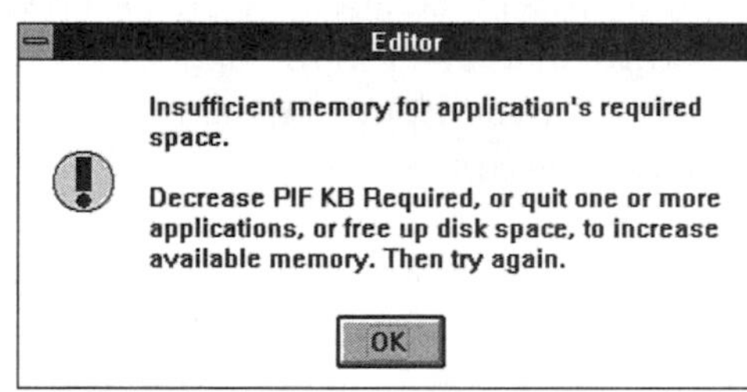

Insufficient memory error message

The reasons for a DOS program not starting are numerous. You can do something about some of the problems, but others may require help from a guru. Should Windows refuse to run a DOS program, try one or all of the following:

Checklist

- ▼ Do as the error message says and close down all other applications (programs) you happen to have open. Don't be tempted to free up disk space by deleting files from your computer's hard drive. This procedure is a bad idea unless you really know what you're doing.

- ▼ Ignore the error message and just try running the DOS program again. Sometimes this method works.

- ▼ At the top of your lungs, let out the most blood-curdling primal scream ever heard and say: "Why the *&^#%^!! won't Windows start my DOS program?!!?" You'll either be helped by some knowledgeable computer person, or you'll be carted off in a tight-fitting white jacket.

Technical mumbo-jumbo about PIFs

DOS programs have no knowledge of this thing called "Windows" and tend to live by their own rules. If you encounter a DOS program that doesn't seem to want to abide by Windows' rules, all that may be wrong with it is an incorrect setting in its PIF (program information file). *PIFs are only used with DOS programs.*

PIFs do exactly what their name says: they provide information about programs. Among the information in a PIF is the minimum amount of memory (that stuff your computer uses to temporarily store data while you're working with it) needed to run a program. If the memory setting is too low, you'll get an "Insufficient memory to run application" error.

If you need to change a PIF, grab the nearest computer nerd and explain your problem. The nerdiest of nerds should be able to change the PIF settings for you so that your DOS program will run.

Slipping Out of Windows to Use a DOS Command

Within the Main group window is a funny little icon labeled MS-DOS Prompt. Double-click on this icon and you suddenly see the C:\> DOS prompt! You are still in Windows; what you have started is a DOS "session"—sort of DOS within Windows.

From the C:\> prompt, you can type the name of most any DOS command you want. It might be easier to run a DOS program or a DOS command from the prompt. If you cut your teeth on DOS, you might miss the old DOS prompt. Or if you want a peek at computer hell (life before Windows) you might want to see the DOS prompt.

I HATE WINDOWS!

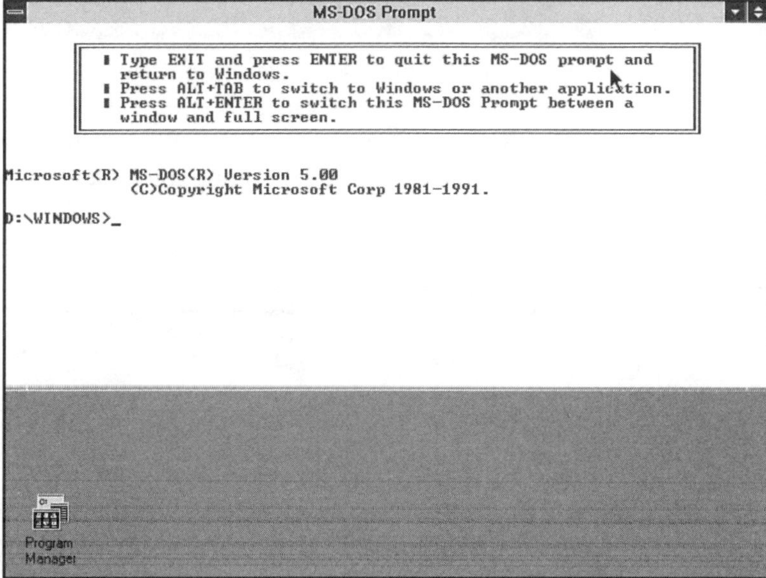
MS-DOS Prompt
Type EXIT and press ENTER to quit this MS-DOS prompt and return to Windows.
Press ALT+TAB to switch to Windows or another application.
Press ALT+ENTER to switch this MS-DOS Prompt between a window and full screen.
Microsoft(R) MS-DOS(R) Version 5.00
(C)Copyright Microsoft Corp 1981-1991.
D:\WINDOWS>_
Program Manager

The MS-DOS prompt

Checklist

- The C:\> prompt you get under Windows lets you run almost any—but not all—DOS program or command you can run when outside Windows. Examples of DOS programs you can't run under Windows include UNDELETE and UNFORMAT.

- When you're ready to end the DOS session and return to Windows, type **EXIT** and press Enter.

- You can return to Windows without ending the DOS session by pressing Ctrl+Esc. This key combination brings you back to the Program Manager, where you can run another program. Get back to the DOS session by clicking on its icon at the bottom of the screen.

continues

Checklist Continued

- Windows must set aside a certain amount of memory when you run a DOS session. If you're done with the DOS session, end it (type **EXIT**, then press Enter) rather than simply switching back to the Program Manager. By ending the DOS session, you free up some memory that another program can use. You can always start another DOS session later on by double-clicking on the MS-DOS Prompt icon again.

CAUTION

The DOS session makes it a little too easy to forget you're really still using Windows. A lot of otherwise intelligent Windows users have forgotten this, and have typed **WIN** at the DOS prompt, rather than **EXIT**. So instead of returning to the Windows that's already running, they start another copy of Windows!

In the older versions of Windows (Version 3.0 and before), this action used to be bad news. Now, Windows displays an error message reminding you that you're already in Windows.

PART IV

Troubleshooting

Includes:

CHAPTER 16

Help! (The 24-Hour Answer Service)

IN A NUTSHELL

- Calling on Windows for help
- Inside the Help window
- Closing the Help window
- Jumping to Help topics
- Searching for topics

When you can't find someone's phone number, what do you do? Call the information operator, of course. Likewise, when you need assistance in Windows—like when you forget which keys to push and when—call Windows' information service: instant on-line Help!

On-line Help is an electronic reference that's always just a mouse click away. It's "on line" because it's instantly available. So the next time you need help with Windows, who ya gonna call?

TIP

It's worth your while to learn how to use Help in Windows. Help for all Windows programs works the same way. Once you learn Help for one program, you know how to use it for all Windows programs.

Information Please!

To get help in the Program Manager, open the Help menu and choose the Contents command. A new window appears—the Help window—and you see a table of contents for the Help system.

Next, click on the topic you want to know more about. For instance, if you want help on arranging windows and icons, click on the topic called Arrange Windows and Icons. A Help window opens with information on the topic you selected.

TIP

As a shortcut, press the F1 key to display Help's table of contents.

Checklist

- If you want help on Help, open Help's Help menu and choose the How to Use Help command. This is sort of a Catch-22, because you already have to know how to use Help to learn how to use Help. (Help!)
- Some dialog boxes have a Help button. Click on this button to display help on the specific dialog box you're using.

The Anatomy of the Help Window

Working through the Help system is sometimes like going into uncharted territory. Before you set off on a journey, take a second to get familiar with the topography of the Help window.

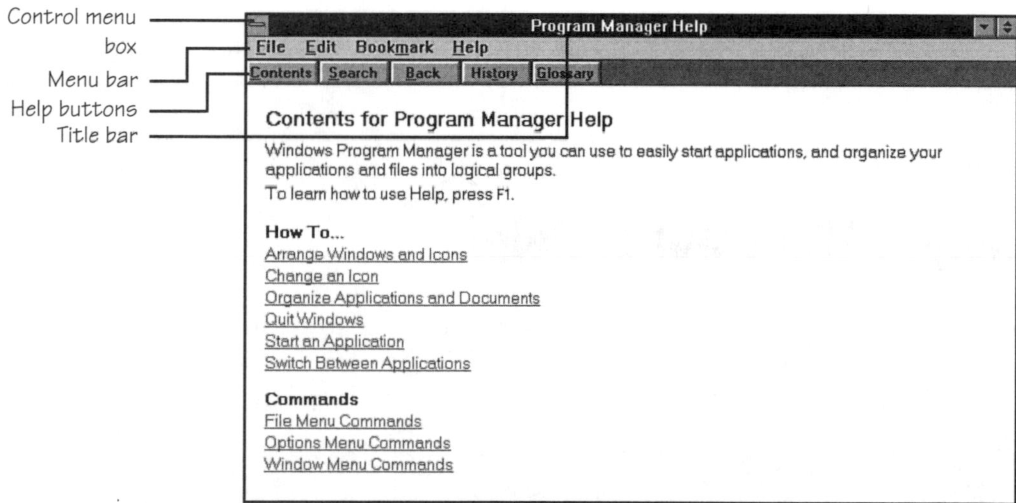

Checklist

▼ The title bar tells you which Help you are using: "Program Manager Help" means that you are getting help with the Program Manager, "File Manager Help" with the File Manager, and so on.

▼ Double-click on the Control menu box to close the Help window.

▼ The menu bar lists menu names. Pertinent menu tricks are covered later in this chapter.

▼ The Help buttons, below the menu bar, are your navigation keys. They let you move through the world of Help.

▼ If the Help window holds more information than it can display, you'll see a scroll bar on the right side of the window. Click on the scroll arrows to display one more line at a time. Or drag the scroll box to scroll at a faster clip.

▼ Help is like any other window. You can change its size, minimize it, maximize it, or move it out of the way. Read Chapter 2 for more details on how to change the size and appearance of windows.

Help! I Want Out of Help!

When you're done using Help, open the File menu in the Help window. Then choose the Exit command. This closes the Help window and returns you to whatever program you were using last.

TIP

As a shortcut, double-click on the Control menu box in the Help window.

Jumping around in Help

Finding the exact help you need may not be as simple as opening the Help window. That's just the first step on the journey. The first Help screen might give you a clue, but what if you want more? What if that's just part of the answer you need?

Windows helps you out by anticipating related questions. It lets you jump to related topics, called *help jumps*. Help jumps are colored (usually green) and underlined. If you have a monochrome (single color) monitor, the help jumps will be shown as regular, black text. Or they might be gray.

To jump to a new entry, just click once on the help jump, and Windows takes you where you want to go.

Checklist

- When you move the mouse over a jump topic, the pointer turns into a pointing hand. If you don't see the hand, the mouse isn't directly over the jump.
- Windows keeps track of the topics you've visited, in case you make a wrong turn somewhere. To go back through the Help topics in reverse order, click on the Help button called "Back." Each time you click, you back up by one topic. When you get back to the topic you're looking for, you can click on some other jump topic to take you down a different road.
- If you want to return to Help's table of contents (the list of main Help topics), click on the Help button labeled "Contents."

TIP

Windows Help also gives you assistance with terms and concepts that might be new to you (like the Buzzwords in this book). If you see what looks like a help jump, but it has a dotted underline instead of a solid one, click it. A little pop-up window appears on your screen. Inside the window is the definition of the term.

To make the pop-up go away, click anywhere in the Help window or press the Esc key.

Searching for Help Topics

(A direct flight)

If you already know what you're looking for, there's no sense journeying through the Help maze to find it. Instead, you can go directly to the topic you want.

To get to the topic you want, click on the Search button in the Help window. (Remember how to get to the Help window? You open the Help menu and choose the Contents command.) The Search dialog box appears, displaying a list of Help subjects.

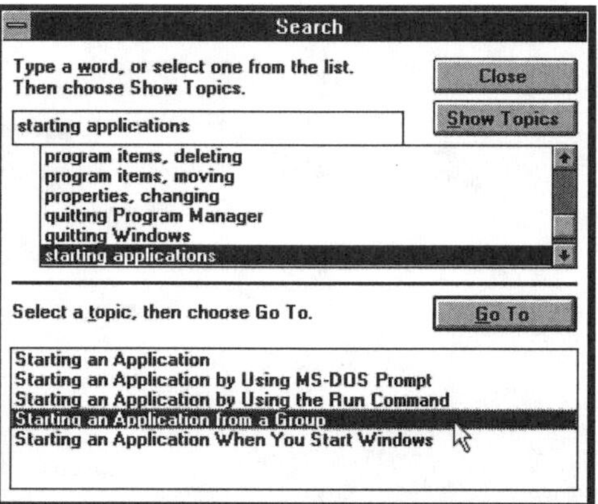

The Search dialog box

Look for the subject you want by using the mouse to scroll through the list. You can also type a subject in the entry blank at the top of the Search dialog box. As you type, Windows zeros in on that subject. If there is no subject with that exact name, Windows stops on the one closest to it alphabetically.

When you find the subject you want, click on it with the mouse to select it. Then click on the Show Topics button. Windows displays a second list with individual topics related to the subject you selected. Click on the topic you want, and then click on the Go To button. Windows takes you directly to that Help topic.

TIP

As a shortcut to using the Show Topics button, you can just double-click on the subject you want. And you can double-click on the topic you want, rather than using the Go To button.

I HATE WINDOWS!

@☆#!
"I HATE THIS!"

The subject or topic I want isn't listed!

You can only search for subjects that the Help writers thought of. Windows Help is not a "database" of topics where you can search for any word you want and find every occurrence of that word in the text. For example, you can't search for "icon" and find all the places where that word is used. You can only look up topics. If "icon" is mentioned in the topic name, you'll find it. If it's not in the topic name, you won't find it.

More and More and More Help

Help is available for most other Windows programs as well. The easiest way to access Help for a particular program is to locate its Help menu, yank it down, and click on the command you want.

Checklist

- Just about every Windows program you have or will buy comes with its own on-line Help system. This includes the programs that come with Windows—Program Manager, Write, Paintbrush, File Manager—and Windows programs you might buy—Excel, Word, PowerPoint, etc.
- Remember that all this Help menu stuff applies to Windows programs. If you're running a DOS program under Windows, it probably won't have a Help menu.

CHAPTER 17

Windows Glitches, Gotchas, and Goofs

IN A NUTSHELL

- Windows almost starts, but doesn't
- I can't see the mouse pointer
- Whenever I move the mouse, the pointer jumps around the screen
- I try to click on a menu command, but the command is grayed out
- I forgot my screen saver password
- I accidentally deleted a program icon

- Windows tells me the computer is low on memory
- I can't see the icons of program windows I have minimized
- I see a bunch of icons at the bottom of the window
- I press Alt+Tab to switch programs, but nothing happens
- Each time I start windows, the Program Manager shows something different
- I'm having trouble double-clicking on icons
- I selected some desktop wallpaper, but the wallpaper doesn't show up

Having general problems with Windows? Is the mouse not working right? Or is the Program Manager playing hide-and-seek with you? Look through this chapter for answers to common Windows glitches. If you're having problems with programs or with files, see Chapters 18 and 19, respectively.

Windows Almost Starts, But Doesn't

Okay, so you type **WIN** and press Enter at the DOS C:\> prompt. Windows looks like it's about to start; it might even display the Windows 3.1 welcome screen. But soon after, the screen goes blank and you're back at the C:\> prompt—an error message may or may not appear—or the welcome screen freezes. (If the welcome screen freezes, press the Reset button on the front of your computer or press Ctrl+Alt+Del.)

Well, friend, you've got problems, right here in River City. (You didn't want to hear that, did you?) The most likely reason Windows isn't starting is that it can't find one or more of the files it needs. Why can't Windows find a file that was there yesterday?

Checklist

- Something happened to your computer's hard disk drive, and the necessary file was damaged.
- You or someone else accidentally erased the file.
- You or someone else changed the innards of the file (such as an "INI" file, which is used to store choices), and Windows doesn't know what to make of the changes.

Repairing this problem can be difficult. If you know a seasoned Windows expert, get on your hands and knees and offer anything if he or she will fix it for you. If you're on your own, you can almost always correct the problem by reinstalling the Windows system onto your computer's hard disk drive. Run the Setup program that's on Disk 1 of the Windows package.

"I HATE THIS!"

Reinstalling undoes all your lovely decorating

When you reinstall Windows you lose all of the customization you've done, such as the color scheme of Windows and the organization of the icons in the Program Manager. Therefore, you should reinstall Windows only as a last resort.

I Can't See the Mouse Pointer

Under normal circumstances, you should always be able to see the pointer for the mouse. But a couple of glitches can cause the pointer to disappear.

Checklist

- If the mouse pointer doesn't appear when you start Windows, the mouse might be unplugged from your computer. Turn your computer off, check the mouse cord, and turn the computer back on. Run Windows again. If that doesn't work, you might not have the right mouse driver software, in which case you need the help of a knowledgeable person.
- If the mouse pointer disappears while you're using Windows, first be sure that it's not simply hiding in the lower right corner (mice like to do that kind of thing, you know). Move the mouse to see whether the pointer reappears.
- If you still can't see the mouse pointer, there is a problem in Windows or one of the programs currently running. You must restart Windows to get the pointer back. Do so by pressing Ctrl+Esc. The Task List dialog box appears. Press the up- or down-arrow key to highlight Program Manager, and press the Enter key. Then press Alt+F4. Press Enter to answer OK to the prompt warning you that you're about to leave Windows. Finally, restart Windows in the usual manner (type **WIN** at the C:\> prompt), and cross your fingers.

Whenever I Move the Mouse, the Pointer Jumps around the Screen

A jumpy mouse is most often caused by a dirty roller ball or an uneven rolling surface.

Checklist

- ▼ If you use a mouse pad, wipe off the pad in case it's dirty.
- ▼ Remove any objects under the pad that may be creating a lump.
- ▼ Pick up the mouse and examine the roller ball. Carefully remove the ball (follow the instructions that came with the mouse), and wipe off the ball with a handkerchief. (A clean handkerchief is best, unless you want to give your cold to your mouse.)
- ▼ With the ball out of the mouse, look inside the mouse. Inside are little rollers or ball bearings. Are these dirty? If so, clean them carefully by rubbing them with a pencil eraser and blowing out the debris with a huff and a puff. When you're done, put the ball back and try the mouse again.

I Try to Click on a Menu Command, But the Command Is Grayed Out

A grayed-out command means that the command is not currently available. No matter how hard you try, clicking on a grayed-out command does nothing.

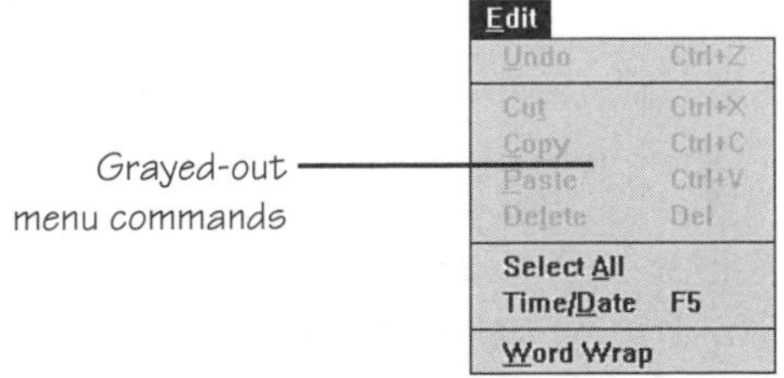

If a menu command is not available, it generally means that choosing the command is not suitable to what you're doing at the moment. Make sure there's not something you should do before you select the command.

For example, suppose that you just started the Windows Write program. If you open the Find menu, you'll see that all the commands in it are grayed out, or "dimmed." The document doesn't have any text, so there isn't anything to find. Type some text, and open the Find menu again. Only one of the commands will be grayed out.

Uh-Oh! I Forgot My Screen Saver Password!

If you forget the password to your screen saver, Windows refuses to reactivate, and the screen saver movie continues. The only thing you can do at this point is turn off your computer or reset it. Unfortunately, if you have any unsaved work, you will lose it.

Run Windows by typing **WIN** at the C:\> DOS prompt and pressing the Enter key.

Now you need to turn the password feature off. After Windows starts and the Program Manager window appears, double-click on the Main group icon, and then double-click on the Control Panel icon. Find the Desktop icon inside the Control Panel window and double-click on it. The Desktop dialog box appears.

Click on the Setup button in the Desktop dialog box, and the Setup dialog box appears. Click on the box that says Password Protected to remove the X. Click on OK to close the Setup dialog box, click on OK to close the Desktop dialog box, and then double-click in the Control menu box of the Control Panel window to close the Control Panel window and return to the Program Manager.

I Accidentally Deleted a Program Icon

It's pretty easy to accidentally delete a program icon you meant to keep. You can't get the old icon back, but you can easily make a new one. Remember that the program icon is not the same as the program file itself. The icon merely points to the program on your hard disk drive. Deleting an icon does not delete the program. See "The Art of Icon Making" in Chapter 9 if you're not sure how to remake a program icon.

Windows Tells Me the Computer Is Low on Memory

Windows needs lots of memory in your computer to operate. When you're low on that memory, an error message may appear. Don't ignore this message; you could end up losing your current work.

If the error message appears, make a note of what it says, and then click on the OK button to clear it.

Checklist

- ▼ If other programs are currently active but you're not using them at the moment, quit them to free up memory for Windows.
- ▼ Check the Task List to see whether you are running multiple copies of a program. If you see a program listed more than once, switch to the other copy and exit the program. Be sure to save any files you are working on.

continues

Checklist Continued

- ▼ If no other programs are active, Windows could be running out of hard disk space. You can check this out in the File Manager. Start the File Manager; then make sure that you've selected drive C. Look at the bottom left corner of the File Manager window, which tells you how much hard disk space is free. If it says anything less than about 5 megabytes (see Chapter 21 if you're not sure what a megabyte is), Windows is running out of room. You need to delete programs and files you no longer need or move files you don't use much to a floppy disk.

- ▼ If there are no other programs running and you have plenty of hard disk space, Windows just screwed up—believe me, it happens. Save anything you're working on, exit Windows in the usual way, and then restart it. The low memory situation should fix itself.

I Can't See the Icons of Program Windows I've Minimized

You're running a program and you minimize it to an icon (by clicking the Minimize button in the upper right corner of the window). You're supposed to be able to see the icon for this minimized window along the bottom edge of your screen, but you don't.

Relax. The icon is there, but it's covered up by another window, probably the Program Manager window. Make the other windows smaller, and you'll be able to see the icon.

Another way you can see the icons of minimized program windows is to press Ctrl+Esc. The Task List pops up, showing you a list of all currently running programs. You can then double-click on the name of the program you're looking for to expand its window. This technique is generally easier than moving and resizing other windows.

I've Got a Bunch of Icons at the Bottom of the Screen

Remember that when you minimize a program, that program is still running. Minimized programs appear as icons along the bottom of the screen. If you are finished with the program, exit it—don't minimize it.

To exit the program, first switch to it. Then look for an Exit command in its File menu. Or double-click on the Control menu box.

I Pressed Alt+Tab to Switch Programs, But Nothing Happened!

The Alt+Tab key combination lets you switch from one currently running program to another. First you hold down Alt; then you press Tab until you see the name of the program you want to switch to (it appears on-screen in a little box). When you release the Alt key, that program is activated. Pressing Alt+Tab again takes you to the next currently running program.

This is a neat trick, but it's also an option that can be turned off. If it gets turned off, pressing Alt+Tab won't do anything. To turn Alt+Tab program switching back on, double-click on the Main group icon, and then double-click the Control Panel icon. Find the Desktop icon in the Control Panel window and double-click on it. The Desktop window appears. Find the Fast Alt+Tab Switching box, and click on it to put an X in the box. The Alt+Tab keys are now activated. Close the Desktop dialog box by clicking on OK. Close the Control Panel window by double-clicking on its Control menu box.

Each Time I Start Windows, the Program Manager Shows Something Different!!

If the Program Manager displays a different arrangement of icons and windows each time you start Windows, the Program Manager is taking a snapshot of the icon and window layout each time you leave Windows.

If you don't want that, set up the icons and windows in the Program Manager the way you like them. Hold down the Shift key, open the File menu, and choose the Exit command. Choosing Exit in this way doesn't actually leave the Program Manager, but records the layout.

Now tell the Program Manager not to save the layout each time you leave Windows: Open the Options menu. The Save Settings on Exit command should have a check mark beside it. Click on the Save Settings on Exit command to remove the check mark.

I'm Having Trouble Double-Clicking on Icons

Not everyone can double-click the mouse at the same speed. Some people are faster double-clickers than others. If you click too slow, Windows thinks you're just clicking, not double-clicking.

Normally, Windows considers it an "official double-click" when you give two clicks within about a half second of one another. But this time delay can be changed:

1. Click once on the Main group icon, and then press Enter.
2. Click once on the Control Panel icon, and then press Enter. The Control Panel window appears.
3. Find the Mouse icon, and click once on it. Press Enter to open the Mouse window.

Mouse window

4. Click on the left arrow in the Double Click Speed scroll bar to increase the amount of time you have to double-click. On the scroll bar, "Slow" means more time between clicks; "Fast" means less time between clicks.
5. Try the new double-click setting by double-clicking inside the Test box. The box turns black if you double-clicked correctly.

6. When you're done, click on the OK button to leave the Mouse dialog box. Enjoy double-clicking on the Control menu box of the Control Panel window, because now you can do it.

Where's the Wallpaper I Thought I Hung?

Windows lets you decorate the desktop (the part behind all the windows) with a picture. The picture is called *wallpaper*, and you can choose it by using the Desktop icon in the Control Panel.

If you hang some wallpaper, but it doesn't seem to show up, you might be trying to spread a too-small piece of it over the entire desktop. Before doing anything, first check whether Windows is in fact displaying some wallpaper by minimizing all the windows you see. Exit whatever programs are running or click on the Minimize button (upper right corner) of all the windows to uncover the desktop, which is always behind the windows. You should see a small bit of wallpaper in the middle of the screen.

CAUTION

If you don't see anything in the middle of the screen, the problem is something else. Maybe you didn't select the wallpaper correctly the first time. Try again.

You need to change the wallpaper from Center to Tile. Double-click on the Main group icon, and then double-click on the Control Panel icon. Find the Desktop icon in the Control Panel window and double-click on it. The Desktop dialog box appears. Click on the Tile option; a black dot appears in its circle. (The Tile option is hard to spot: it's in the Wallpaper box.) Click on OK, and then double-click on the Control menu box in the upper left corner of the Control Panel window to close it. The wallpaper should now be properly spread over the entire desktop.

CHAPTER 18

Splat! There Goes My Program!

IN A NUTSHELL

- Windows says it can't find my program
- My program doesn't respond to the keyboard or the mouse
- Nothing happens when I press the Alt key to show a menu
- The time and/or date is wrong in the Windows Clock
- When I run a DOS program the screen flashes, and I'm returned to Windows
- When I start a program, its window always shrinks to an icon

- Whenever I start a program, the Program Manager window shrinks to an icon
- My program beeps at me whenever I do something wrong
- My program runs too s-l-o-w-l-y
- Windows won't let me leave

Most of the time, running programs is as simple as a click-click here and a click-click there. However, once in a great while you might have a problem with a program. When you have such a problem, look through this chapter for the solution.

Windows Says It Can't Find My Program

You probably clicked on an icon for a program that doesn't exist. Remember that program icons in the Program Manager merely point to the program files on your computer's hard disk drive. The icon is not the program file itself.

Checklist

- The program may no longer be on your computer's hard disk drive. Did you or someone else accidentally delete it? If so, you must copy the program file back onto the hard drive.

- You might have moved the program to a different directory on the computer's hard disk drive. Accidentally moving a file isn't as hard as it sounds when using the File Manager. You may have meant to *copy* a program file, for example, but ended up moving it instead. Use the File Manager's Search command (from the File menu) to find the file. Then move the program file back into its original directory.

▼ You might have entered the path or name of the file incorrectly when creating the program icon. You can edit the path and name for the program icon easily enough, as Chapter 9 describes.

My Program Doesn't Respond to the Keyboard or the Mouse

If you can't get your program moving, try these things:

Checklist

▼ If the mouse pointer is the shape of an hour glass, the program is busy with something. Wait until it turns back into its regular shape.

▼ If the program seems to be doing something, but the pointer is not an hour glass—this happens sometimes—wait to see whether the program finishes whatever it's doing. A minute should be long enough. If you still get no response, try one of these other tips.

▼ If a menu is selected (the menu is shown in a different color but isn't pulled down), press the Esc key to deselect the menu.

▼ If you try the preceding tricks but the program still fails to respond to anything, the program probably "broke" Windows. Try the following, but only as a last resort (because you'll lose any work you haven't saved): press Ctrl+Esc. The Task List dialog box appears. Click on the program that's not responding and then click on the End Task button.

continues

Checklist Continued

- ▼ If the preceding idea doesn't do the trick, click on the window of the program that's not responding, hold down the Ctrl and Alt keys, and then press the Del key. If Windows can stop the sleeping program, it displays a message with the name of the program. Press the Enter key to stop the program and return to Windows. If that doesn't work, you'll have to restart your computer.

Nothing Happens When I Press the Alt Key to Show a Menu

If you're using the keyboard method of accessing commands in menus (pressing Alt and a letter key), Windows might not respond by displaying the menu. In most cases, this lack of response means that Windows is busy doing something else. Try the following:

Checklist

- ▼ If the mouse pointer is the shape of an hourglass, wait until it turns back into its regular shape.
- ▼ If a dialog box is displayed, close it first.
- ▼ Make sure that you're pressing the right letter to open the menu you want. The underlined character in the menu names shows you the letter key to press, such as F for the File menu. Nothing will happen if you press a letter key that doesn't correspond to a menu.

CHAPTER 18

The Time and/or Date is Wrong in the Windows Clock

The Windows Clock program gets the time and date information from your computer. Your computer hasn't the slightest idea what the time really is. You have to tell it. If you haven't set the clock in a while, it'll probably be a little off. And if you have never set it, who knows what time the computer thinks it is.

You can use Windows to set the time and date in your computer. Follow these steps:

1. Double-click on the Main group icon.
2. Double-click on the Control Panel program icon. The Control Panel window opens.
3. Find the Date/Time icon and double-click on it. The Date & Time dialog box appears.

Date & Time dialog box

4. Click inside the Date entry box on the part you want to change. Click on the up or down arrows to set the correct date.
5. Click inside the Time entry box on the part you want to change. Then click on the up or down arrows to set the correct time.

6. Click on OK to set the date and time.

7. Double-click on the Control menu box in the upper left corner of the Control Panel window to close the window.

When I Run a DOS Program, the Screen Flashes and I'm Returned to Windows

Some DOS commands aren't commands at all; they're programs. Many of these DOS programs display some sort of on-screen text after you run them. Immediately after displaying the text, the program ends and you're returned to the C:\> prompt. Most of the programs in the DOS directory on your computer's hard disk drive behave like this. Examples are TREE, CHKDSK, FIND, and ATTRIB. If you try to run these DOS programs from Windows, the program runs and then it ends. When it ends, you're immediately returned to Windows before you can see the result of whatever the program did. How annoying! But there is a cure.

Don't use the Run command in the Program Manager or double-click on the program name in the File Manager to run the DOS program. Instead, double-click on the Main group icon. Find the MS-DOS Prompt icon and double-click on it. Windows starts a DOS session and displays the C:\> DOS prompt. Type the name of the program you want to run and press the Enter key. When the program is done, type **EXIT** and press Enter. You're returned to Windows.

When I Start a Program, Its Window Always Shrinks to an Icon

Normally when you start a Windows program, its window opens. But if the program immediately turns into an icon, someone has monkeyed with the properties for the icon that starts the program.

Here's how to fix it: In the Program Manager, click once on the icon. Open the File menu and choose the Properties command. The Program Item Properties dialog box appears. The Run Minimized option box has an X in it, which means that when you run the program, it automatically shrinks to an icon. Click inside the Run Minimized box to remove the X, and click on OK to close the Program Item Properties dialog box.

Whenever I Start a Program, the Program Manager Window Shrinks to an Icon

Most folks like to have the Program Manager stay just the way they left it when they run a program. But Program Manager has an option that automatically shrinks the Program Manager window to an icon when you run a program.

If this is happening to you, and you don't like it, return to the Program Manager and open the Options menu. The Minimize on Use command will have a check mark beside it. Choose this command to remove the check mark and turn the option off. Now, whenever you run a program, the Program Manager window stays the way it is. So there.

My Program Beeps at Me Whenever I Do Something Wrong

Some programs like to get on your nerves by beeping at you whenever you do something wrong. Windows Write is a good example of a program with this type of annoying behavior. For example, if you try to use the cursor keys to move the flashing insertion point bar beyond the text in the document, the computer sounds an annoying beep, as if to say, "You dummy! You can't do that!!"

You can't fix beep-happy programs, but you can turn off the blasted beeping for *all* programs. Follow these steps:

1. Double-click on the Main group icon.
2. Double-click on the Control Panel icon. The Control Panel window opens.
3. Find the Sound icon and double-click on it. The Sound dialog box appears.

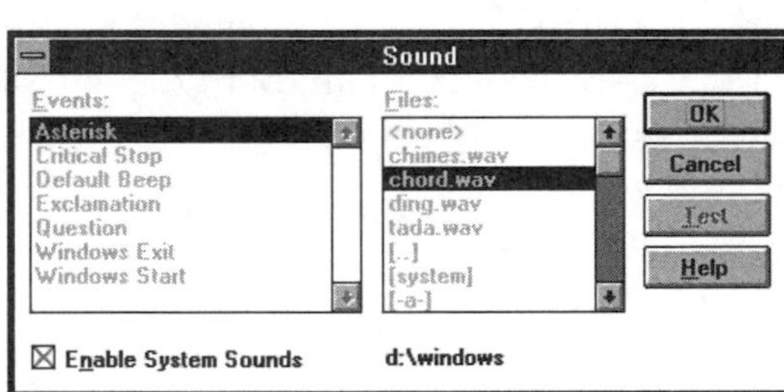

Sound dialog box

4. Click on the Enable System Sounds box to remove the X that's inside it.
5. Click on OK to close the Sound dialog box.

6. Double-click on the Control menu box in the upper left corner of the Control Panel window. The Control Panel window closes.

Unfortunately, turning off the beeps also turns off all other sounds.

My Program Runs S-L-O-W-L-Y, Like a 45 rpm Record Playing at 33 1/3

If a program begins to run very slowly—much more slowly than usual—Windows might be running out of memory. Try one or all of the following:

Checklist

- Close any programs you're not using right now. Any improvement? If not, go to the next idea.
- Close the program you're using, after saving any changes in your current work. Any improvement? If not, go to the next idea.
- Leave Windows, and then restart your computer. This action almost always returns your computer to normal.

I'm all out of ideas. If the slowness persists, it could be an indication of a more serious problem with your computer or with your Windows setup. Have the nearest qualified computer expert look into the matter.

Help! Windows Won't Let Me Leave!

If you try to exit Windows, but see this message

```
Application still active
Quit the application before quitting Windows
```

it means there's a program—usually a DOS program—that's still running. You must exit the program before you can leave Windows.

If you can't see any program that's currently running, Windows is confused. Double-check that there are no remaining programs by pressing Ctrl+Esc to view the Task List dialog box. The only program you should see is Program Manager. If you see another program, click on it and then choose the Switch To command. You can now exit the program in the usual way. If you don't see another program, you have to leave Windows by turning your computer off.

CHAPTER 19

Files and Disks That Go Bump in the Night

IN A NUTSHELL

- ▼ Holy cow! I just accidentally deleted a file!!
- ▼ I can't find the files for the wallpaper or screen savers
- ▼ I don't see the file I want
- ▼ I'm in the right directory, but still don't see the file I want
- ▼ I saved that file yesterday, but today I can't find it
- ▼ Windows tells me that the file I want to open is already in use

- Windows tells me that the disk I want to use isn't formatted
- Windows tells me there's no disk in the drive, but I know it's there
- My floppy disk makes grinding noises whenever I start the File Manager
- The File Manager tells me: "Access denied"
- The File Manager tells me: "No application is associated with this file"
- I can't close the File Manager window

If your disks and files are giving you fits—they sass back or won't stay put—look at this chapter for relief. This chapter helps you find the answer to the popular question "Where is that $#!%! file?"

Holy Cow! I Just Accidentally Deleted a File!!

The more you use your computer, the more chance you have of making a BIG mistake like accidentally deleting a file. Over the years I must have deleted hundreds of files I didn't mean to. It happens to all of us, regardless of computer experience, IQ, or Dunn and Bradstreet rating.

If you accidentally delete a file, you should stop using your computer at once. The reason: Although the file may no longer appear in the File Manager's File List, the contents of the file still remain on your computer's hard disk drive. If you save any more files, they might overwrite the data of the file you accidentally erased. Once the data has been overwritten, the file can never be brought back from the accidental dead, at least not in one piece.

If you do delete a file by mistake, here are your choices:

Checklist

- If there's a computer guru in your office, ask that person for help in getting the accidentally deleted file back.
- If no one is around to help you, and you absolutely must have the file back, you can try to "undelete" it yourself. If your computer uses MS-DOS Version 5.0 or later, you're in luck because it comes with an "undelete" program called UNDELETE. Using the UNDELETE program is beyond the intentions of this book, but you'll find an explanation in the companion book *I Hate DOS*. If you don't have MS-DOS Version 5.0, you'll need to purchase a utility program for the job. Talk to your local software dealer.
- Forget about the file. You probably didn't need it anyway. (Follow this one at your own risk!)

EXPERTS ONLY

Don't know which version of DOS you're using?

Double-click on the Main group icon, then double-click on the MS-DOS Prompt icon. When the C:\> prompt appears, type **VER** and press Enter. DOS will tell you what version you are using. You want it to have a number equal to or greater than 5.00. Type **EXIT** and press Enter to get back to Windows.

I Can't Find the Files for the Wallpaper or Screen Savers

Windows doesn't require you to copy every single one of its files when you install it onto your hard disk drive. Some files, like files for wallpaper and screen savers, are optional. You (or someone else) had the choice of whether or not you wanted to copy these files onto your computer's hard disk drive when installing Windows on your computer.

If you try to use the wallpaper or screen-saver features of Windows, but there are no wallpaper or screen-saver files, you'll have to copy them from the original disks that came with your Windows package. The job isn't that hard to do, but if you don't feel up to it, ask the nearest computer geek to help you.

Where, Oh Where, Has My Little File Gone?

You're using the File Manager, and you've spent hours looking for a file in the File List—well maybe not hours, but it sure seems like it. No matter how hard you look, you can't find the file you want. What gives?

Odds are you're looking in the wrong directory in your computer's hard disk drive, or maybe even on the wrong disk.

Checklist

- To look in another directory, find its folder in the Directory Tree and click on it (if you don't see the Directory Tree, open the View menu and choose the Tree and Directory command).

- To see what's on another disk drive, insert the disk and click on one of the drive icons. For example, to look at floppy drive B, put a disk in drive B and click on the B icon.

- The same thing applies if you're using the Open dialog box to find a document file that you want to open. To take a look inside another directory, first double-click on the C:\ folder; that shows you all the directories on the disk. Then double-click on the folder of the directory you want to see. To see what's on another *disk*, click on the down arrow beside the Drives box, and then click on the drive you want.

I'm in the Right Directory, But I Still Don't See the File I Want

You're using the Open dialog box to find the document file you want to open. You know you're looking in the right directory, but the file is not listed in file list box. Now what?

The Open dialog box is probably using a "file name pattern" that excludes the file you want. A file name pattern consists of one or more wild-card characters.

BUZZWORDS

WILD CARD

A wild card is a special character that represents any other character. Windows (and DOS) use two wild-card characters: the asterisk (*), sometimes called "star," and the question mark (?).

Like a wild card in poker, a wild card in a file name is a substitute for any other character. By putting wild cards together in creative and ingenious ways, you can ask Windows to show only those files that match the desired pattern. For example, type ***.DOC** in the File Name entry blank in the Open dialog box and press the Enter key. Windows shows only those files with the extension .DOC. All other file names are excluded.

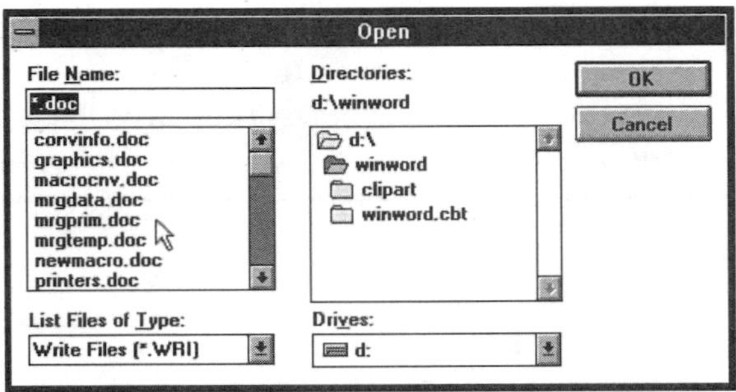

Displaying only *.DOC files

Windows won't show you a file if it doesn't match the file name pattern specified in the File Name entry blank. To show all files, type ***.*** in the Entry Blank and press Enter. You should now be able to spot that file.

I Saved That File Yesterday, But Today I Can't Find It

If you know you saved a file, but now you can't find it, odds are you saved it in a different directory than the one you're looking in right now. Try looking in a different directory or on a different drive. Or search for the file.

The File Manager program lets you search through your computer's hard disk in the wink of an eye. If it finds the file you're looking for, it tells you where the little devil has been hiding.

1. Click on the C:\ folder in the Directory Tree of the File Manager.

2. Open the File menu and choose the Search command. The Search dialog box opens.

3. Make sure that there's an X in the Search All Subdirectories check box. If there is no X, click in the box to put one there.

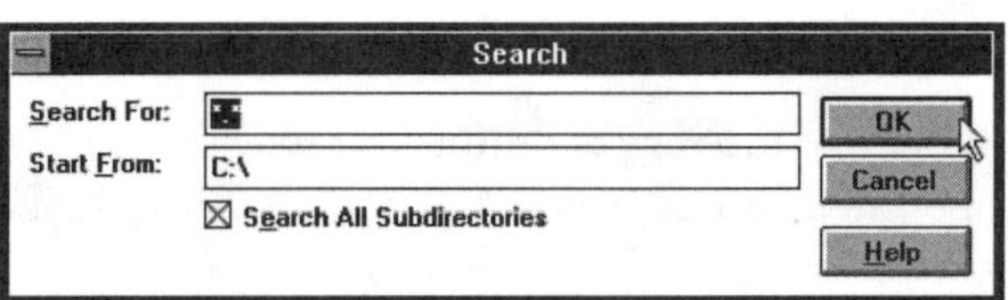

The Search dialog box

4. Double-click inside the Search For entry blank, and press the Del key to remove any text that's already there.

5. Type the name of the file you want to find.

6. Click on the OK button.

   The File Manager roots through all the directories on your computer's hard disk drive. The search will be very fast, but the speed will depend on how many directories and files your computer's hard disk drive contains.

   When and if the file is found, the Search Results window appears. The file name is shown, as well as its full path. The path tells you which directory (or directories) the file is located in. Write down or memorize this path. Then double-click on the Control menu box in the Search Results window to close it.

Windows Tells Me That the File I Want to Open Is Already in Use

Suppose that you're using the Windows Write program. You go to open a document, but Windows tells you:

```
This file is already in use
```

The error message is telling you that the file you tried to open is already open in another program. Click on OK to make the error message go away.

Checklist

- Maybe the document is already open in Notepad or some other program. You will have to find out where the document is being used, and close it.
- Maybe someone else on your network has the document open. You'll have to wait until that person closes the file before you can open it.

Windows Tells Me That the Disk I Want to Use Isn't Formatted

You get a floppy disk from a friend, and you pop into your computer's floppy disk drive. In the File Manager you click on the drive button to see the files on the disk. But instead of a drive window, you get a big, fat error message that says, "The disk in drive A is not formatted. Do you

want to format it now?" (Of course, you might see *B* instead of *A*, if you're using floppy drive B.)

CAUTION

For heaven's sake, don't click on the Yes button! Until you figure out why Windows is having trouble reading the disk, you DO NOT want to format it. Click on No if you see the "Do you want to format it now?" question.

Okay, so you clicked on No (you don't want to format the disk), and you're left scratching your head. Here are some possible causes for the problem:

Checklist

- You incorrectly inserted the disk into the disk drive. Take it out, make sure that you're inserting the disk into the drive properly, and try again.
- Sometimes the disk doesn't "set" itself properly when you insert it into the disk drive. Take it out and try again.
- The disk you got is actually blank. Your friend is trying to pull a fast one on you by sending you a new, unformatted disk. Ask for a replacement disk (and get a new friend).
- The disk you got is actually blank, but your friend is innocent. She really meant to send you a good disk, and it was all a big mistake. Ask for a replacement disk (and forgive your friend).
- The disk isn't meant for the IBM PC or a compatible computer. Is the disk for the Apple Macintosh or Commodore Amiga computers, by any chance? If so, you can't use it in your computer. Ask for a disk you can use.

continues

Checklist Continued

- ▼ There's something wrong with the disk, and your computer can't read its contents. (Disks can "lose" data if they are damaged or mishandled during mailing.) Ask for a replacement disk.
- ▼ The disk was formatted on a floppy disk drive that has a higher capacity than the one you are using. Ask for a replacement disk that has been formatted in the capacity you can use. Or ask the boss for a better computer! (Flip ahead to Chapter 21 if you're not sure about all this disk capacity stuff.)
- ▼ The disk drive is dirty. Either you or the office computer janitor will have to use a cleaning kit to clean the disk drive. These kits are available at most computer stores.

TIP

If you insert a blank disk and *do* want to format it, first be really sure that you want to. The information on the disk will be deleted once you format the disk. If you're sure that you want to format the disk, click on the Yes button.

Windows Tells Me There's No Disk in the Drive, But I Know It's There

If you try to get a reading from a disk that's in a floppy drive, but Windows tells you there's no disk in the drive, be sure that you closed the drive latch if you're using a 5 1/4-inch disk drive. The most probable cause, however, is that you inserted the disk backward or upside down. This is alarmingly easy to do with 5 1/4-inch disks. So, take the disk out of the drive, orient it correctly, and slip it back in.

If Windows still says that there's no disk in the drive, something might be wrong with the disk. Try a disk you *know* is good.

If the problem persists, there's a good chance something's wrong with your computer. It might need to be serviced.

My Floppy Disk Makes Grinding Noises Whenever I Start the File Manager

If your floppy disk drive makes a "shisk-shisk-shisk" sound whenever the File Manager starts, it means that at some previous time when you used the File Manager, you opened a drive window for your floppy drive.

The File Manager remembers that it displayed a drive window for your floppy drive and is trying to show it again. It can't though, because there is no disk in the drive. All you get is the noise of the File Manager trying to read the disk in the drive, but failing.

If you want the File Manager to stop reading the floppy drive whenever you run it, select the hard drive. Then, holding down the Shift key, open the File menu and choose the Exit command. This saves the current window layout, but doesn't leave the File Manager.

TIP

The File Manager is set up so that it remembers the layout each time you leave it. If you don't want that, open the Options menu and look at the Save Settings on Exit command. If it has a check mark beside it, the option is turned on and the File Manager records the layout each time you leave. Choose the Save Settings on Exit command to remove the check mark and turn off the option.

The File Manager Tells Me "Access Denied" When I Try to Copy a File to a Floppy Disk

Access is denied? What is this, an automatic teller machine at a bank? Why won't the File Manager let you copy your file to your floppy disk?!

There are two possible and completely understandable reasons:

Checklist

- ▼ The floppy disk's cup runneth over. It can't accept any more data. Click on OK to make the message go away. You'll either have to use another disk, or delete one or more files on the disk to make room for more.
- ▼ The floppy disk is write-protected. All floppy disks can be protected to prevent you from accidentally changing or deleting files. Click on OK to make the message go away. Then take the disk out of the drive, remove the write-protection tab, and try again. Chapter 21 gives you more details on write-protected disks.

When I Double-Click on a File in the File Manager, I'm Told That "No application is associated with this file." What Does That Mean?

The File Manager keeps a list of "associated" document files and the programs they belong to. The association is based on the file name

extension, such as .DOC or .TXT. That way, when you double-click on a document file that has a .DOC or .TXT (or whatever) extension, Windows starts the program that created the document, then opens the document into that program.

If you double-click on a file in the File Manager and you're told that "No application is associated with this file," it means that Windows doesn't know which program created the file, so it obviously can't run that program. Click OK to make the error message go away. Try running the program from the Program Manager, as explained in Chapter 9.

I Can't Close the File Manager Window

When you start the File Manager, a window is automatically opened. One window must remain open at all times. If only one window is open and you try to double-click on its Control menu box, nothing happens.

Why are you trying to close that window, anyway? If you want to change what the window shows, just select a new drive or directory, as described in Chapter 7. If you want to exit the File Manager, open the File menu and choose the Exit command.

PART V

Stuff That Didn't Fit Anywhere Else

Includes:

CHAPTER 20

Different Flavors of Windows

IN A NUTSHELL

- ▼ Windows 3.0
- ▼ Windows for Workgroups
- ▼ Windows NT
- ▼ IBM OS/2

Throughout this book I've concentrated on Version 3.1 of Windows. Yet there are other variations of Windows out there, and you may encounter them. These other Windows are similar to Windows 3.1, but not exact, so things work a little differently in them.

I can't give step-by-step instructions for all the variations on the Windows theme. That would make this book three times the size that it is, not to mention a lot more expensive. Just the same, you should be aware of the different Windows versions out there, in case you ever run across one or two of them.

If you're sure that you have Windows 3.1, and you aren't planning on changing versions (nor is your company forcing such a change), skip this chapter.

Windows 3.0

(Old and gray)

Windows has been around since 1985, but it really didn't "take off" until May of 1990, when Microsoft unveiled Version 3.0. Windows 3.0 was a lot prettier than the previous versions, and it could do a lot more.

Despite the advances made in Windows 3.0, it was still pretty rough around the edges, and Microsoft came out with an update, Version 3.1, in April of 1992. This book is written for version 3.1 of Windows, although a lot of the material also applies to Windows 3.0.

A lot, but not everything.

TIP

If you're still using Windows 3.0, you should think about getting an upgrade to Version 3.1. Windows 3.1 is faster and adds a number of new features, like TrueType fonts, sound, a vastly improved File Manager, and a better Program Manager.

If you're stuck with Windows 3.0, you'll have to make the best of it. Much of the information and step-by-step instructions in this book applies to both Windows 3.0 and 3.1, but you might need to make adjustments here and there.

Windows for Workgroups

(The "social" Windows)

If you use a computer in an office, there's about a 40-percent chance that all the computers are linked together in a network.

BUZZWORDS

NETWORK

A network is a bunch of computers hooked together so that you can share files, programs, and printers with the other computers.

And if you're on a network, you might be using the network version of Windows, called Windows for Workgroups (WFW). Windows for Workgroups is almost identical to regular Windows (we're talking Version 3.1 here), except that it's designed from the inside out for use

on networks. You can use Windows for Workgroups to fetch files created by someone else and stored on another computer's hard disk drive. In fact, you can even use *programs* that are on another computer.

You can do any of the following things to tell whether you're using Windows for Workgroups:

Checklist

- ▼ In the Program Manager, open the Help menu and choose the About Program Manager command. The dialog box that opens will say "Microsoft Windows for Workgroups", rather than "Microsoft Windows Program Manager".
- ▼ When you start Windows, look at the logo screen that appears. It'll say either "Windows for Workgroups 3.1" or "Windows 3.1".
- ▼ Phone up the network guru at work and say, "Are we using Windows for Workgroups or just regular, old-fashioned Windows here?"

Windows NT

(Windows to be)

There's a new Windows on the horizon—a future product that's not out yet, even though tens of thousands of people are already using it. How's that for confusing!

The new Windows is called NT. The NT stands for *new technology*, and it's still in the making. Microsoft has provided early copies of NT to users and developers in an effort to squash any "bugs" that might remain and to forge support for the product.

Windows NT runs only on the fastest computers and is primarily designed to be used as the "server" in a big, company-wide network. A really big hard disk drive in the server computer contains most or all of the programs and documents you and your coworkers will use.

BUZZWORDS

SERVER

A server is a central computer in a network that all users are connected to.

Although Windows NT is not yet a retail product sold by Microsoft, you already may have encountered it at the office, because your company might be testing it. If you have seen Windows NT, you know that it works a lot differently than the Windows described in this book. If you use Windows NT, you should refer to the instruction manual that came with it, not this book.

Windows NT was supposed to be out by now, but has been delayed due to one technical glitch or another. It might be out by the time you read this, but I'm not about to take bets on it. If and when NT does come out, your company may switch to it. If you're already familiar with the regular Windows, you'll have to learn a few new tricks to use Windows NT.

IBM's OS/2

(The Windows that's not really Windows)

And then there's a Windows that not really Windows: it's OS/2, developed by IBM. OS/2 is a new operating system for your computer. It replaces the usual operating system, MS-DOS (although MS-DOS can

remain on your computer if you want it to). OS/2 provides the same kind of graphical user interface—or GUI ("gooey")—that Windows does. Programs appear in windows, commands are in menus, and you can start programs by double-clicking on icons.

As an added advantage, OS/2 Versions 2.0 and 2.1 can run most Windows programs. For example, you can run Windows Write and the File Manager on OS/2. You don't have to have the rest of the Windows system to run a Windows program.

Checklist

- OS/2 can also run programs written specifically for it. Right now there aren't too many programs written just for OS/2, but IBM hopes there will be more in the near future.

- Because of OS/2's triple personality—it can run Windows, DOS, and OS/2 programs—OS/2 is gaining in popularity in many businesses. If you use it at your office, you might be running Windows programs under it.

- When running under OS/2, Windows programs behave exactly the same way they do when running under Windows. In fact, you may not even be aware you're using a Windows program in OS/2. If you're not sure whether you're using OS/2 or Windows, ask—just make sure to mention that you're asking "for a friend" of yours. You don't want to look dumb!

- Versions of OS/2 prior to 2.0 could not run Windows programs. Furthermore, Version 2.0 of OS/2 can only run Windows 3.0 programs. If you have a Windows program written specifically for Windows 3.1, you need OS/2 2.1 or later.

CHAPTER 21

Everything You Always Wanted to Know about Computers (But Were Smart Enough Not to Ask!)

IN A NUTSHELL

- The parts that make up a computer
- The CPU, microprocessor brain, and memory
- All about keyboards
- Seeing what's going on with the monitor
- The hard disk drive
- Floppy disks: having your data and taking it with you

- The mouse in the computer house
- Printers
- Extra stuff you can add to your computer
- DOS makes it all work

Maybe you are brand-spanking new to personal computers and don't know anything about them or what they're made of. Or you're not new, but maybe no one ever explained the pieces and parts that make up a computer. In this chapter, you'll learn the basics about personal computers, their component parts, and other such goodies.

The PC in PC

The term "personal computer" means any computer used by an individual. A personal computer is different from the big computers with blinky lights that you see in old movies. These computers had to be shared among a lot of people and required all sorts of eggheaded scientists just to keep them running.

There are lots of kinds of personal computers, but the ones I'm talking about are made by IBM or by someone else who is using the same design as the IBM machines. These computers are generically called "PCs"; the PC stands for—you guessed it!—personal computer. (Never mind that PC also stands for "politically correct" and a jillion other things.)

IBM made the first PC in 1981, and it's been copied and improved on ever since by hundreds of companies. Because all PCs can trace their family tree to the first IBM-made PC, they are sometimes called "IBM compatible" computers, or "clones."

Non-IBM or IBM-Compatible PCs

The PC (made by IBM or otherwise) isn't the only "personal computer" in the world. Other companies make personal computers, like the Apple Macintosh computer or the Commodore Amiga. These are personal computers, too, but they don't run Windows or any type of Windows software.

Parts Is Parts

Your car is made from individual parts. It consists of wheels, axles, a frame, an engine, seats, doors, windows, electrical wiring, and bunch of other junk. Taken apart, the car doesn't look like much. But when you put everything together, you can drive it to work.

Your computer is similar. The computer is made from individual parts, all put together so that you can use Windows. Here are the major parts:

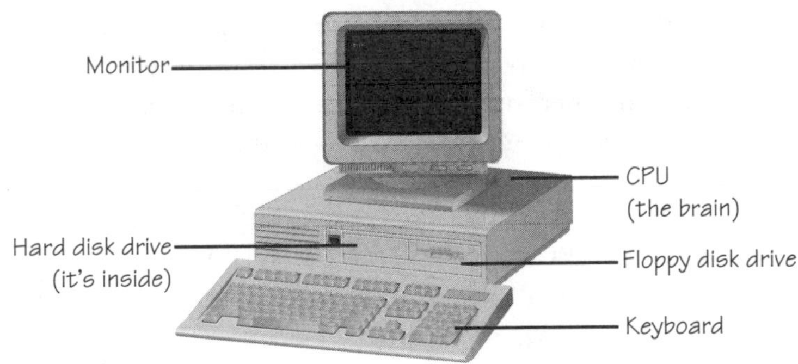

Other computer parts you might have are a printer and a mouse (if you plan to use Windows a lot, you would be crazy not to get a mouse). We will discuss both of these in a little while.

The Brain

The main part of the computer is the CPU.

BUZZWORDS

CPU

CPU stands for *central processing unit*. It's a holdover term from when computers took up entire rooms (you know, the kind you see in 1950s sci-fi flicks). The portion of the computer that had the so-called thinking part was the central processing unit.

Checklist

- Inside your computer is a big, square-shaped board, with all sorts of electronic gizmos soldered into it. This board—called "the motherboard" by computer geeks—contains a very important component: the *microprocessor*.
- The microprocessor is the "brain" of the computer. It's the part that does the actual thinking (if you can call it thinking); the other electronic doodads inside the computer help the microprocessor do its thing.
- Microprocessors are numbered 8086, 8088, 80286, 80386, and 80486—the greater the number, the better and faster the machine. Usually the microprocessor is referred to by the last three digits: 286, 386, 486.

- ▼ You probably have a 386 or 486, because you need a 386 or better to run Windows.
- ▼ The microprocessor name might also include letters, such as SX and DX. An SX microprocessor runs a bit slower; a DX runs at full strength.
- ▼ Microprocessors are rated by clock speeds—33MHz, 50MHz, 66MHz. The faster the better.
- ▼ Clock speeds aren't a reliable guide to system performance when you are comparing two different microprocessors. But when you're comparing two systems that use the same microprocessor, they are.

MHz

MHz stands for *megahertz*, the unit of measurement used to clock the speed of a computer. One megahertz is equal to "one million cycles per second," which seems like a lot, but computers have a lot of data to crunch.

Thanks for the Memories

Your computer has to remember bits and pieces of information as the microprocessor does its thinking. Your computer does have a memory and uses it to remember data. This memory is completely electronic; when you turn the computer off, the stuff inside the memory just disappears.

When you try to remember something, you don't have to start with stuff you learned when you were born and work your way to the present. You

can pick through the cobwebs of your brain to find just the thing you want to know about, like whether your wedding anniversary is on the 20th or 21st of the month.

Being able to pull out anything from your brain without having to go through the stuff from one end to the other is called "random access." The memory inside your computer is the same way. There might be lots of information in there, but the microprocessor can fetch just the part it wants. That's why the memory in your computer is called *random-access memory*, often shortened to just RAM.

Checklist

- The more RAM in your computer, the more data the microprocessor can get to at once, so the more complex things your computer can do.
- RAM is measured in kilobytes (K or KB) and megabytes (M or MB). One kilobyte equals about 1,000 characters. One megabyte equals around 1,000,000 characters. To run Windows at a respectable pace, you should have 4M of RAM. 8M would be fabulous.
- In most cases, you can add memory to your computer to improve its performance. (Get a Windows whizz to do it for you.)

The Keyboard

(Bossing your computer around)

The keyboard is your main link to the computer. The keyboard lets you give commands so that your computer knows what you expect of it.

CHAPTER 21

Keyboards for IBM PC and compatible computers have changed in the past years. Early models started with 83 keys; now most of them have 101 or 102 keys. The extra keys make it easier to do special things with your computer.

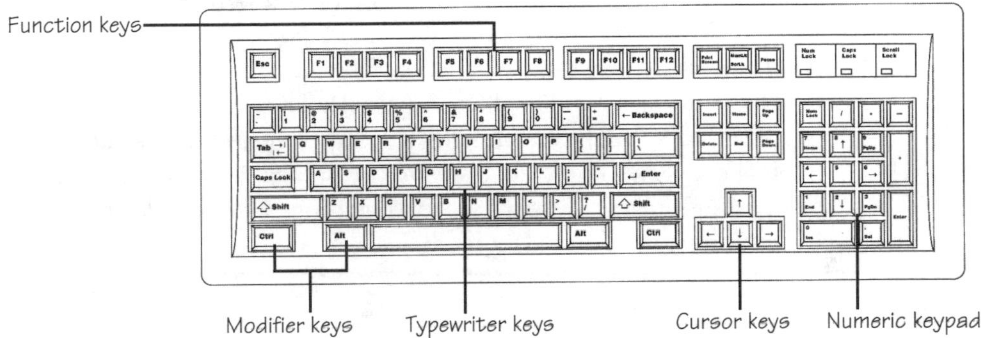

Checklist

- *Typewriter keys*. These are the same keys you find on a typewriter, including the alphabet keys and the number keys above them, the big space bar at the bottom, and the assorted symbol keys.
- *Function keys*. These keys are either along the left side or the top (or both) of the keyboard and are labeled F1 through F10 (keyboards with 100 or more keys have two extra function keys, F11 and F12). Function keys do different things in different programs, usually for shortcuts to commands.
- *Numeric keypad*. On the right side of the keyboard is a separate set of number keys, as well as add, subtract, multiply, and divide keys. The keypad lets you enter numbers faster.
- *Cursor keys*. These keys are sometimes mixed with the numeric keypad (in which case the keys serve double-duty) or they are

continues

separate keys placed between the typewriter keys and the numeric keypad. The cursor keys let you move an on-screen, this-is-where-I'm-at cursor. If you're typing text, for example, the cursor shows you where the text will go when you press a letter key.

- *Presto-chango keys*. Also called *modifier keys*, these are labeled Alt (for Alternate) and Ctrl (for Control). These keys are pressed with other keys, much like pressing the Shift key and the "a" key to make an "A." There are also *other keys*: Ins, Del, Home, and End. Various programs use these keys for things such as deleting text or moving around in a document.

Two Keys You Should Never Forget

The two most important keys on the keyboard are

- *Enter*. On a typewriter, this is the same as the Return key. Enter tells the computer you're done and ready to move on.
- *Esc*. A typewriter doesn't have a key that's equivalent to the Esc key. The Esc (Escape) key tells the computer that you've changed your mind and want to "escape."

EXPERTS ONLY

Dig them crazy key names!

I can hear you now: "Where did they come up with those stupid-sounding names for the keys?" The answer is simple: the names were inherited.

EXPERTS ONLY

When IBM developed the PC, they saw it as a way to connect PCs to big "mainframe" computers, used by the government and big banks, that sort of thing. So the keys on the PC keyboard were modeled after the keys on the mainframe keyboards. Keys like F1, Esc, Ctrl, and Alt meant something to the operators of those old clunky mainframes.

Today, the names of the keys remain, but they are called upon to do whatever things the Windows programmers want them to do.

The Monitor

(Seeing where the computer is screwing up)

You need some way to see what the computer is doing. That's the job of the monitor. The name comes from what it does: it lets you monitor the goings-on in your computer.

Checklist

- Like TV sets, computer monitors come in all sorts of shapes, sizes, and types.
- A common size is 14 inches, measured diagonally from one corner to the opposite corner (like a TV). It's an approximate measurement—give or take a half inch or so.
- And like TV sets, monitors for computers come in black and white or color. The black-and-white models aren't always black and

continues

Checklist Continued

white, and because of that, they're called *monochrome* monitors. Monochrome means "one color." That one color can be black or green or yellow. Most Windows users have a full-color monitor.

- Computer monitors differ in the sharpness of the picture they display. This sharpness is expressed in "dots" across the screen, horizontally and vertically. The sharpness is called the *resolution*. A common resolution for monitors used with Windows is 640 dots side to side and 480 dots top to bottom.
- Some lucky Windows users have monitors with 1,024 dots horizontally and 768 dots vertically. That's over 40 percent more dots than the common resolution (640 by 480). You can imagine how much clearer the picture is with all those extra dots.

EXPERTS ONLY

Acronym Heaven

Instead of talking about dots all the time and who has more, computer geeks use code to describe the sharpness of their monitors. Here's how to decipher the code:

Code Word	Dots Horizontally	Dots Vertically
EGA	640	200
VGA	640	480
Super VGA	1024	768
Hercules	720	348

The code words are actually monitor standards first developed by IBM. The standards help you buy equipment that will work with your computer.

CHAPTER 21

The Hard Disk Drive

(The "U-Stor" of your computer)

There's not enough random access memory (RAM) in your computer to store all the programs you use and data you'll make. Besides, remember what happens to the data in RAM when the computer gets turned off? It goes away.

Your computer uses what's called a *hard disk drive* for long-term storage of data and programs. The hard disk drive gets its name because the magnetic disks inside it are made of metal—and therefore hard.

Checklist

- Your computer's hard disk drive is about the size of a Sony Walkman, and it can store millions and millions of pieces of information.
- The amount of information a hard disk can store is measured in megabytes—just like memory. One megabyte equals about 1,000,000 characters.
- Hard disk drives differ in the exact amount of memory they can store. A typical hard disk drive for Windows can store 120 million characters of information—that is, 120M.
- Other hard disk drives might hold more or less data. The smallest practical hard disk drive for use with the Windows system holds 60 megabytes. There are some super-duper drives that can store 650 megabytes or more.
- To give you an idea of how much memory 650 megabytes really is, if each byte (character) in the hard disk is a typewritten letter, and you stack them all on top of one another, the letters would reach over 1,500 miles into the sky!

I HATE WINDOWS!

@☆#!
"I HATE THIS!"

Memory and hard disks are not the same things

Mistaking the amount of memory (RAM) you have with the amount of hard disk space you have is a common mistake. If you say you have 1 megabyte of disk space when you mean RAM, computer geeks will snicker. Keep in mind that although the same measuring stick is used for both, RAM and hard disks are entirely different. You'll always have lots more hard disk space than RAM.

The Floppy Disk

The data in your computer's hard disk drive stays with your computer. The magnetic disk is permanently sealed inside the hard drive, and the drive is bolted to the busty innards of your computer.

What if you want to share some data with a friend? You don't have to ship your whole computer—just the data. Put the data on a floppy disk, and send the disk!

Floppy disks also let you get information (like a program or a file) from another source and put it on your hard disk.

Checklist

- A floppy disk get its name because the magnetic disk is made of plastic and is flexible—you know, floppy. The disk itself is placed in a protective covering, which can be flexible vinyl or hard plastic. Either way, it's still a "floppy" because the floppy part refers to the disk itself, not its outside skin.

- ▼ Floppy drives are placed at the front of the computer so you can easily reach them. You slip the floppy disk into the disk drive slot, and away you go.
- ▼ Floppy disks come in two sizes—sizes that don't "fit all." If your floppy disk drive is made to hold the one size, you can't use the other.
- ▼ 5 1/4-inch disks have a big hole in the middle and a flexible vinyl covering.
- ▼ 3 1/2-inch disks have a round, metal piece in the middle, a metal "slide" on one end, and a hard plastic covering.
- ▼ In addition to matching the size of the disk to the size of the drive, you also must use the right disk capacity, as described next.

One Size Doesn't Fit All

To make matters even more complicated, both floppy disk sizes can store different amounts of data. The amount of data you can store is called the "capacity."

BUZZWORDS

CAPACITY

Capacity is the amount of information you can store on a disk and is measured in kilobytes (K or KB) or megabytes (M or MB).

Take a look at the following table to get a rough idea of how floppy disks stack up. Note that the Text Equivalent column tells you how many

pages of double-spaced text can be stored on the disk; the number of pages is approximate. The Label Code column tells you what you'll see on the disk box or label.

Size	Capacity	Text Equivalent	Label Code
5 1/4"	360K	220 pages	DS/DD
5 1/4"	1.2M	740 pages	HD
3 1/2"	720K	440 pages	DS/DD
3 1/2"	1.44M	880 pages	HD

Checklist

- Most disks are labeled either by their capacity in bytes, such as 360K, or by the label code, as shown in the preceding table.
- The label code refers to the disk's *density*. Density is the recording method used to cram stuff onto the disk. DD (double-density) disks store less than HD (high-density) disks.
- The label code probably also says DS. This stands for *double-sided* and indicates absolutely nothing, since all disks are now double-sided (both sides of the disk are usable).
- Out of the box, a 5 1/4-inch floppy disk doesn't leave you many clues as to whether its capacity is 360K or 1.2M. It's nearly impossible to tell just by looking at it—except of course, if you look at the label, which should say what kind of disk it is. Be sure not to cover up the disk label with another label of your own.

- ▼ It's a little easier to tell the difference between 720K and 1.44M 3 1/2-inch floppy disks. If it's a high-capacity disk, it should have a little window in two of its corners, near where the label goes. If the disk is low-capacity, you'll see only one window.
- ▼ Floppy disk drives that can take high-capacity disks can also take low-capacity ones. However, floppy disk drives that can take only low-capacity disks can take only low-capacity disks.

Inserting and Ejecting Disks

To insert a disk, hold the disk with the label up and toward you; then slide it into the drive.

Checklist

- ▼ 5 1/4-inch disks go into the drive label up, with the label nearest you. If the drive is mounted into your computer sideways, turn the disk so that the label is still nearest you, but is facing the disk-lock latch. Once you push the disk all the way in, turn the latch to lock the disk in the drive.
- ▼ 3 1/2-inch disks also go into the drive label up, with the label nearest you (the metal "slide" part goes in first). Push the disk all the way in until it snaps into place.
- ▼ Don't try to cram a disk into the drive. If it doesn't go in smoothly, something is wrong. Does the drive already have a disk in it? Is the disk latch open on 5 1/4-inch drives?

continues

Checklist Continued

- Putting a 5 1/4-inch disk into the drive backward or upside down won't cause any permanent damage, but your computer won't be able to use the disk. However, *inserting a 3 1/2-inch disk into the drive incorrectly can damage both the disk and the drive!* So be careful.

To eject a disk from a 5 1/4-inch drive, open the latch. The disk should pop out a bit. Slide the disk out the rest of the way.

To eject a disk from a 3 1/2-inch drive, push the button. The disk will pop out so that you can grab it.

Protecting the Disk (Safe Data)

A floppy disk can be protected to prevent you or anyone from accidentally erasing or altering the data it contains. To protect a disk, you use a *write-protect tab.*

Checklist

- For 5 1/4-inch disks, the write-protect tab is a piece of special tape. Put the tab over the "notch" in the side of the disk. If you don't have the tabs, you can use regular tape. With the tab in place, you can't place new data on the disk or erase existing data.

- For 3 1/2-inch disks, the write-protect tab is a piece of plastic you slide up or down in a little window in the corner of the disk. When the plastic covers the window, the disk is not write-protected. If you slide the plastic so that you can see through the window, you can't place new data on the disk or erase existing data.

▼ If you see an error message that reads “This disk is write-protected” (or something similar), you’ll know what’s going on. You need to take the disk out of the floppy drive, remove the write-protect tab, and try again.

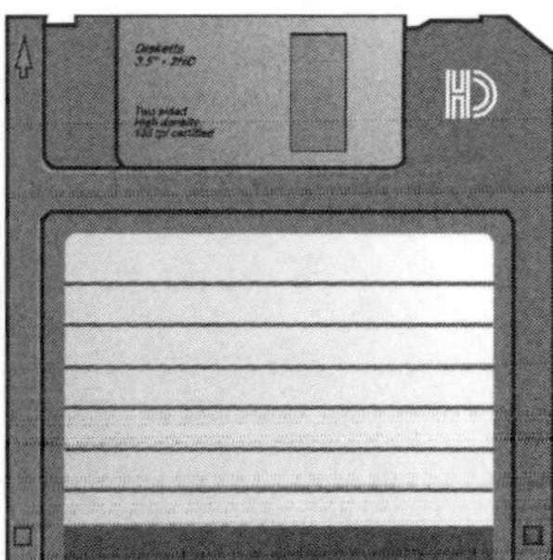

Checklist

- On the top of the mouse is a set of buttons—either two or three, depending on the design of the mouse. First you move the mouse to point at something on the computer's screen; then press one of the buttons, usually the left, to tell the computer that you're ready to do something.

- Not all computers are equipped with a mouse. A mouse is not absolutely required to use most computer programs, including Windows, but it sure is handy. If you want to use Windows, you should seriously consider getting a mouse for your computer.

- The mouse isn't the only "pointing device" you can get for your computer. Another option is something called a *trackball*. These are popular in arcade games; you roll a ball back and forth to move the game hero on the screen.

The Printer

For years the "experts" have been telling us that the office of the future would be paperless. Everything would be electronic. No more paper letters, paper memos, paper reports. No more jamming reams of paper into a file cabinet. No more trips to the paper recycler to get rid of the rejects.

Hah!

If anything, there's more paper flying around the office than ever before. If you use a computer to create documents, you have to have a way to get your work on paper. That's the job of the printer. The computer tells

the printer what characters to print and how to print them. The printer then produces an image on a piece of paper and shoots it out to you.

There are lots of different kinds of printers these days. Odds are that your office is equipped with a laser printer. In the case of a laser printer, the laser isn't some death ray that will blow up your boss's office (too bad); it's a light source for printing the images that will appear on the paper.

Other kinds of printers include the dot-matrix, the inkjet, and the daisy-wheel. In the end, they all do about the same thing, although they go about it in different ways.

The Extras

So far we've talked about the parts your computer must have to operate (mouse and printer excluded). But you can cram even more junk on your computer to increase its capabilities. Here are some of the things you can get for your computer—some you might already have; some you might get in the future, if you ever get that check from Ed McMahon and Publishers Clearing House.

Checklist

- *Telephone modem*. Lets you connect to other computers over the phone line.
- *Fax/phone modem*. Combines a telephone modem with a fax. You can talk to other computers, and you can send or receive faxes. You don't need a separate fax machine.
- *Network*. Connects to other computers in your office. Once connected, you can share programs and data.

continues

Checklist Continued

- *Tape backup drive*. Saves all the data stored on your hard disk drive, and does it fairly quickly. Just pop a tape cassette into the drive, and make a copy of all the programs and data on your computer's hard disk drive. That way, if anything happens to your hard disk drive, you have a backup copy on tape.

The Disk Operating System Ties It All Together

Making sure that all the parts of your computer are working together as they should be is something called the *disk operating system*, or DOS (rhymes with "boss"). The most popular disk operating system for personal computers is sold by Microsoft (they're the ones who make Windows) and goes by the name of MS-DOS—the MS stands for Microsoft.

You've probably heard of DOS and how it's hard to learn. Well, you heard right. And you were probably thinking that Windows would keep you from having to worry about DOS on your computer. Not quite.

Even though you're using Windows, your computer still needs DOS for all of its housekeeping chores. Windows insulates you from a lot of the nitty-gritty of DOS, so for the most part, you don't even have to worry it's there. But every once in a while, you have to deal with some DOS reality, like when you're using the File Manager to create a directory but have to obey DOS's rules for naming it.

PART VI

Quick & Dirty Dozens

Includes:

12 Cool Things Nobody Knows You Can Do with Windows

12 Heart-Stopping Windows Messages and What to Do about Them

12 Common Mistakes in Windows

12 Best Windows Shortcuts

12 Mystifying Acronyms and What They Mean

12 Super Simple Ways to Customize Windows

I HATE WINDOWS

Quick & Dirty Dozens

IN A NUTSHELL

- 12 cool things nobody knows you can do with Windows
- 12 heart-stopping Windows messages and what to do about them
- 12 common mistakes in Windows
- 12 best Windows shortcuts
- 12 mystifying acronyms and what they mean
- 12 super simple ways to customize Windows

12 Cool Things Nobody Knows You Can Do with Windows

1. **Cheat at Solitaire**

   The Windows Solitaire game lets you deal out one card at a time, or three at a time. The three-at-a-time version is harder and more challenging, because there's a chance that the card you really need won't get dealt. If you're playing the three-at-a-time version, here's a trick that forces Solitaire to deal the next card in the deck. Press down the Ctrl, Alt, and Shift keys while you click on the deck. Just make sure that no one is watching.

2. **Start 'er up!**

   Let Windows be your butler and automatically start a program when you start Windows. In the Program Manager, find the icon for the program you want automatically started. Be sure that the StartUp group icon is in view (move windows around if it's not). Hold down the Ctrl key and drag the program icon on top of the StartUp group icon. This puts a copy of the program icon into the StartUp group. The original icon remains.

   The next time you start Windows, your program starts too.

   You can put as many programs as you want in the StartUp group, and Windows will run them all when it first starts. But you should keep the number of programs to a minimum; Windows runs faster that way.

3. **Stashing a start-up program**

   Putting a program icon into the StartUp group icon automatically runs that program when Windows starts. But what if you don't

want the program's window hogging the view right off the bat? Maybe you'd like to run the program, but hide its window until you're ready for it.

After copying the program icon to the StartUp group, double-click on the StartUp group icon. Click once on the program icon, then press Alt+Enter. The Program Item Properties dialog box appears. Click inside the Run Minimized box to put an X there. Click OK.

Now when Windows starts, the program runs, but its window is shrunk to an icon at the bottom of the screen. Double-click on this icon to expand the window.

4. Hey bud, you got the time?

The Windows Clock is a good program to put in the StartUp group and run automatically when Windows first starts. With the Clock on-screen, you'll always know the time.

If you want the Clock to appear in a window, be sure the Run Minimized box is not Xed, as explained above in #3.

You can keep the Clock window (or icon) on the top of your other windows at all times by setting the Always on Top option. Run the Clock program by double-clicking on its icon (in the Accessories group window). If the Clock appears as an icon, click on the icon. Then click the Always on Top command to put a check mark beside it. If the clock appears as a window, click on its Control menu box (upper left corner). Then click on the Always on Top command to put a check mark beside it.

5. The funny characters you meet in Windows

Many fonts (text styles) you use in Windows come with all sorts of special characters, like round dots for bullets, upside-down question

marks, foreign characters, you name it. You get these characters by pressing and holding the Alt key, then tapping out a number using the numeric keypad on the right side of your keyboard (be sure the Num Lock light is on; if it isn't, press the Num Lock key).

For example, to insert a 1/4 character, press Alt+0188. Le'go of the Alt key. The 1/4 character pops up (not all Windows programs support the Alt+0xxx trick, but most do). See the Special Characters appendix in the user's guide that comes with Windows for a list of the characters you can create.

6. Hot diggety dog, hot keys!

Forget double-clicking on icons to start programs. An easier and quicker method is to tell Windows that you want to use a "hot key" to start a program. Here's how:

Find the icon for the program you want to make a hot key for—say the Windows Write program. Click on the icon, then press Alt+Enter. The Program Item Properties dialog box appears. Click inside the Shortcut Key entry blank. Now press the letter or number key you want to use to start the program. Windows automatically adds the Ctrl and Alt keys to the list. For example, if you press the W key, the Shortcut key entry looks like Ctrl+Alt+W. Click OK when you're done.

To start Windows Write, press Ctrl+Alt+W instead of double-clicking on the Windows Write icon.

7. Was that 1,778,987 or 1,787,789?

You've got this really big number in the Calculator program, see, and you want to put the number in a letter you're writing with the Windows Write program. Don't waste time jotting it down on a piece of paper or trying to memorize it. Use the Windows copy-and-paste feature instead.

With the result you want showing in the Calculator, open the Edit menu and choose Copy. Now click on the window of the program you want to put the number in. Inside that program (say, Windows Write), open the Edit menu and choose Paste. The number from the Calculator program appears.

8. Documents can have icons, too

You can make a Program Manager icon for your favorite document. When you double-click on a document icon, you run the program that created the document, and open the document into the program so you can work on it. Use this trick to make an icon for a document you use a lot, like maybe your resume! (Just kidding....)

To make an icon for a document, click once on the icon of the program that made the document. Make a copy of that icon by pressing the Ctrl key and dragging the copy to a new place in the group window. Now press Alt+Enter; the Program Item Properties dialog box for the new icon appears.

Click inside the Command Line entry blank and press the right-arrow key until the flashing cursor is at the end of the line. Then type a space, followed by the file name of the document you want to use. Include the path of the file so that Windows is sure to find it. Click on OK. Then click on the document icon to start the program and the document.

This technique works for most, but not all, Windows programs. If you try it and it doesn't work, the program you're using doesn't support this trick.

9. Instant Control Panel icons (just add water)

Double-click, double-click, double-click! Getting to a Control Panel program is a major pain in the butt. It would be much easier

if you could just drag out a favorite Control Panel icon—say like the Color icon—and put it in the Main group window so that you don't have to open the Control Panel window every time you want to use it. But you can't. Windows won't let you.

But you *can* make copies of the icons in the Control Panel. Putting these icons in the Main group window lets you bypass the Control Panel icon altogether, saving you some time and some double-clicks. Here's how to copy a Control Panel icon to the Main group window: Double-click on the Main icon to open it, and then click once on the Control Panel icon. Hold down the Ctrl key and drag a copy of the Control Panel icon elsewhere in the Main window. Click on the copy you just made, and then press Alt+Enter to open the Program Item Properties dialog box for the new icon.

Click inside the Command Line entry blank and press the right-arrow key until the flashing cursor is at the end of the line, to the right of *control.exe*. Then type a space, followed by the name of the Control Panel program you want to use, so that the entry blank shows the same text you see in the Command Line column of the following table (be sure to put in the spaces, as shown). While you're at it, change the Description entry blank to match the text in the Description column in the table below. Click on the OK button when you are done.

Program	Command Line	Description
Color	control.exe main.cpl color	Color
Fonts	control.exe main.cpl fonts	Fonts
Ports	control.exe main.cpl ports	Ports
Mouse	control.exe main.cpl mouse	Mouse

Program	Command Line	Description
Desktop	control.exe main.cpl desktop	Desktop
Keyboard	control.exe main.cpl keyboard	Keyboard
Printers	control.exe main.cpl printers	Printers
International	control.exe main.cpl international	International
Date/Time	control.exe main.cpl date/time	Date/Time
Network	control.exe main.cpl network	Network
386 Enhanced	control.exe cpwin386.cpl	386 Enhanced
Drivers	control.exe drivers.cpl	Drivers
Sound	control.exe snd.cpl	Sound

10. Changing those boring Control Panel icons

If you follow the preceding trick, you'll find that the icon for all the Control Panel programs are the same. You can change the icon if you want.

Click on the Control Panel program icon you created in the above trick. Press Alt+Enter to display the Program Item Properties dialog box. Click Change Icon. The Change Icon dialog box appears. In the File Name entry blank, delete the current entry and type one of the file names listed below; then press Enter. Click on the icon; then click OK. Click OK to close the Program Item Properties dialog box. (The MAIN.CPL file contains a whole raft of icons for the Control Panel programs. Click on the one you want.)

Control Panel Program	Control Panel File Name
Color	main.cpl
Fonts	main.cpl
Ports	main.cpl
Mouse	main.cpl
Desktop	main.cpl
Keyboard	main.cpl
Printers	main.cpl
International	main.cpl
Date/Time	main.cpl
Network	main.cpl
386 Enhanced	cpwin386.cpl
Drivers	drivers.cpl
Sound	snd.cpl

11. **Doin' the old copy-and-paste with DOS**

You already know that you can copy and paste text between Windows programs, but did you know you can do the same thing with DOS programs? Well, you can. But there's a "gotcha": you have to be running Windows in 386 Enhanced Mode. If you're not sure which mode Windows is running in, open the Help menu in the Program Manager and choose the About Program Manager command. A dialog box shows you the current operating mode of Windows.

To paste text to a DOS program, first copy it from the source program. Run the DOS program or switch to it (press Ctrl+Esc to display the Task List, and double-click on the DOS program). In order to paste the text, you must put the DOS program into a window: do that by pressing Alt+Enter. Click on the Control menu box in the upper left corner of the window, click on Edit, and then click on Paste. Press Alt+Enter again to make the DOS program full-screen.

To copy text from a DOS program, make the program into a window by pressing Alt+Enter. Click on the Control menu box, click on Edit, and then click on Mark. Use the mouse to drag over the text you want to copy; then press Enter. Press Alt+Enter again to make the DOS program full-screen. You can now paste the text into another program, DOS or Windows.

12. **See the Windows movie (bring your own popcorn)**

Few people know that Windows comes with a movie. Well, at least the credits for a movie. It's called the "gang screen," because it shows the gang of lunatics that developed Windows. Follow these steps:

1. In the Program Manager, open the Help menu and choose About Program Manager. The About Program Manager dialog box appears.

2. Hold down the Ctrl and Shift keys, double-click on the Microsoft logo in the dialog box, then click on OK.

3. Once again, open the Help menu and choose About Program Manager.

4. And once again, hold down the Ctrl and Shift keys, double-click on the Microsoft logo in the dialog box, and click on OK.

5. For the third time, open the Help menu and choose About Program Manager.

6. Last but not least, hold down the Ctrl and Shift keys and double-click on the Microsoft logo.

One of four "presenters" appears—among them multibillionaire and Head Nerd, Bill Gates. A little box shows you the names of all the folks who worked on Windows. This list goes on forever, over and over. Click on OK when you get sick of watching it.

12 Heart-Stopping Windows Messages and What to Do about Them

1. "General Protection Fault"

This error message is the granddaddy of all Windows error messages. It means that something messed up big time. It's caused by some mistake in Windows or the program you're using.

In most cases, this error message includes an OK button; click OK to make the message go away. The program you were using will probably end abruptly, and any work you haven't saved will be lost. After any general protection fault, you should leave Windows and restart it.

In some cases, clicking on OK isn't enough. If clicking on OK doesn't seem to do anything, you will need to reset your computer. Press the computer's Reset button or press Ctrl+Alt+Del. If that doesn't work, turn your computer off. Wait 10 seconds; then turn the computer back on.

Depending on the glitch, the General Protection Fault error message gives you the option of "ignoring" the error by pressing the Ignore button. This is a misnomer. You really can never ignore the error, because odds are that Windows or the program you're using won't be able to continue. You should click on the Ignore button just the same to see if anything happens. If Windows and/or your program comes back to life, save your work. Since Windows is often left in an unstable state after a general protection fault, you should exit and restart Windows. This puts everything back to normal.

2. **"System Violation Error"**

This error occurs only when a DOS program gives you fits. Click OK to make the error message go away. The DOS program will end, and any unsaved work you've done with it will be lost. After a system violation error, you should leave Windows and restart it.

3. **Application Execution Error: "Unexpected DOS Error #11"**

This is one of several Application Execution Error messages you might see when trying to run a DOS program. If you get this error message, it usually means there's a bad or missing Windows file required for running a DOS program. The problem can sometimes be fixed simply by restarting the DOS program. You might also have some luck if you leave Windows and restart it. Click on OK to make the error message go away.

If these measures fail, it could indicate that one or more Windows files are missing or damaged. You or the Windows guru at your office might have to reinstall Windows to set things straight.

4. **Application Execution Error: "Cannot find file xxx..."**

You see this message when Windows can't find the program you want to run (the "xxx" stands for the name of the program). The error message will rear its ugly head if you double-click on an icon for a program that's no longer on your computer's hard disk drive. You also get it if you specify the wrong path or program name in the Run dialog box.

To fix the error, be sure that the program is on the computer's hard disk drive and that you have the correct path and name.

5. "System Error. Cannot read from Drive x" or "Error Selecting Drive. There is no disk in Drive x"

Windows displays this error message when it can't read a disk drive (the *x* is the letter of the drive it can't read, such as A or B). Two buttons appear: Cancel and Retry (in some cases only the Cancel button will appear). Make sure that you have a disk in the drive, and then click on Retry to have Windows reread the disk drive. If the error happens again, it could mean a problem with the program you're using or with your disk drive. Click on Cancel one or more times until the error message goes away.

6. "Disk is full"

This error message appears if there's no more room on a disk to store the file you want to save. Click on OK to close the error message box.

If you're saving a file onto a floppy disk, replace the disk with one that has more room on it, or make room on the disk by removing other files. If you're saving a file onto the computer's hard disk drive, you'll need to remove some files to make room.

7. "Insufficient memory to run this application. Quit one or more Windows applications and then try again."

With this error message, Windows is telling you that there isn't enough unused memory available in your computer to continue working. Click on OK to close the error message box; then do as Windows says: quit any Windows programs you happen to be running but not using, and try again.

This error message can also occur when there's plenty of unused memory left in your computer, but when something called "system resources" are running low. You can fix this problem by leaving Windows and restarting it.

Windows will tell you how much free memory and system resources are available; just open the Help menu in the Program Manager and choose the About Program Manager command. The memory is listed in KB, which means *kilobytes* (thousands of bytes). The more the merrier. The amount of system resources is listed as a percentage. Trouble is abrewing when this figure dips below 30 percent.

8. "Extremely low on memory. Close an application and try again."

Windows is telling you that there is little or no unused memory available to run your program, and that doing anything else could cause bigger problems. Click on OK to make the error message go away. Immediately quit any programs you are not actively using, and close any Program Manager windows that don't need to be opened. Try to run the program again. If this doesn't work, leave Windows and restart it.

9. "xxx cannot be initialized"

This error message appears when Windows can't run a program (the "xxx" is the name of a program). Click OK to close the error message box.

Here are the main reasons this error message appears:

- There's not enough unused memory in your computer. Quit other programs and try again.
- There aren't enough "system resources" available to Windows (see #7). Quit other programs and try again. You might have to leave Windows and restart it.
- One or more files that go with the program are missing or damaged. You'll need to reinstall the program. Get help from a Windows guru.

10. "Share violation"

This error message appears when you try to open or save a document file that's already being used in another program. Click OK to close the error message box. Close the document in the other program. If you're on a network, someone else in the office might be using the document. You'll have to wait until that person closes the document before you can use it.

You may or may not encounter the "Share violation" error message. You'll only see it if the SHARE program was run before Windows started (the SHARE program is most often run automatically, when your computer starts). If SHARE wasn't run, the "Share violation" error message won't appear.

11. Start-up error: "Cannot find the system initialization file needed to run Windows. You need to run the setup program again."

If you get this message when you try to start Windows, it means that the very critical SYSTEM.INI file cannot be found or is damaged. After the error message appears, you're left at the DOS C:\> prompt.

If this error occurs, try starting Windows again. If that doesn't work, try restarting your computer. Still no luck? You'll need to run the Windows Setup program to reinstall stuff.

You can avoid this problem by always keeping an extra copy of the SYSTEM.INI file. Copy it onto a floppy disk and store the disk in a safe place. Every so often, recopy the file to make sure it's up-to-date. Then, if the SYSTEM.INI file is ever missing or mangled, you have the copy to bail you out.

12. **The "no nuthin" error**

This isn't an error message at all. In fact, it's just the opposite—the absence of an error message when a mondo error has occurred during your attempt to start Windows. Windows looks like it's about to start, but fails part way through—no error message, nuthin. Either the opening Windows screen freezes on your monitor, or you're left staring at the DOS C:\> prompt. In some cases, a message of some type flashes on the screen, but not long enough for you to read what it says. Gee, thanks.

If this happens, it's usually because some aspect of your computer was changed—like maybe you replaced the display. It can also happen when one or more critical Windows files are missing or damaged. Try starting Windows again. If it still won't run, restart your computer. Sometimes, it's just a momentary glitch and the problem fixes itself when you restart the computer.

Should Windows continue putting up a fight, you or the office computer mascot will need to run the Windows Setup program. Windows might have to be installed all over again. Aren't computers fun?!

12 Common Mistakes in Windows

1. Where, oh where, has my Program Manager gone?!

When you click on the Minimize button in the Program Manager window, you reduce the window to an icon. The icon settles at the bottom of your screen. Some folks shriek with despair that the Program Manager has "disappeared," but that's not the case. To see the full Program Manager window, just double-click on the Program Manager icon at the bottom of the screen. If you can't see the icon because you've got another program maximized, minimize that program, too.

2. Group icons: the fewer the better

In the Program Manager, icons for programs have to be put inside group icons. Most programs you add to Windows create their own program icon, and for good measure, create a separate group icon to hold it. This isn't a good idea on two counts: it causes group icon clutter in the Program Manager, and each time you open a different group icon into a window, a little bit of your computer's memory is used up (you get that memory back when you leave Windows at the end of the day).

It's far better to consolidate program icons into just a small handful of groups. You can always create your own groups and move icons around, so there is no reason to settle for the groups that programs create when you install them on your computer's hard disk drive.

3. Once is enough

Windows lets you run two or more programs at the same time. Some of these programs might be able to open the same kinds of document files; for example, the programs Windows Write and

Notepad can both open text files. That's fine, but you want to avoid opening the same document file more than once at the same time (if the DOS SHARE program was loaded before Windows started, Windows won't even let you do this).

Why is this important? Suppose that you open the same document file at the same time in two different programs, but you forgot that you did that. You make changes to the document in one of the programs, then save the document. Later that day, you make different changes in the other program, and save the file again. What happens is that the changes you made in the first program are lost, because the second program used the original document, not the revised one.

4. Windows is not Grand Central Station

One of the most enticing features of Windows is that it lets you run more than one program at a time. But really, folks, there's a limit to the number of programs that Windows can juggle at once. The absolute number of programs you can run at one time depends on the programs you're using and the particulars about your computer. But a good rule of thumb is to limit the number of concurrently running programs to five or less, preferably three or less. And whenever possible, run just one program at a time. Windows works a lot faster that way.

5. DOS programs in Standard Mode: "I don't do Windows"

Windows has two operating modes, depending on the kind of computer you have: there's Standard Mode and 386 Enhanced Mode. 386 Enhanced Mode is the one that offers all the great little tricks when you're using DOS programs. So if you're running Windows in Standard Mode, you won't be able to do things like shrink the DOS program into a window.

How can you tell which mode you're in? In the Program Manager, open the Help menu and choose the About Program Manager command. The About Program Manager dialog box lists the mode, either Standard or 386 Enhanced.

6. One size doesn't fit all

Windows that are "maximized"—that is, zoomed to their absolute limits—can't be resized, because they don't have window borders. If you want to make the window smaller, you first have to "restore" it ("restore" is a bad word for this, but I didn't invent it) by clicking on the Restore button in the upper right corner of the window. The Restore button has two arrows on it. Once it's restored, the window shrinks to less than full size, and you can drag its borders to resize it.

7. My Windows desktop is gone?

Underneath all the windows and icons is the *desktop*. The desktop is a permanent part of Windows and never takes five for a smoke, so you can always count on it being there. But there are times when you might think it's disappeared.

This can happen if you maximize the Program Manager window to full size. The desktop disappears, as do the icons for any currently running programs (the icons are placed at the bottom of the screen). Don't panic, because everything is still where it used to be; it's just hidden by the overgrown Program Manager window. To see the Windows desktop, click on the Restore button in the upper right corner of the Program Manager window.

8. Where the heck am I?

Double-click on the MS-DOS Prompt icon (in the Main program group) to get the C:\> prompt in DOS. You can type any DOS

command you want. Though it looks like you're back to boring old DOS, Windows is still running. You're just on a DOS break, that's all.

A common mistake is forgetting that you're still in Windows. Your natural inclination is to start Windows by typing **WIN** at the DOS prompt. Fortunately, Windows is smarter than that and gently tells you that Windows is already running. To get back to Windows, type **EXIT** and press Enter at the DOS prompt.

9. The window you can never close

The File Manager must show at least one drive window. You can open additional drive windows, then close them, but the last one can never be closed. It doesn't matter which drive is displayed in the window. This rule applies to both floppy disk drives and hard disk drives.

On the other hand, you can minimize any and all drive windows. This reduces the drive window to an icon, which appears inside the File Manager. To see the window again, just double-click on its icon.

10. All that work, and for nothing

You've spent long, hard hours perfecting your Program Manager window and icon layout. Everything is in its place, and all the icons are neatly organized. But the next time you use the Program Manager, the icons are all mixed up again. Wha' happened?

No doubt the Save Settings on Exit option is turned off (you can check this by opening the Options menu in the Program Manager; if there's no check mark beside the Save Settings on Exit command, the option is turned off). When this option is on, the

Program Manager takes a snapshot of the layout of the Program Manager before exiting Windows. The next time you start Windows, you get the same layout you last had.

To turn this option back on so that everything in the Program Manager stays in its place, open the Options menu and choose the Save Settings on Exit command. This places a check mark next to the option to indicate that it's on now.

11. Program icons in groups only, please

The Program Manager only lets you place icons for programs inside groups. You cannot move program icons into the main Program Manager window or onto the Windows desktop. If you try such nonsense, the mouse pointer turns into a circle-and-slash, meaning "Forget it, pal."

12. Says Windows, "If the Program Manager goes, I go!"

The Program Manager is your ticket into Windows. When Windows starts, the Program Manager is the first one there. It stands to reason, then, that the Program Manager is the last one to leave. It stands to reason even more that if you try to close the main Program Manager window, what you're really doing is saying, "I want out of Windows." Indeed, if you double-click on the Program Manager's Control menu box, Windows will ask if you want to end the session. Click on Cancel to stay in Windows; click on OK to exit.

If you want to get the Program Manager window out of the way, you should minimize it. This reduces the Program Manager window to an icon, which is placed at the bottom of the screen. You can view the whole window again by double-clicking on this icon.

12 Best Windows Shortcuts

1. Make a new program icon, clickity-click

To make a new program icon without using the File menu in the Program Manager, simply hold down the Alt key while you double-click in the blank portion of a group window. The Program Item Properties dialog box appears, in which you can fill in the details about the icon.

2. It's no drag to drop

Here's a real easy way to create a program icon: Run the File Manager program, and find the program you want to make an icon for. If the File Manager window isn't already smaller than full-screen, make it so by clicking the Restore button in the upper right corner. Adjust the size of the File Manager window so that you can see both the program file you want and the group window that will contain the new icon. Now click on the program file in the File Manager, and drag it (hold the mouse button while you move the mouse) into the group window. Voilà! Instant program icon. This technique is called "drag and drop."

By the way, you don't have to open the group into a window to use the drag-and-drop technique. You can just drop the program file over a group icon.

3. Don't forget the Task List

An oft-forgotten tool of Windows is the Task List dialog box, which you display by pressing Ctrl+Esc. Using the Task List, you can switch to another currently running program by double-clicking on the program's name. You can also stop programs (click on the End Task button), organize windows (click on the Tile or Cascade button), and more.

4. Favorite programs run themselves

When you use Windows, if you use a particular program most or all of the time, put its icon into the StartUp group. That way, when Windows starts, the program starts, too.

To place a program icon into the StartUp group, open the group that contains the program icon you want. Hold down the Ctrl key and use the mouse to drag the icon on top of the StartUp group icon. This copies the program icon into the StartUp group.

5. And don't forget the wonders of the almighty DOS prompt

You can automatically start your favorite Windows programs by specifying them at the DOS prompt. Normally, you start Windows by typing **WIN** and pressing Enter at the DOS prompt. To automatically run a program and start Windows at the same time, type **WIN** and a space and the name of the program, such as

WIN WRITE

Then press the Enter key. This starts the Windows Write program. You might need to include the path of the program if the program file is not in the WINDOWS directory.

6. The mystery of the Control menu boxes solved

Ever wonder why the Control menu boxes for windows are shown with a long or a short dash? The long dash represents the space bar on your keyboard—the dash is long because the space bar key is long. The short dash represents the hyphen key on your keyboard. You use these keys, along with the Alt key, as keyboard shortcuts to display the Control menus.

- To display the Control menu for a program (a long dash), press Alt+Space bar.
- To display the Control menu for a window that's within a program window (a short dash), press Alt+Hyphen.

7. Hands off that mouse!

When you're on a roll, typing away with the speed of a woodpecker, the last thing you want to do is stop to use the mouse just to minimize or maximize a window. Use these keyboard alternatives instead:

- To maximize a window (make it full-screen), press Alt+Space bar and then press X.
- To minimize a window (make it an icon), press Alt+Space bar and then press N.

8. Asterisks are wild

Suppose that you need to select a number of files in the File Manager all at once (maybe you want to delete them all or copy them to another disk). If the files share something common in their names—like if they all end with the extension .DOC—you can use the * (asterisk) "wild card" character to select all the files that match a particular pattern.

First, click on the directory folder that contains the files you want. Then open the File menu and choose the Select Files command. The Select Files dialog box appears. Type the wild-card pattern you

want to use. The * character means "any characters." For example, *.DOC finds all files that end with .DOC, and REPORT*.TXT will find files that have the extension .TXT and begin with REPORT, such as REPORT1.TXT and REPORTXX.TXT. (If you need a wild card for just a single character, use ? instead of *.)

Click on Select and then click on Close. All the files that matched the pattern you specified are shown selected.

9. No-drag icon copying

To copy a program icon in the Program Manager without using the mouse to drag it from one group window to another, do this: Click on the icon you want to copy and press the F8 key. The Copy Program Item dialog box appears. Click on the down arrow beside the To Group box; click on the program group you want to copy the icon to; then click OK. The icon is copied.

You can *move* icons in a similar fashion. Press the F7 key instead of the F8 key.

10. Speed-searching through files

Where there are lots of files in a file list, Windows shows them in a scrolling list box. You can use the up- and down-arrow keys or the scroll bars to hunt through the list to find the file you want.

There's an even faster way of thumbing through list boxes, if you know the first character of the file you're looking for: click once on the file list; then press the key for the first letter of the file name. Suppose that the file is called LETTER.DOC. Just type **L**. Windows takes you to the first file that begins with *L*. Keep pressing the key to go to the next file that begins with that letter.

11. Leave a program, pronto

To end a program without touching the mouse, press Alt+F4. Just like when you choose the Exit command from the File menu, the program will ask you to save your work if you haven't done so already.

12. Double-click no more

All programs are shown in a window. And some programs create even more windows inside that window. Examples are the group windows in the Program Manager and drive windows in the File Manager.

To quickly close one of these windows without using the mouse, just press Ctrl+F4.

12 Mystifying Acronyms and What They Mean

1. WYSIWYG

Stands for: What You See Is What You Get

Pronounced: "whizzy-wig"

It means: What you see on the computer's screen is identical, or nearly identical, to what you'll get on paper. Applies mostly to things like word processing programs that show you exactly how the text will look when printed.

2. RAM

Stands for: Random-Access Memory

Pronounced: "ram"

It means: The memory inside your computer that stores programs and data while you work with them. The stuff inside RAM is lost when you turn your computer off. Compare that to a magnetic disk, which remembers its contents for as long as you want.

3. ROM

Stands for: Read-Only Memory

Pronounced: "rhomm" (rhymes with "prom")

It means: A special kind of memory that your computer uses for basic operating instructions. This memory is permanent (it never goes away) and you can't change it—hence the name "read only."

4. CPU

Stands for: Central Processing Unit

Pronounced: "see-pee-you"

It means: The main part of your computer; the box that all the computer junk goes into.

5. GUI

Stands for: Graphical User Interface

Pronounced: "gooey"

It means: A way for you to work with your computer by using pictures and on-screen "objects" (like icons and windows) rather than text commands.

6. ASCII

Stands for: (Never mind what it stands for. That's not important.)

Pronounced: "ask-ee"

It means: A standard way to store and retrieve text characters, like the letter A or the "(" symbol. ASCII has been in use since the early Teletype days. Personal computers just picked it up and claimed the standard for their own.

7. OLE

Stands for: Object Linking and Embedding

Pronounced: "oh-lay" or "oh-ell-ee"

It means: An automatic way that Windows programs can share data. With OLE, you can put a table from an electronic spreadsheet program into your word processor document. If you want to change the contents of the table, you just double-click on the table, and Windows will start up the electronic spreadsheet program. Make the change, and the data is automatically updated in the word processor document.

8. DDE

Stands for: Dynamic Data Exchange

Pronounced: "dee-dee-ee"

It means: Another automatic way that Windows programs can share data, but you can't double-click on something and have it start another program. DDE is what Windows 3.0 used. OLE is what Windows 3.1 uses; it expands on DDE.

9. GPF

Stands for: General Protection Fault

Pronounced: "gee-pee-eff"

It means: Windows just had a meltdown. The "General Protection Fault" error message means that Windows or the currently running program just disrupted your computer. Quite often, you have to leave Windows to set things straight. In Windows 3.0 a GPF was called a UAE—Unrecoverable Application Error.

10. DOS

Stands for: Disk Operating System

Pronounced: "doss" (rhymes with "boss")

It means: The control system for your computer. DOS controls the way your computer works with the monitor, keyboard, disk drives, and all the other junk (called "hardware") attached to the computer.

11. PC

Stands for: Personal Computer

Pronounced: "pee-see"

It means: A computer you can use for your very own, and maybe even fit on your desk. For that reason, they are sometimes called "desktop computers." They used to be called "microcomputers," but only real geeks use that term these days.

12. DLL

Stands for: Dynamic Link Library

Pronounced: "dee-ell-ell"

It means: A special kind of file used by other Windows programs. Just about all the big Windows programs have at least one DLL file, and this file is often really big.

12 Super Simple Ways to Customize Windows

1. Dealer, get me a new deck!

Tired of the same ol' card backs in the Windows Solitaire game? Change them!

In Solitaire, open the Game menu and choose the Deck command. The Select Card Back dialog box appears, showing you several new card backs you can use. (None are marked, drat!) Click on the card back you want; then click OK.

2. Clean mousie droppings

For a neat effect, turn on "mouse trails." Then whenever you move the mouse, you'll see a fading trail of arrows. Stop the mouse, and the trail soon disappears. To turn on mouse trails, double-click on the Main group; then double-click on the Control Panel icon. Find the Mouse icon inside the Control Panel window, and double-click on it. Click inside the Mouse Trails box to put an X inside it; then click on OK. Close the Control Panel window by double-clicking its Control menu box. Repeat the process to turn mouse trails off.

The mouse trails feature actually has some benefit. If you're using a laptop computer with a liquid crystal display, the mouse trails make it easier to see where the mouse is as you move it.

3. Lefties unite!

Lefties (politically correct term: "persons of the left-handed persuasion") aren't forgotten where Windows is concerned. An option lets you switch the right and left mouse buttons, so that the index finger is always used for the important stuff (for righties, the index finger controls the left mouse button, the one that does 99.9999 percent of the work in Windows).

To swap the mouse buttons, double-click on the Main group; then double-click on the Control Panel icon. Find the Mouse icon inside the Control Panel window, and double-click on it. Click inside the Swap Left/Right Buttons box to put an X inside it, and click on OK. Close the Control Panel window by double-clicking its Control menu box.

4. Changing the keyboard repeat

Are you a keyboard leadfoot? Do you get lots of rreeaappeeaatteedd characters as you type? If you do, you'll want to change the key repeat rate. Here's how: Double-click on the Main group; then double-click on the Control Panel icon. Find the Keyboard icon inside the Control Panel window, and double-click on it. Use the mouse to slide the Repeat Rate scroll bar from Fast to Slow. To test the new setting, click inside the Test entry blank and type something. Click OK when you're done messing around. Close the Control Panel window by double-clicking on its Control menu box.

5. Personalized wallpaper

Add your initials to your favorite Windows wallpaper. That way everyone knows whose computer they're using when they sit behind your desk.

You use the Windows Paintbrush program to add your initials to the wallpaper picture. To do that, double-click on the Accessories group; then double-click on Paintbrush. Open the wallpaper picture by opening the File command and choosing the Open command. In the Open dialog box that appears, find the wallpaper picture file you use (such as MARBLE.BMP). Click on the file; then click OK.

Click on the Text icon (labeled *ABC*); then click over the spot where you want to add your initials. Open the Text menu and

choose the Fonts command to change the style of the text. When you're done adding your initials, save the file by opening the File menu and choosing the Save command. Leave Paintbrush by choosing Exit from the File menu.

Next time you start Windows, your initials will appear.

6. Say the password!

Here's a way to keep people from monkeying with your computer while you're away from your desk. If you use Windows' screen saver feature, you can make up a password that must be typed before the screen saver movie will end.

To set the password, double-click on the Main group; then double-click on the Control Panel icon. Find the Desktop icon inside the Control Panel window, and double-click on it. The Desktop dialog box appears. Click on the Setup button, then inside the Password Protected box to put an X there. Click on the Set Password button. Type the password in the second and third entry blanks; then click on OK three times. Close the Control Panel window by double-clicking on its Control menu box.

Now, whenever the screen saver is activated, you must type the password to get back into Windows.

Be sure to remember your password!

7. Make mine vermilion

Why settle for the stock colors when you can blend your own? You're changing the colors of Windows elements by using the Color dialog box (double-click on Main, then Control Panel, then Color). If you're looking for that special hue for the windows title bar, go ahead and mix up your own.

To create a custom color, click on the Color Palette button to expand the Color dialog box; then click the Define Custom Colors button. Use the mouse to drag around inside the big color palette. The cross shows you the color you've mixed up. Click on one of the empty Custom Colors boxes; then click on Add Color. That color appears in the Custom Colors box. You can now apply that color to whatever screen element you want.

8. More and more icons

Windows comes with a gazillion icons you can use for your boring old DOS program. Okay, so a gazillion is a slight exaggeration, but there are lots of 'em available, including icons for such DOS favorites as Lotus 1-2-3, WordPerfect, WordStar, and dBASE.

To change the appearance of one of the DOS program icons in the Program Manager, hold down the Alt key and double-click on the icon. The Program Item Properties dialog box appears. Click on the Change Icon button. In the File Name entry box, type **MORICONS.DLL** (if it isn't already) and press Enter. All the icons in this special file are shown. Use the scroll bars to find the icon you want to use; then click on it. Click OK to leave this dialog box. Click OK again in the Program Item Properties dialog box.

9. Hot Foot the Print Manager

Are your documents taking forever to print? You can speed things up a bit by changing an option in the Print Manager program. Double-click on the Main group; then double-click on the Print Manager icon. The Print Manager window appears. Open the Options menu and choose the High Priority command. This places a higher priority on printing than other Windows tasks.

10. **You mean we were supposed to meet for lunch?!**

Never miss an important meeting again. Have Windows remind you of important events by marking them in the Calendar program. Here's how: Double-click on the Accessories group; then double-click on the Calendar icon. The Calendar program window opens. Open the View menu and choose the Month command to see the whole month at a glance. Double-click on the day of your appointment.

If your appointment is scheduled on the hour, click beside the hour. If the appointment is scheduled for another time, open the Options menu and choose the Special Time command. Enter the time of day, click on the AM or PM button, and then click on Insert. Type a short description of the appointment. Finally, open the Alarm menu and choose Set.

The alarm is now set; however, the Calendar program must be running for you to hear the alarm. Minimize the Calendar program by clicking on its Minimize button. If you use the Calendar a lot, put its icon in the StartUp group window. That way, the Calendar program will automatically run whenever you start Windows.

11. **Be your own director**

If you use Windows' screen saver feature, you can be your own director of the screen saver movies. Most of the screen saver movies let you change their speed, alter colors, or pick a different cast of characters.

To change a screen saver setting, double-click on the Main group; then double-click on the Control Panel icon. In the Control Panel window, double-click on the Desktop icon. Click on the down arrow beside the Screen Saver Name box, and click on the screen

saver you want to use. Next, click on the Setup button. The Setup dialog box appears.

Inside this dialog box are all the settings you can make to that particular screen saver (the contents of the box depends on the screen saver movie you've selected). For example, if you've opted for the Starfield Simulation screen saver, you can set the "warp speed" from slow to fast to simulate cruising through the outer reaches of the universe, and you can set the "starfield density" so that you're smack dab in the center of a galaxy with either gobs of stars or just a few.

12. A two-tone clock

The Windows clock displays the time either in the old-fashioned analog (big hand, little hand) style or in the new-fangled digital style. This is but one of the ways you can customize the Clock the way you want it.

To customize the clock, get it going by double-clicking on the Accessories group and double-clicking on the Clock icon. Most of the Clock options are on the Settings menu. Open this menu to change such things as the clock face (analog or digital); the font you want to use to tell time; whether you want to show the date, the seconds, or both; and whether you want to hide the title and borders of the Clock window. (To show the title and borders, double-click anywhere in the Clock window.)

One additional option you can choose to customize the clock is found in the Control menu. Click on the Control menu box in the Clock window; then click on Always on Top if you want the Clock window to appear over all other windows, even when you're working in another program.

Buzzwords

active window The window currently getting the attention. Clicking on the mouse or typing on the keyboard affects the active window. Only one window can be active at a time.

application A type of program you use to create something, like a letter or a spreadsheet. The word *application* (or "app") is often used as a synonym for *program.*

application window A window that contains a program.

AUTOEXEC.BAT A special file used by your computer when the computer first starts. You can make changes to the contents of the AUTOEXEC.BAT file if you want to.

bit map A collection of dots that makes up a picture. Each dot is a "bit," and they are "mapped" out in a certain way to make the finished picture.

boot The techie term for "starting up your computer."

button A visual object used in dialog boxes that works just like a push button on a telephone or on some other mechanical gadget. Click on the button with the mouse and a command is carried out.

cascading windows Windows that are automatically arranged in a neat overlapping stack. The Program Manager in Windows is one of several programs that gives you the option of cascading your windows. See also *tiling windows*.

check box A visual object used in dialog boxes to denote an option you can turn on or off. It works like a check box in a fill-in form at a doctor's office. Put a check in the box if you want to have your tonsils taken out. Leave it blank if you don't.

click Pressing once on the left mouse button.

Clipboard The place where Windows temporarily stores data (like text and pictures) so that you can retrieve the data later. The Clipboard makes the cut-and-paste feature of Windows possible.

Control menu box An icon that most windows have, located in the top left corner (shown with a short or long dash, depending on what kind of window it is). Clicking on it once opens the Control menu, which lets you move and size the window, among other tasks.

CPU Stands for *central processing unit,* a term held over from when computers took up entire rooms, and each part of the computer was in a separate compartment. The portion of the computer that had the so-called thinking part was the central processing unit. Now CPU refers to the system box itself.

current directory The directory that Windows is working with at the moment. If you can see files, those files are the ones in the current directory.

cursor The flashing vertical bar that tells you where the text will appear when you type on the keyboard. In Windows, the cursor is often called the "insertion point."

default The standard choice. You don't have to make any changes if you just want the default settings.

desktop The imaginary table where Windows places program windows and icons.

dialog box A special kind of window that appears when you select some commands. The dialog box confirms an action or displays further options.

directory Like a folder. An indication of where your files are kept on disk. Computer hard disk drives are divided into directories to make it

easier to store and locate files. The specific directories in the hard disk drive in your computer is completely up to you.

directory path The trail your computer must follow to find a particular file. The directory path includes whatever directories a particular file is in.

directory tree The conceptual layout of directories on a disk; it looks a little like an inverted tree, with the root on top and the branches (other directories) coming out from it. The directory structure is sometimes called a "tree."

document A file you create with a program.

document window A window that contains text or other data information. Usually the document window is displayed within a program window.

DOS Stands for *disk operating system*, which is the software that makes your computer work.

DOS prompt Typically the letter of the current disk drive and name of the current directory. DOS is known as a "command-driven system," meaning that you must type special commands to tell DOS what you want to do. DOS tells you that it's ready to accept these commands by displaying the DOS prompt. For computers with hard disk drives, the prompt is often signified as C:\>. Of course, the actual characters of the prompt can vary.

double-click Pressing twice on the left mouse button in rapid succession.

DPI Stands for *dots per inch*. Printers really print with dots. The more dots the printer can cram into an inch, the sharper the printed page will be.

drag Pressing and holding the mouse button while moving the mouse.

drag-and-drop A feature of Windows in which you can drag an icon over something and "drop" it into place, usually into a group window in the Program Manager.

Enhanced Mode One of two modes that Windows operates under, depending on the technical aspects of your computer. Enhanced Mode (also called "386 Enhanced Mode") offers the most features and capabilities. The other mode is Standard Mode.

entry blank A visual object used in a dialog box that works like an entry blank in a form. You type text in the blank to answer a question. In a dialog box, you click inside an entry blank and then type in the information. Also called a "text box."

error message A comment that Windows displays to tell you that something is wrong.

executable file Another name for a program.

file A self-contained module that holds data. Files are stored for safekeeping on a disk.

file association A Windows feature that lets you associate a document file with the program you created it in. That way, when you double-click on the document file to open it, Windows automatically starts the program that made the document.

file extension The part of the file name that appears after the period. The extension can be up to three characters long and usually indicates what type of file it is. For instance, the extension .DOC indicates document files. When naming a file, adding the period and extension is optional.

folder The conceptual equivalent to a directory on a disk drive. The folder is often used in Windows to denote a directory, because folders hold related documents.

font The design of typewritten characters.

format This term can mean either of two things: (1) To prepare a disk so that it can hold data. The formatting process divides the disk into tracks; once the tracks are there, data can be recorded on the disk. (2) To add special effects to word processing documents, like letters and memos, to make them look better. These effects include different kinds of text styles and alignments.

function keys Special-purpose keys on your computer's keyboard. They are labeled F1 through F12 (some keyboards only have 10 function keys) and are placed along the top of the keyboard or on the left side (or both). These keys work differently, depending on which program you are using.

graphical user interface The way Windows works with you, using visual objects—such as dialog boxes, pull-down menus, and windows—rather than commands you have to memorize and type. Windows is a graphical user interface, or *GUI*—affectionately pronounced "gooey."

group window A window you can open in the Program Manager to access program icons. The Program Manager lets you separate program icons into groups so that the icons are easy to find. Also called *group*.

group icon In the Program Manager, a group window reduced to an icon to keep it out of the way when you don't need it. You double-click on the group icon to reopen it into a window, allowing you to see the program icons inside.

hardware The mechanical portion of your computer, such as the monitor and the keyboard. The "software" is the programs.

icon A pictorial representation of something, usually of a program on your computer's hard disk drive.

insertion point The politically correct term for the flashing vertical bar that tells you where the text will appear when you use the keyboard to type characters. Also called the "cursor."

install To load Windows and DOS programs into your computer by copying their files from one or more diskettes to your computer's hard disk drive.

laser printer The most popular type of printer used in businesses. It works like a copier and uses laser light (or some other controllable light source) to "paint" an image onto a piece of paper.

list box An item in a dialog box that contains a list of things, most often a list of files. You can use the mouse or the keyboard to sift through the list to find the file you want.

maximize To enlarge a window so that it fills up your entire screen.

menu A display that Windows uses to hold commands. The menus are placed along the top of the program window, but are "closed" so that they're out of the way. Using the mouse or the keyboard, you can open the menu to see the commands inside.

menu bar The strip along the top of a program window that contains the menus.

minimized To shrink a window so that it appears on-screen as an icon.

mouse A mechanical device you use to control the pointer that appears on your computer screen. When you move the mouse on the desk, the on-screen pointer moves correspondingly.

operating system The software your computer uses to operate. DOS is the most common operating system in use today.

option button In a dialog box, a circle-shaped option that is grouped together with other options buttons; you can choose only one option button in the group. They are sometimes referred to as "radio buttons" because they work like the station-changing buttons on a car radio.

PC Stands for *personal computer*. A PC is intended to be used by one person or, at most, a small number of people.

password A word that only you know. It lets you gain access to Windows, but blocks unauthorized people.

PIF Stands for *program information file*, a special kind of file Windows uses to keep track of the special needs of DOS programs. PIFs are used only for DOS programs, not Windows programs.

pixel Stands for *picture element*—a dot. The Windows screen is really made up of a series of dots, most commonly 640 dots (pixels) wide by 480 dots high. Your system might have more dots or less dots, depending on the kind of monitor you are using. The more dots there are, the better the picture looks.

point To move the mouse to point out an object on-screen. When you move the mouse, an on-screen arrow (called the "pointer") moves correspondingly.

pointer The on-screen arrow you control with the mouse. The pointer isn't always shaped like an arrow. It changes depending on what Windows is doing.

program A set of instructions that your computer uses to perform some task. The computer follows each instruction in turn, until the program ends. The word *application* and *program* mean the same thing.

program icon An icon that represents a program on your computer's hard disk drive. Program icons are contained inside group icons in the Program Manager.

RAM Stands for *random-access memory*, the stuff your computer uses to hold programs and data while it's working with them. When you turn your computer off, the information in RAM is erased.

root The main directory on disk. Inside this root directory (which never has a specific name) are all the files and other directories of the disk.

restore To change a window between full-screen (maximized) and partial-screen.

run To start a program.

select To click on something in Windows, like an icon, a menu, a window, or some text.

scroll bar The part of a window along the right or bottom edge that lets you pan its contents when there's more inside the window than can be shown at once. Scroll bars are also used in file lists.

software The programs you run on your computer. Windows is considered software. See *hardware*.

Standard Mode See *Enhanced Mode*.

subdirectory A directory placed inside another directory on your hard disk drive.

system resources A small portion of your computer's memory that Windows sets aside to store important details about itself. When this memory is filled up, Windows is said to be "out of system resources."

Task List A dialog box you can display by pressing Ctrl+Esc (hold down the Ctrl key and then press Esc). The Task List lets you easily switch over to any other program currently running in Windows.

task switching To jump from program to program when you have more than one program running at the same time.

tiling windows Windows that are automatically arranged in a neat, side-by-side arrangement. The Program Manager in Windows is among one of several programs that gives you the option of tiling windows. See *cascading windows*.

TrueType A type of font that Windows uses to display and print characters in different sizes and shapes, allowing you to print text in a variety of different looks and styles.

utility program A special kind of computer program designed to make using your computer easier and better.

wild card A special character that represents any other character. Windows (and DOS) use two wild-card characters: the asterisk (sometimes called "star") and the question mark.

window A self-contained on-screen box that contains different types of things, such as a program, a document, or a set of program icons.

WYSIWYG An acronym for "what you see is what you get." This term, pronounced "wizzy-wig," refers to how closely the printed version of a document looks like the version you see on-screen.

I HATE WINDOWS

Index

Symbols

A-B

C

E

F

G

I HATE WINDOWS!

M

N-O

P

I HATE WINDOWS!

Q-R

S

T

U

V-Z

I HATE WINDOWS!